Essays

By

Ralph Waldo Emerson

Essays
by Ralph Waldo Emerson

ISBN: 978-93-60460-34-1
Published by

DOUBLE 9 BOOKS

2/13-B, Ansari Road
Daryaganj, New Delhi – 110002
info@double9books.com
www.double9books.com
Tel. 011-40042856

ABOUT THE AUTHOR

Ralph Waldo Emerson was an American essayist, speaker, philosopher, abolitionist, and poet who lived from May 25, 1803 to April 27, 1882. He went by his middle name, Waldo. He led the transcendentalist movement in the middle of the 1800s. People looked up to him as a supporter of freedom and critical thinking, as well as a wise critic of how society and conformity can make people feel bad about themselves. He was called "the most gifted of the Americans" by Friedrich Nietzsche, and Walt Whitman called him his "master." Emerson slowly moved away from the religious and social beliefs of his time. In his 1836 essay "Nature," he formulated and explained the theory of transcendentalism. After this, in 1837, he gave a speech called "The American Scholar." Oliver Wendell Holmes Sr. thought it was America's "intellectual Declaration of Independence." Emerson was born on May 25, 1803, in Newbury, Massachusetts. His parents were Ruth Haskins and the Rev. William Emerson, who was a Unitarian preacher. He was named for Ralph, his mom brother, and Rebecca Waldo, his dad great-grandmother. William, Edward, Robert Bulkeley, and Charles were the other four sons who lived to adulthood. Ralph Waldo was the second of these boys to do so.

CONTENTS

LIFE OF EMERSON

Ralph Waldo Emerson was born in Boston, May 25, 1803. He was descended from a long line of New England ministers, men of refinement and education. As a school-boy he was quiet and retiring, reading a great deal, but not paying much attention to his lessons. He entered Harvard at the early age of fourteen, but never attained a high rank there, although he took a prize for an essay on Socrates, and was made class poet after several others had declined. Next to his reserve and the faultless propriety of his conduct, his contemporaries at college seemed most impressed by the great maturity of his mind. Emerson appears never to have been really a boy. He was always serene and thoughtful, impressing all who knew him with that spirituality which was his most distinguishing characteristic.

After graduating from college he taught school for a time, and then entered the Harvard Divinity School under Dr. Channing, the great Unitarian preacher. Although he was not strong enough to attend all the lectures of the divinity course, the college authorities deemed the name Emerson sufficient passport to the ministry. He was accordingly "approbated to preach" by the Middlesex Association of Ministers on October 10, 1826. As a preacher, Emerson was interesting, though not particularly original. His talent seems to have been in giving new meaning to the old truths of religion. One of his hearers has said: "In looking back on his preaching I find he has impressed truths to which I always assented in such a manner as to make them appear new, like a clearer revelation." Although his sermons were always couched in scriptural language, they were touched with the light of that genius which avoids the conventional and commonplace. In his other pastoral duties Emerson was not quite so successful. It is characteristic of his deep humanity and his dislike for all fuss and commonplace that he appeared to least advantage at a funeral. A connoisseur in such matters, an old sexton, once remarked that on such occasions "he did not appear at ease at all. To tell the truth, in my opinion, that young man was not born to be a minister."

Emerson did not long remain a minister. In 1832 he preached a sermon in which he announced certain views in regard to the communion service which were disapproved by a large part of his congregation. He found it impossible to continue preaching, and, with the most friendly feelings on both sides, he parted from his congregation.

A few months later (1833) he went to Europe for a short year of travel. While abroad, he visited Walter Savage Landor, Coleridge and Wordsworth, and Thomas Carlyle. This visit to Carlyle was to both men a most interesting experience. They parted feeling that they had much intellectually in common. This belief fostered a sympathy which, by the time they had discovered how different they really were, had grown so strong a habit that they always kept up their intimacy. This year of travel opened Emerson's eyes to many things of which he had previously been ignorant; he had profited by detachment from the concerns of a limited community and an isolated church.

After his return he began to find his true field of activity in the lecture-hall, and delivered a number of addresses in Boston and its vicinity. While thus coming before the open public on the lecture platform, he was all the time preparing the treatise which was to embody all the quintessential elements of his philosophical doctrine. This was the essay *Nature,* which was published in 1836. By its conception of external Nature as an incarnation of the Divine Mind it struck the fundamental principle of Emerson's religious belief. The essay had a very small circulation at first, though later it became widely known.

In the winter of 1836 Emerson followed up his discourse on Nature by a course of twelve lectures on the "Philosophy of History," a considerable portion of which eventually became embodied in his essays. The next year (1837) was the year of the delivery of the *Man Thinking, or the American Scholar* address before the Phi Beta Kappa Society at Cambridge.

This society, composed of the first twenty-five men in each class graduating from college, has annual meetings which have called forth the best efforts of many distinguished scholars and thinkers. Emerson's address was listened to with the most profound interest. It declared a sort of intellectual independence for America. Henceforth we were to be emancipated from clogging foreign influences, and a national literature was to expand under the fostering care of the Republic.

These two discourses, *Nature* and *The American Scholar,* strike the keynote of Emerson's philosophical, poetical, and moral teachings. In fact he had, as every great teacher has, only a limited number of principles and theories to teach. These principles of life can all be enumerated in twenty words—self-reliance, culture, intellectual and moral independence, the divinity of nature and man, the necessity of labor, and high ideals.

Emerson spent the latter part of his life in lecturing and in literary work. His son, Dr. Edward Emerson, gave an interesting account of how these lectures were constructed. "All through his life he kept a journal. This book, he said, was his 'Savings Bank.' The thoughts thus received and garnered in his journals were indexed, and a great many of them appeared in his published works. They were religiously set down just as they came, in no order except chronological, but later they were grouped, enlarged or pruned, illustrated, worked into a lecture or discourse, and, after having in this capacity undergone repeated testing and rearranging, were finally carefully sifted and more rigidly pruned, and were printed as essays."

Besides his essays and lectures Emerson left some poetry in which is embodied those thoughts which were to him too deep for prose expression. Oliver Wendell Holmes in speaking of this says: "Emerson wrote occasionally in verse from his school-days until he had reached the age which used to be known as the grand climacteric, sixty-three.... His poems are not and hardly can become popular; they are not meant to be liked by the many, but to be dearly loved and cherished by the few.... His occasional lawlessness in technical construction, his somewhat fantastic expressions, his enigmatic obscurities hardly detract from the pleasant surprise his verses so often bring with them.... The poetic license which we allow in the verse of Emerson is more than excused by the noble spirit which makes us forget its occasional blemishes, sometimes to be pleased with them as characteristic of the writer."

Emerson was always a striking figure in the intellectual life of America. His discourses were above all things inspiring. Through them many were induced to strive for a higher self-culture. His influence can be discerned in all the literary movements of the time. He was the central figure of the so-called transcendental school which was so prominent fifty years ago, although he always rather held aloof from any enthusiastic participation in the movement.

Emerson lived a quiet life in Concord, Massachusetts. "He was a first-rate neighbor and one who always kept his fences up." He traveled extensively on his lecturing tours, even going as far as England. In *English Traits* he has recorded his impressions of what he saw of English life and manners.

Oliver Wendell Holmes has described him in this wise: "His personal appearance was that of the typical New Englander of college-bred ancestry. Tall, spare, slender, with sloping shoulders, slightly stooping in his later years, with light hair and eyes, the scholar's complexion, the prominent, somewhat arched nose which belongs to many of the New England sub-species, thin lips, suggestive of delicacy, but having nothing like primness, still less of the rigidity which is often noticeable in the generation succeeding next to that of the men in their shirt-sleeves, he would have been noticed anywhere as one evidently a scholarly thinker astray from the alcove or the study, which were his natural habitats. His voice was very sweet, and penetrating without any loudness or mark of effort. His enunciation was beautifully clear, but he often hesitated as if waiting for the right word to present itself. His manner was very quiet, his smile was pleasant, but he did not like explosive laughter any better than Hawthorne did. None who met him can fail to recall that serene and kindly presence, in which there was mingled a certain spiritual remoteness with the most benignant human welcome to all who were privileged to enjoy his companionship."

Emerson died April 27, 1882, after a few days' illness from pneumonia. Dr. Garnett in his excellent biography says: "Seldom had 'the reaper whose name is Death' gathered such illustrious harvest as between December 1880 and April 1882. In the first month of this period George Eliot passed away, in the ensuing February Carlyle followed; in April Lord Beaconsfield died, deplored by his party, nor unregretted by his country; in February of the following year Longfellow was carried to the tomb; in April Rossetti was laid to rest by the sea, and the pavement of Westminster Abbey was disturbed to receive the dust of Darwin. And now Emerson lay down in death beside the painter of man and the searcher of nature, the English-Oriental statesman, the poet of the plain man and the poet of the artist, and the prophet whose name is indissolubly linked with his own. All these men passed into eternity laden with the spoils of Time, but of none of them could it be said, as of Emerson, that the most shining intellectual glory and the most potent intellectual force of a continent had departed along with him."

CRITICAL OPINIONS OF EMERSON
AND HIS WRITINGS

Matthew Arnold, in an address on Emerson delivered in Boston, gave an excellent estimate of the rank we should accord to him in the great hierarchy of letters. Some, perhaps, will think that Arnold was unappreciative and cold, but dispassionate readers will be inclined to agree with his judgment of our great American.

After a review of the poetical works of Emerson the English critic draws his conclusions as follows:

"I do not then place Emerson among the great poets. But I go farther, and say that I do not place him among the great writers, the great men of letters. Who are the great men of letters? They are men like Cicero, Plato, Bacon, Pascal, Swift, Voltaire—writers with, in the first place, a genius and instinct for style.... Brilliant and powerful passages in a man's writings do not prove his possession of it. Emerson has passages of noble and pathetic eloquence; he has passages of shrewd and felicitous wit; he has crisp epigram; he has passages of exquisitely touched observation of nature. Yet he is not a great writer.... Carlyle formulates perfectly the defects of his friend's poetic and literary productions when he says: 'For me it is too ethereal, speculative, theoretic; I will have all things condense themselves, take shape and body, if they are to have my sympathy.' ...

" .... Not with the Miltons and Grays, not with the Platos and Spinozas, not with the Swifts and Voltaires, not with the Montaignes and Addisons, can we rank Emerson. No man could see this clearer than Emerson himself. 'Alas, my friend,' he writes in reply to Carlyle, who had exhorted him to creative work,—'Alas, my friend, I can do no such gay thing as you say. I do not belong to the poets, but only to a low department of literature,— the reporters; suburban men.' He deprecated his friend's praise; praise 'generous to a fault' he calls it; praise 'generous to the shaming of me,— cold, fastidious, ebbing person that I am.'"

After all this unfavorable criticism Arnold begins to praise. Quoting passages from the Essays, he adds:

"This is tonic indeed! And let no one object that it is too general; that more practical, positive direction is what we want.... Yes, truly, his insight is admirable; his truth is precious. Yet the secret of his effect is not even in these; it is in his temper. It is in the hopeful, serene, beautiful temper wherewith these, in Emerson, are indissolubly united; in which they work and have their being.... One can scarcely overrate the importance of holding fast to happiness and hope. It gives to Emerson's work an invaluable virtue. As Wordsworth's poetry is, in my judgment, the most important done in verse, in our language, during the present century, so Emerson's Essays are, I think, the most important work done in prose.... But by his conviction that in the life of the spirit is happiness, and by his hope that this life of the spirit will come more and more to be sanely understood, and to prevail, and to work for happiness,—by this conviction and hope Emerson was great, and he will surely prove in the end to have been right in them.... You cannot prize him too much, nor heed him too diligently."

Herman Grimm, a German critic of great influence in his own country, did much to obtain a hearing for Emerson's works in Germany. At first the Germans could not understand the unusual English, the unaccustomed turns of phrase which are so characteristic of Emerson's style.

"Macaulay gives them no difficulty; even Carlyle is comprehended. But in Emerson's writings the broad turnpike is suddenly changed into a hazardous sandy foot-path. His thoughts and his style are American. He is not writing for Berlin, but for the people of Massachusetts.... It is an art to rise above what we have been taught.... All great men are seen to possess this freedom. They derive their standard from their own natures, and their observations on life are so natural and spontaneous that it would seem as if the most illiterate person with a scrap of common-sense would have made the same.... We become wiser with them, and know not how the difficult appears easy and the involved plain.

"Emerson possesses this noble manner of communicating himself. He inspires me with courage and confidence. He has read and seen but conceals the labor. I meet in his works plenty of familiar facts, but he does not employ them to figure up anew the old worn-out problems: each stands on a new spot and serves for new combinations. From everything he sees the direct line issuing which connects it with the focus of life....

" .... Emerson's theory is that of the 'sovereignty of the individual.' To discover what a young man is good for, and to equip him for the path he is to strike out in life, regardless of any other consideration, is the great duty to which he calls attention. He makes men self-reliant. He reveals to the eyes of the idealist the magnificent results of practical activity, and unfolds before the realist the grandeur of the ideal world of thought. No man is to allow himself, through prejudice, to make a mistake in choosing the task to which he will devote his life. Emerson's essays are, as it were, printed sermons—all having this same text.... The wealth and harmony of his language overpowered and entranced me anew. But even now I cannot say wherein the secret of his influence lies. What he has written is like life itself—the unbroken thread ever lengthened through the addition of the small events which make up each day's experience."

Froude in his famous "Life of Carlyle" gives an interesting description of Emerson's visit to the Carlyles in Scotland:

"The Carlyles were sitting alone at dinner on a Sunday afternoon at the end of August when a Dumfries carriage drove to the door, and there stepped out of it a young American then unknown to fame, but whose influence in his own country equals that of Carlyle in ours, and whose name stands connected with his wherever the English language is spoken. Emerson, the younger of the two, had just broken his Unitarian fetters, and was looking out around him like a young eagle longing for light. He had read Carlyle's articles and had discerned with the instinct of genius that here was a voice speaking real and fiery convictions, and no longer echoes and conventionalisms. He had come to Europe to study its social and spiritual phenomena; and to the young Emerson as to the old Goethe, the most important of them appeared to be Carlyle.... The acquaintance then begun to their mutual pleasure ripened into a deep friendship, which has remained unclouded in spite of wide divergences of opinion throughout their working lives."

Carlyle wrote to his mother after Emerson had left:

"Our third happiness was the arrival of a certain young unknown friend named Emerson, from Boston, in the United States, who turned aside so far from his British, French, and Italian travels to see me here! He had an introduction from Mill and a Frenchman (Baron d'Eichthal's nephew) whom John knew at Rome. Of course, we could do no other than welcome him; the rather as he seemed to be one of the most lovable creatures in himself we had ever looked on. He stayed till next day with us, and talked and heard to his heart's content, and left us all really sad to part with him."

In 1841 Carlyle wrote to John Sterling a few words apropos of the recent publication of Emerson's essays in England:

"I love Emerson's book, not for its detached opinions, not even for the scheme of the general world he has framed for himself, or any eminence of talent he has expressed that with, but simply because it is his own book; because there is a tone of veracity, an unmistakable air of its being *his*, and a real utterance of a human soul, not a mere echo of such. I consider it, in that sense, highly remarkable, rare, very rare, in these days of ours. Ach Gott! It is frightful to live among echoes. The few that read the book, I imagine, will get benefit of it. To America, I sometimes say that Emerson, such as he is, seems to me like a kind of New Era."

John Morley, the acute English critic, has made an analytic study of Emerson's style, which may reconcile the reader to some of its exasperating peculiarities.

"One of the traits that every critic notes in Emerson's writing is that it is so abrupt, so sudden in its transitions, so discontinuous, so inconsecutive. Dislike of a sentence that drags made him unconscious of the quality that French critics name *coulant*. Everything is thrown in just as it comes, and sometimes the pell-mell is enough to persuade us that Pope did not exaggerate when he said that no one qualification is so likely to make a good writer as the power of rejecting his own thoughts.... Apart from his difficult staccato, Emerson is not free from secondary faults. He uses words that are not only odd, but vicious in construction; he is sometimes oblique and he is often clumsy; and there is a visible feeling after epigrams that do not always come. When people say that Emerson's style must be good and admirable because it fits his thought, they forget that though it is well that a robe should fit, there is still something to be said about its cut and fashion.... Yet, as happens to all fine minds, there came to Emerson ways of expression deeply marked with character. On every page there is set the strong stamp of sincerity, and the attraction of a certain artlessness; the most awkward sentence rings true; and there is often a pure and simple note that touches us more than if it were the perfection of elaborated melody. The uncouth procession of the periods discloses the travail of the thought, and that, too, is a kind of eloquence. An honest reader easily forgives the rude jolt or unexpected start when it shows a thinker faithfully working his way along arduous and unworn tracks. Even at the roughest, Emerson often interjects a delightful cadence. As he says of Landor, his sentences are cubes which will stand firm, place them how or where you will. He criticised Swedenborg for being superfluously explanatory, and having an exaggerated feeling of the ignorance of men. 'Men take truths of this nature,' said Emerson, 'very fast;' and his own style does no doubt very boldly take this capacity for granted in us. In 'choice and pith of diction,' again, of which Mr. Lowell speaks, he hits the mark with a felicity that is almost his own in this generation. He is terse, concentrated, and free from the important blunder of mistaking intellectual dawdling for meditation. Nor in fine does his abruptness ever impede a true urbanity. The accent is homely and the apparel plain, but his bearing has a friendliness, a courtesy, a hospitable humanity, which goes nearer to our hearts than either literary decoration or rhetorical unction. That modest and lenient fellow-feeling which gave such charm to his companionship breathes in his gravest writing, and prevents us from finding any page of it cold or hard or dry."

E.P. Whipple, the well-known American critic, wrote soon after Emerson's death:

"But 'sweetness and light' are precious and inspiring only so far as they express the essential sweetness of the disposition of the thinker, and the essential illuminating power of his intelligence. Emerson's greatness came from his character. Sweetness and light streamed from him because they were *in* him. In everything he thought, wrote, and did, we feel the presence of a personality as vigorous and brave as it was sweet, and the particular radical thought he at any time expressed derived its power to animate and illuminate other minds from the might of the manhood, which was felt to be within and behind it. To 'sweetness and light' he therefore added the prime quality of fearless manliness.

"If the force of Emerson's character was thus inextricably blended with the force of all his faculties of intellect and imagination, and the refinement of all his sentiments, we have still to account for the peculiarities of his genius, and to answer the question, why do we instinctively apply the epithet 'Emersonian' to every characteristic passage in his writings? We are told that he was the last in a long line of clergymen, his ancestors, and that the modern doctrine of heredity accounts for the impressive emphasis he laid on the moral sentiment; but that does not solve the puzzle why he unmistakably differed in his nature and genius from all other Emersons. An imaginary genealogical chart of descent connecting him with Confucius or Gautama would be more satisfactory.

"What distinguishes *the* Emerson was his exceptional genius and character, that something in him which separated him from all other Emersons, as it separated him from all other eminent men of letters, and impressed every intelligent reader with the feeling that he was not only 'original but aboriginal.' Some traits of his mind and character may be traced back to his ancestors, but what doctrine of heredity can give us the genesis of his genius? Indeed, the safest course to pursue is to quote his own words, and despairingly confess that it is the nature of genius 'to spring, like the rainbow daughter of Wonder, from the invisible, to abolish the past, and refuse all history.'"

CHRONOLOGICAL LIST OF EMERSON'S PRINCIPAL WORKS

Nature	1836
Essays (First Series)	1841
Essays (Second Series)	1844
Poems	1847
Miscellanies	1849
Representative Men	1850
English Traits	1856
Conduct of Life	1860
Society and Solitude	1870
Correspondence of Thomas Carlyle and R.W. Emerson	1883

THE AMERICAN SCHOLAR

This address was delivered at Cambridge in 1837, before the Harvard Chapter of the Phi Beta Kappa Society, a college fraternity composed of the first twenty-five men in each graduating class. The society has annual meetings, which have been the occasion for addresses from the most distinguished scholars and thinkers of the day.

Mr. President and Gentlemen,

I greet you on the recommencement of our literary year. Our anniversary is one of hope, and, perhaps, not enough of labor. We do not meet for games of strength[1] or skill, for the recitation of histories, tragedies, and odes, like the ancient Greeks; for parliaments of love and poesy, like the Troubadours;[2] nor for the advancement of science, like our co-temporaries in the British and European capitals. Thus far, our holiday has been simply a friendly sign of the survival of the love of letters amongst a people too busy to give to letters any more. As such it is precious as the sign of an indestructible instinct. Perhaps the time is already come when it ought to be, and will be, something else; when the sluggard intellect of this continent will look from under its iron lids and fill the postponed expectation of the world with something better than the exertions of mechanical skill. Our day of dependence, our long apprenticeship to the learning of other lands, draws to a close. The millions that around us are rushing into life cannot always be fed on the sere remains of foreign harvests.[3] Events, actions arise that must be sung, that will sing themselves. Who can doubt that poetry will revive and lead in a new age, as the star in the constellation Harp, which now flames in our zenith, astronomers announce, shall one day be the pole-star[4] for a thousand years?

In the light of this hope I accept the topic which not only usage but the nature of our association seem to prescribe to this day,—the American Scholar. Year by year we come up hither to read one more chapter of his biography. Let us inquire what new lights, new events, and more days have thrown on his character, his duties, and his hopes.

It is one of those fables which out of an unknown antiquity convey an unlooked-for wisdom, that the gods, in the beginning, divided Man into men, that he might be more helpful to himself; just as the hand was divided into fingers, the better to answer its end.[5]

The old fable covers a doctrine ever new and sublime; that there is One Man,—present to all particular men only partially, or through one faculty; and that you must take the whole society to find the whole man. Man is not a farmer, or a professor, or an engineer, but he is all. Man is priest, and scholar, and statesman, and producer, and soldier. In the *divided* or social state these functions are parceled out to individuals, each of whom aims to do his stint[6] of the joint work, whilst each other performs his. The fable implies that the individual, to possess himself, must sometimes return from his own labor to embrace all the other laborers. But, unfortunately, this original unit, this fountain of power, has been so distributed to multitudes, has been so minutely subdivided and peddled out, that it is spilled into drops, and cannot be gathered. The state of society is one in which the members have suffered amputation from the trunk and strut about so many walking monsters,—a good finger, a neck, a stomach, an elbow, but never a man.

Man is thus metamorphosed into a thing, into many things. The planter, who is Man sent out into the field to gather food, is seldom cheered by any idea of the true dignity of his ministry. He sees his bushel and his cart, and nothing beyond, and sinks into the farmer, instead of Man on the farm. The tradesman scarcely ever gives an ideal worth to his work, but is ridden[7] by the routine of his craft, and the soul is subject to dollars. The priest becomes a form; the attorney a statute-book; the mechanic a machine; the sailor a rope of the ship.

In this distribution of functions the scholar is the delegated intellect. In the right state he is *Man Thinking*. In the degenerate state, when the victim of society, he tends to become a mere thinker, or, still worse, the parrot of other men's thinking.

In this view of him, as Man Thinking, the whole theory of his office is contained. Him Nature solicits with all her placid, all her monitory pictures. [8] Him the past instructs. Him the future invites. Is not indeed every man a student, and do not all things exist for the student's behoof? And, finally, is not the true scholar the only true master? But as the old oracle said, "All things have two handles: Beware of the wrong one."[9] In life, too often, the scholar errs with mankind and forfeits his privilege. Let us see him in his school, and consider him in reference to the main influences he receives.

I. The first in time and the first in importance of the influences upon the mind is that of nature. Every day, the sun;[10] and, after sunset, Night and her stars. Ever the winds blow; ever the grass grows. Every day, men and women, conversing, beholding and beholden.[11] The scholar must needs stand wistful and admiring before this great spectacle. He must settle its value in his mind. What is nature to him? There is never a beginning, there is never an end, to the inexplicable continuity of this web of God, but always circular power returning into itself.[12] Therein it resembles his own spirit, whose beginning, whose ending, he never can find,—so entire, so boundless. Far too as her splendors shine, system on system shooting like rays, upward, downward, without center, without circumference,—in the mass and in the particle, Nature hastens to render account of herself to the mind. Classification begins. To the young mind everything is individual, stands by itself. By and by it finds how to join two things and see in them one nature; then three, then three thousand; and so, tyrannized over by its own unifying instinct, it goes on tying things together, diminishing anomalies, discovering roots running under ground whereby contrary and remote things cohere and flower out from one stem. It presently learns that since the dawn of history there has been a constant accumulation and classifying of facts. But what is classification but the perceiving that these objects are not chaotic, and are not foreign, but have a law which is also a law of the human mind? The astronomer discovers that geometry, a pure abstraction of the human mind, is the measure of planetary motion. The chemist finds proportions and intelligible method throughout matter; and science is nothing but the finding of analogy, identity, in the most remote parts. The ambitious soul sits down before each refractory fact; one after another reduces all strange constitutions, all new powers, to their class and their law, and goes on forever to animate the last fiber of organization, the outskirts of nature, by insight.

Thus to him, to this school-boy under the bending dome of day, is suggested that he and it proceed from one Root; one is leaf and one is flower; relation, sympathy, stirring in every vein. And what is that root? Is not that the soul of his soul?—A thought too bold?—A dream too wild? Yet when this spiritual light shall have revealed the law of more earthly natures,—when he has learned to worship the soul, and to see that the natural philosophy that now is, is only the first gropings of its gigantic hand,—he shall look forward to an ever-expanding knowledge as to a becoming creator.[13] He shall see that nature is the opposite of the soul, answering to it part for part. One is seal and one is print. Its beauty is the beauty of his own mind. Its laws are the laws of his own mind. Nature then becomes to him the measure of his attainments. So much of nature as he is ignorant of, so much of his own mind does he not yet possess. And, in fine, the ancient precept, "Know thyself,"[14] and the modern precept, "Study nature," become at last one maxim.

II. The next great influence into the spirit of the scholar is the mind of the Past,—in whatever form, whether of literature, of art, of institutions, that mind is inscribed. Books are the best type of the influence of the past, and perhaps we shall get at the truth,—learn the amount of this influence more conveniently,—by considering their value alone.

The theory of books is noble. The scholar of the first age received into him the world around; brooded thereon; gave it the new arrangement of his own mind, and uttered it again. It came into him life; it went out from him truth. It came to him short-lived actions; it went out from him immortal thoughts. It came to him business; it went from him poetry. It was dead fact; now, it is quick thought. It can stand, and it can go. It now endures, it now flies, it now inspires.[15] Precisely in proportion to the depth of mind from which it issued, so high does it soar, so long does it sing.

Or, I might say, it depends on how far the process had gone, of transmuting life into truth. In proportion to the completeness of the distillation, so will the purity and imperishableness of the product be. But none is quite perfect. As no air-pump can by any means make a perfect vacuum,[16] so neither can any artist entirely exclude the conventional, the local, the perishable from his book, or write a book of pure thought, that shall be as efficient, in all respects, to a remote posterity, as to contemporaries, or rather to the second age. Each age, it is found, must write its own books; or rather, each generation for the next succeeding. The books of an older period will not fit this.

Yet hence arises a grave mischief. The sacredness which attaches to the act of creation, the act of thought, is instantly transferred to the record. The poet chanting was felt to be a divine man. Henceforth the chant is divine also. The writer was a just and wise spirit. Henceforward it is settled the book is perfect; as love of the hero corrupts into worship of his statue. Instantly the book becomes noxious.[17] The guide is a tyrant. We sought a brother, and lo, a governor. The sluggish and perverted mind of the multitude, always slow to open to the incursions of Reason, having once so opened, having once received this book, stands upon it, and makes an outcry if it is disparaged. Colleges are built on it. Books are written on it by thinkers, not by Man Thinking, by men of talent, that is, who start wrong, who set out from accepted dogmas, not from their own sight of principles. Meek young men grow up in libraries, believing it their duty to accept the views which Cicero, which Locke,[18] which Bacon,[19] have given; forgetful that Cicero, Locke and Bacon were only young men in libraries when they wrote these books.

Hence, instead of Man Thinking, we have the bookworm. Hence the book-learned class, who value books, as such; not as related to nature and the human constitution, but as making a sort of Third Estate[20] with the world and soul. Hence the restorers of readings,[21] the emendators,[22] the bibliomaniacs[23] of all degrees. This is bad; this is worse than it seems.

Books are the best of things, well used; abused, among the worst. What is the right use? What is the one end which all means go to effect? They are for nothing but to inspire.[24] I had better never see a book than to be warped by its attraction clean out of my own orbit, and made a satellite instead of a system. The one thing in the world of value is the active soul,— the soul, free, sovereign, active. This every man is entitled to; this every man contains within him, although in almost all men obstructed, and as yet unborn. The soul active sees absolute truth and utters truth, or creates. In this action it is genius; not the privilege of here and there a favorite, but the sound estate of every man.[25] In its essence it is progressive. The book, the college, the school of art, the institution of any kind, stop with some past utterance of genius. This is good, say they,—let us hold by this. They pin me down.[26] They look backward and not forward. But genius always looks forward. The eyes of man are set in his forehead, not in his hindhead. Man hopes. Genius creates. To create,—to create,—is the proof of a divine presence. Whatever talents may be, if the man create not, the pure efflux of the Deity is not his;[27]—cinders and smoke there may be, but not yet flame. There are creative manners, there are creative actions, and creative words; manners, actions, words, that is, indicative of no custom or authority, but springing spontaneous from the mind's own sense of good and fair.

On the other part, instead of being its own seer, let it receive always from another mind its truth, though it were in torrents of light, without periods of solitude, inquest, and self-recovery; and a fatal disservice[28] is done. Genius is always sufficiently the enemy of genius by over-influence. [29] The literature of every nation bear me witness. The English dramatic poets have Shakespearized now for two hundred years.[30]

Undoubtedly there is a right way of reading, so it be sternly subordinated. Man Thinking must not be subdued by his instruments. Books are for the scholar's idle times. When he can read God directly, the hour is too precious to be wasted in other men's transcripts of their readings.[31] But when the intervals of darkness come, as come they must,—when the soul seeth not, when the sun is hid and the stars withdraw their shining,—we repair to the lamps which were kindled by their ray, to guide our steps to the East again, where the dawn is.[32] We hear, that we may speak. The Arabian proverb says, "A fig-tree, looking on a fig-tree, becometh fruitful."

It is remarkable, the character of the pleasure we derive from the best books. They impress us ever with the conviction that one nature wrote and the same reads. We read the verses of one of the great English poets, of Chaucer,[33] of Marvell,[34] of Dryden,[35] with the most modern joy,— with a pleasure, I mean, which is in great part caused by the abstraction of all *time* from their verses. There is some awe mixed with the joy of our surprise, when this poet, who lived in some past world, two or three hundred years ago, says that which lies close to my own soul, that which I also had well-nigh thought and said. But for the evidence thence afforded to the philosophical doctrine of the identity of all minds, we should suppose some pre-established harmony, some foresight of souls that were to be, and some preparation of stores for their future wants, like the fact observed in insects, who lay up food before death for the young grub they shall never see.

I would not be hurried by any love of system, by any exaggeration of instincts, to underrate the Book. We all know that as the human body can be nourished on any food, though it were boiled grass and the broth of shoes, so the human mind can be fed by any knowledge. And great and heroic men have existed who had almost no other information than by the printed page. I only would say that it needs a strong head to bear that diet. One must be an inventor to read well. As the proverb says, "He that would bring home the wealth of the Indies must carry out the wealth of the Indies." There is then creative reading as well as creative writing. When the mind is braced by labor and invention, the page of whatever book we read becomes luminous with manifold allusion. Every sentence is doubly significant, and the sense of our author is as broad as the world. We then see, what is always true, that as the seer's hour of vision is short and rare among heavy days and months, so is its record, perchance, the least part of his volume. The discerning will read, in his Plato[36] or Shakespeare, only that least part,— only the authentic utterances of the oracle;—all the rest he rejects, were it never so many times Plato's and Shakespeare's.

Of course there is a portion of reading quite indispensable to a wise man. History and exact science he must learn by laborious reading. Colleges, in like manner, have their indispensable office,—to teach elements. But they can only highly serve us when they aim not to drill, but to create; when they gather from far every ray of various genius to their hospitable halls, and by the concentrated fires set the hearts of their youth on flame. Thought and knowledge are natures in which apparatus and pretension avail nothing. Gowns[37] and pecuniary foundations,[38] though of towns of gold, can never countervail the least sentence or syllable of wit.[39] Forget this, and our American colleges will recede in their public importance, whilst they grow richer every year.

III. There goes in the world a notion that the scholar should be a recluse, a valetudinarian,[40]—as unfit for any handiwork or public labor as a penknife for an axe. The so-called "practical men" sneer at speculative men, as if, because they speculate or *see*, they could do nothing. I have heard it said that the clergy—who are always, more universally than any other class, the scholars of their day—are addressed as women; that the rough, spontaneous conversation of men they do not hear, but only a mincing[41] and diluted speech. They are often virtually disfranchised; and indeed there are advocates for their celibacy. As far as this is true of the studious classes, it is not just and wise. Action is with the scholar subordinate, but it is essential. Without it he is not yet man. Without it thought can never ripen into truth. Whilst the world hangs before the eye as a cloud of beauty, we cannot even see its beauty. Inaction is cowardice, but there can be no scholar without the heroic mind. The preamble[42] of thought, the transition through which it passes from the unconscious to the conscious, is action. Only so much do I know, as I have lived. Instantly we know whose words are loaded with life, and whose not.

The world—this shadow of the soul, or *other me*, lies wide around. Its attractions are the keys which unlock my thoughts and make me acquainted with myself. I launch eagerly into this resounding tumult. I grasp the hands of those next me, and take my place in the ring to suffer and to work, taught by an instinct that so shall the dumb abyss[43] be vocal with speech. I pierce its order; I dissipate its fear;[44] I dispose of it within the circuit of my expanding life. So much only of life as I know by experience, so much of the wilderness have I vanquished and planted, or so far have I extended my being, my dominion. I do not see how any man can afford, for the sake of his nerves and his nap, to spare any action in which he can partake. It is pearls and rubies to his discourse. Drudgery, calamity, exasperation, want, are instructors in eloquence and wisdom. The true scholar grudges every opportunity of action passed by, as a loss of power.

It is the raw material out of which the intellect molds her splendid products. A strange process too, this by which experience is converted into thought, as a mulberry-leaf is converted into satin.[45] The manufacture goes forward at all hours.

The actions and events of our childhood and youth are now matters of calmest observation. They lie like fair pictures in the air. Not so with our recent actions,—with the business which we now have in hand. On this we are quite unable to speculate. Our affections as yet circulate through it. We no more feel or know it than we feel the feet, or the hand, or the brain of our body. The new deed is yet a part of life,—remains for a time immersed in our unconscious life. In some contemplative hour it detaches itself from the life like a ripe fruit,[46] to become a thought of the mind. Instantly it is raised, transfigured; the corruptible has put on incorruption.[47] Henceforth it is an object of beauty, however base its origin and neighborhood. Observe, too, the impossibility of antedating this act. In its grub state it cannot fly, it cannot shine, it is a dull grub. But suddenly, without observation, the selfsame thing unfurls beautiful wings, and is an angel of wisdom. So is there no fact, no event, in our private history, which shall not, sooner or later, lose its adhesive, inert form, and astonish us by soaring from our body into the empyrean.[48] Cradle and infancy, school and playground, the fear of boys, and dogs, and ferules,[49] the love of little maids and berries, and many another fact that once filled the whole sky, are gone already; friend and relative, profession and party, town and country, nation and world, must also soar and sing.[50]

Of course, he who has put forth his total strength in fit actions has the richest return of wisdom. I will not shut myself out of this globe of action, and transplant an oak into a flower-pot, there to hunger and pine; nor trust the revenue of some single faculty, and exhaust one vein of thought, much like those Savoyards,[51] who, getting their livelihood by carving shepherds, shepherdesses, and smoking Dutchmen, for all Europe, went out one day to the mountain to find stock, and discovered that they had whittled up the last of their pine-trees. Authors we have, in numbers, who have written out their vein, and who, moved by a commendable prudence, sail for Greece or Palestine, follow the trapper into the prairie, or ramble round Algiers, to replenish their merchantable stock.

If it were only for a vocabulary, the scholar would be covetous of action. Life is our dictionary.[52] Years are well spent in country labors; in town; in the insight into trades and manufactures; in frank intercourse with many men and women; in science; in art; to the one end of mastering in all their facts a language by which to illustrate and embody our perceptions. I learn immediately from any speaker how much he has already lived, through the poverty or the splendor of his speech. Life lies behind us as the quarry from whence we get tiles and copestones for the masonry of to-day. This is the way to learn grammar. Colleges and books only copy the language which the field and the work-yard made.

But the final value of action, like that of books, and better than books, is that it is a resource. That great principle of Undulation in nature, that shows itself in the inspiring and expiring of the breath; in desire and satiety; in the ebb and flow of the sea; in day and night; in heat and cold; and, as yet more deeply ingrained in every atom and every fluid, is known to us under the name of Polarity,—these "fits of easy transmission and reflection," as Newton[53] called them, are the law of nature because they are the law of spirit.

The mind now thinks, now acts, and each fit reproduces the other. When the artist has exhausted his materials, when the fancy no longer paints, when thoughts are no longer apprehended and books are a weariness,—he has always the resource *to live*. Character is higher than intellect. Thinking is the function. Living is the functionary. The stream retreats to its source. A great soul will be strong to live, as well as strong to think. Does he lack organ or medium to impart his truth? He can still fall back on this elemental force of living them. This is a total act. Thinking is a partial act. Let the grandeur of justice shine in his affairs. Let the beauty of affection cheer his lowly roof. Those "far from fame," who dwell and act with him, will feel the force of his constitution in the doings and passages of the day better than it can be measured by any public and designed display. Time shall teach him that the scholar loses no hour which the man lives. Herein he unfolds the sacred germ of his instinct, screened from influence. What is lost in seemliness is gained in strength. Not out of those on whom systems of education have exhausted their culture comes the helpful giant to destroy the old or to build the new, but out of unhandselled[54] savage nature; out of terrible Druids[55] and Berserkers[56] come at last Alfred[57] and Shakespeare. I hear therefore with joy whatever is beginning to be said of the dignity and necessity of labor to every citizen. There is virtue yet in the hoe and the spade,[58] for learned as well as for unlearned hands. And labor is everywhere welcome; always we are invited to work; only be this limitation observed, that a man shall not for the sake of wider activity sacrifice any opinion to the popular judgments and modes of action.

I have now spoken of the education of the scholar by nature, by books, and by action. It remains to say somewhat of his duties.

They are such as become Man Thinking. They may all be comprised in self-trust. The office of the scholar is to cheer, to raise, and to guide men by showing them facts amidst appearances. He plies the slow, unhonored, and unpaid task of observation. Flamsteed[59] and Herschel,[60] in their glazed observatories, may catalogue the stars with the praise of all men, and, the results being splendid and useful, honor is sure. But he, in his private observatory, cataloguing obscure and nebulous[61] stars of the human mind, which as yet no man has thought of as such,—watching days and months sometimes for a few facts; correcting still his old records,—must relinquish display and immediate fame. In the long period of his preparation he must betray often an ignorance and shiftlessness in popular arts, incurring the disdain of the able who shoulder him aside. Long he must stammer in his speech; often forego the living for the dead. Worse yet, he must accept— how often!—poverty and solitude. For the ease and pleasure of treading the old road, accepting the fashions, the education, the religion of society, he takes the cross of making his own, and, of course, the self-accusation, the faint heart, the frequent uncertainty and loss of time, which are the nettles and tangling vines in the way of the self-relying and self-directed; and the state of virtual hostility in which he seems to stand to society, and especially to educated society. For all this loss and scorn, what offset? He is to find consolation in exercising the highest functions of human nature. He is one who raises himself from private considerations and breathes and lives on public and illustrious thoughts. He is the world's eye. He is the world's heart. He is to resist the vulgar prosperity that retrogrades ever to barbarism, by preserving and communicating heroic sentiments, noble biographies, melodious verse, and the conclusions of history. Whatsoever oracles the human heart, in all emergencies, in all solemn hours, has uttered as its commentary on the world of actions,—these he shall receive and impart. And whatsoever new verdict Reason from her inviolable seat pronounces on the passing men and events of to-day,—this he shall hear and promulgate.

These being his functions, it becomes him to feel all confidence in himself, and to defer never to the popular cry. He and he only knows the world. The world of any moment is the merest appearance. Some great decorum, some fetich[62] of a government, some ephemeral trade, or war, or man, is cried up[63] by half mankind and cried down by the other half, as if all depended on this particular up or down. The odds are that the whole question is not worth the poorest thought which the scholar has lost in listening to the controversy. Let him not quit his belief that a popgun is a popgun, though the ancient and honorable[64] of the earth affirm it to be the crack of doom. In silence, in steadiness, in severe abstraction, let him hold by himself; add observation to observation, patient of neglect, patient of reproach, and bide his own time,—happy enough if he can satisfy himself alone that this day he has seen something truly. Success treads on every right step. For the instinct is sure that prompts him to tell his brother what he thinks. He then learns that in going down into the secrets of his own mind he has descended into the secrets of all minds. He learns that he who has mastered any law in his private thoughts is master to that extent of all men whose language he speaks, and of all into whose language his own can be translated. The poet, in utter solitude remembering his spontaneous thoughts and recording them, is found to have recorded that which men in cities vast find true for them also. The orator distrusts at first the fitness of his frank confessions, his want of knowledge of the persons he addresses, until he finds that he is the complement[65] of his hearers;—that they drink his words because he fulfills for them their own nature; the deeper he dives into his privatest, secretest presentiment, to his wonder he finds this is the most acceptable, most public and universally true. The people delight in it; the better part of every man feels—This is my music; this is myself.

In self-trust all the virtues are comprehended. Free should the scholar be,—free and brave. Free even to the definition of freedom, "without any hindrance that does not arise out of his own constitution." Brave; for fear is a thing which a scholar by his very function puts behind him. Fear always springs from ignorance. It is a shame to him if his tranquility, amid dangerous times, arise from the presumption that like children and women his is a protected class; or if he seek a temporary peace by the diversion of his thoughts from politics or vexed questions, hiding his head like an ostrich in the flowering bushes, peeping into microscopes, and turning rhymes, as a boy whistles to keep his courage up. So is the danger a danger still; so is the fear worse. Manlike let him turn and face it. Let him look into its eye and search its nature, inspect its origin,—see the whelping of this lion,—which lies no great way back; he will then find in himself a perfect comprehension of its nature and extent; he will have made his hands meet on the other side, and can henceforth defy it and pass on superior. The world is his who can see through its pretension. What deafness, what stone-blind custom, what overgrown error you behold is there only by sufferance,—by your sufferance. See it to be a lie, and you have already dealt it its mortal blow.

Yes, we are the cowed,—we the trustless. It is a mischievous notion that we are come late into nature; that the world was finished a long time ago. As the world was plastic and fluid in the hands of God, so it is ever to so much of his attributes as we bring to it. To ignorance and sin it is flint. They adapt themselves to it as they may; but in proportion as a man has any thing in him divine, the firmament flows before him and takes his signet[66] and form. Not he is great who can alter matter, but he who can alter my state of mind. They are the kings of the world who give the color of their present thought to all nature and all art, and persuade men, by the cheerful serenity of their carrying the matter, that this thing which they do is the apple which the ages have desired to pluck, now at last ripe, and inviting nations to the harvest. The great man makes the great thing. Wherever Macdonald[67] sits, there is the head of the table. Linnæus[68] makes botany the most alluring of studies, and wins it from the farmer and the herb-woman: Davy,[69] chemistry; and Cuvier,[70] fossils. The day is always his who works in it with serenity and great aims. The unstable estimates of men crowd to him whose mind is filled with a truth, as the heaped waves of the Atlantic follow the moon.[71]

For this self-trust, the reason is deeper than can be fathomed,—darker than can be enlightened. I might not carry with me the feeling of my audience in stating my own belief. But I have already shown the ground of my hope, in adverting to the doctrine that man is one. I believe man has been wronged; he has wronged himself. He has almost lost the light that can lead him back to his prerogatives. Men are become of no account. Men in history, men in the world of to-day, are bugs, are spawn, and are called "the mass" and "the herd." In a century, in a millenium, one or two men;[72] that is to say, one or two approximations to the right state of every man. All the rest behold in the hero or the poet their own green and crude being,—ripened; yes, and are content to be less, so *that* may attain to its full stature. What a testimony, full of grandeur, full of pity, is borne to the demands of his own nature, by the poor clansman, the poor partisan, who rejoices in the glory of his chief! The poor and the low find some amends to their immense moral capacity, for their acquiescence in a political and social inferiority.[73] They are content to be brushed like flies from the path of a great person, so that justice shall be done by him to that common nature which it is the dearest desire of all to see enlarged and glorified. They sun themselves in the great man's light, and feel it to be their own element. They cast the dignity of man from their downtrod selves upon the shoulders of a hero, and will perish to add one drop of blood to make that great heart beat, those giant sinews combat and conquer. He lives for us, and we live in him.

Men such as they[74] are very naturally seek money or power; and power because it is as good as money,—the "spoils," so called, "of office." And why not? For they aspire to the highest, and this, in their sleep-walking, they dream is highest. Wake them and they shall quit the false good and leap to the true, and leave governments to clerks and desks. This revolution is to be wrought by the gradual domestication of the idea of Culture. The main enterprise of the world for splendor, for extent, is the upbuilding of a man. Here are the materials strewn along the ground. The private life of one man shall be a more illustrious monarchy, more formidable to its enemy, more sweet and serene in its influence to its friend, than any kingdom in history. For a man, rightly viewed, comprehendeth[75] the particular natures of all men. Each philosopher, each bard, each actor has only done for me, as by a delegate, what one day I can do for myself. The books which once we valued more than the apple of the eye, we have quite exhausted. What is that but saying that we have come up with the point of view which the universal mind took through the eyes of one scribe; we have been that man, and have passed on. First, one, then another, we drain all cisterns, and waxing greater by all these supplies, we crave a better and a more abundant food. The man has never lived that can feed us ever. The human mind cannot be enshrined in a person who shall set a barrier on any one side to this unbounded, unboundable empire. It is one central fire, which, flaming now out of the lips of Etna, lightens the capes of Sicily, and now out of the throat of Vesuvius, illuminates the towers and vineyards of Naples. It is one light which beams out of a thousand stars. It is one soul which animates all men.

But I have dwelt perhaps tediously upon this abstraction of the Scholar. I ought not to delay longer to add what I have to say of nearer reference to the time and to this country.

Historically, there is thought to be a difference in the ideas which predominate over successive epochs, and there are data for marking the genius of the Classic, of the Romantic, and now of the Reflective or Philosophical age.[76] With the views I have intimated of the oneness or the identity of the mind through all individuals, I do not much dwell on these differences. In fact, I believe each individual passes through all three. The boy is a Greek; the youth, romantic; the adult, reflective. I deny not, however, that a revolution in the leading idea may be distinctly enough traced.

Our age is bewailed as the age of Introversion.[77] Must that needs be evil? We, it seems, are critical. We are embarrassed with second thoughts. [78] We cannot enjoy anything for hankering to know whereof the pleasure consists. We are lined with eyes. We see with our feet. The time is infected with Hamlet's unhappiness,—

"Sicklied o'er with the pale cast of thought."[79]

Is it so bad then? Sight is the last thing to be pitied. Would we be blind? Do we fear lest we should outsee nature and God, and drink truth dry? I look upon the discontent of the literary class as a mere announcement of the fact that they find themselves not in the state of mind of their fathers, and regret the coming state as untried; as a boy dreads the water before he has learned that he can swim. If there is any period one would desire to be born in, is it not the age of Revolution; when the old and the new stand side by side and admit of being compared; when the energies of all men are searched by fear and by hope; when the historic glories of the old can be compensated by the rich possibilities of the new era? This time, like all times, is a very good one, if we but know what to do with it.

I read with some joy of the auspicious signs of the coming days, as they glimmer already through poetry and art, through philosophy and science, through church and state.

One of these signs is the fact that the same movement[80] which effected the elevation of what was called the lowest class in the state assumed in literature a very marked and as benign an aspect. Instead of the sublime and beautiful, the near, the low, the common, was explored and poetized. That which had been negligently trodden under foot by those who were harnessing and provisioning themselves for long journeys into far countries, is suddenly found to be richer than all foreign parts. The literature of the poor, the feelings of the child, the philosophy of the street, the meaning of household life, are the topics of the time. It is a great stride. It is a sign—is it not?—of new vigor when the extremities are made active, when currents of warm life run into the hands and the feet. I ask not for the great, the remote, the romantic; what is doing in Italy or Arabia; what is Greek art, or Provençal minstrelsy; I embrace the common, I explore and sit at the feet of the familiar, the low. Give me insight into to-day, and you may have the antique and future worlds. What would we really know the meaning of? The meal in the firkin; the milk in the pan; the ballad in the street; the news of the boat; the glance of the eye; the form and the gait of the body;—show me the ultimate reason of these matters; show me the sublime presence of the highest spiritual cause lurking, as always it does lurk, in these suburbs and extremities of nature; let me see every trifle bristling with the polarity that ranges it instantly on an eternal law;[81] and the shop, the plow, and the ledger referred to the like cause by which light undulates and poets sing;—and the world lies no longer a dull miscellany and lumber-room, but has form and order: there is no trifle, there is no puzzle, but one design unites and animates the farthest pinnacle and the lowest trench.

This idea has inspired the genius of Goldsmith,[82] Burns,[83] Cowper,[84] and, in a newer time, of Goethe,[85] Wordsworth,[86] and Carlyle.[87] This idea they have differently followed and with various success. In contrast with their writing, the style of Pope,[88] of Johnson,[89] of Gibbon,[90] looks cold and pedantic. This writing is blood-warm. Man is surprised to find that things near are not less beautiful and wondrous than things remote. The near explains the far. The drop is a small ocean. A man is related to all nature. This perception of the worth of the vulgar is fruitful in discoveries. Goethe, in this very thing the most modern of the moderns, has shown us, as none ever did, the genius of the ancients.

There is one man of genius who has done much for this philosophy of life, whose literary value has never yet been rightly estimated:—I mean Emanuel Swedenborg.[91] The most imaginative of men, yet writing with the precision of a mathematician, he endeavored to engraft a purely philosophical Ethics on the popular Christianity of his time. Such an attempt of course must have difficulty which no genius could surmount. But he saw and showed the connexion between nature and the affections of the soul. He pierced the emblematic or spiritual character of the visible, audible, tangible world. Especially did his shade-loving muse hover over and interpret the lower parts of nature; he showed the mysterious bond that allies moral evil to the foul material forms, and has given in epical parables a theory of insanity, of beasts, of unclean and fearful things.

Another sign of our times, also marked by an analogous political movement, is the new importance given to the single person. Everything that tends to insulate the individual—to surround him with barriers of natural respect, so that each man shall feel the world is his, and man shall treat with man as a sovereign state with a sovereign state—tends to true union as well as greatness. "I learned," said the melancholy Pestalozzi,[92] "that no man in God's wide earth is either willing or able to help any other man." Help must come from the bosom alone. The scholar is that man who must take up into himself all the ability of the time, all the contributions of the past, all the hopes of the future. He must be an university of knowledges. If there be one lesson more than another that should pierce his ear, it is—The world is nothing, the man is all; in yourself is the law of all nature, and you know not yet how a globule of sap ascends; in yourself slumbers the whole of Reason; it is for you to know all; it is for you to dare all. Mr. President and Gentlemen, this confidence in the unsearched might of man belongs, by all motives, by all prophecy, by all preparation, to the American Scholar. We have listened too long to the courtly muses of Europe. The spirit of the American freeman is already suspected to be timid, imitative, tame. Public and private avarice make the air we breathe thick and fat. The scholar is decent, indolent, complaisant. See already the tragic consequence. The mind of this country, taught to aim at low objects, eats upon itself. There is no work for any one but the decorous and the complaisant. Young men of the fairest promise, who begin life upon our shores, inflated by the mountain winds, shined upon by all the stars of God, find the earth below not in unison with these, but are hindered from action by the disgust which the principles on which business is managed inspire, and turn drudges, or die of disgust, some of them suicides. What is the remedy? They did not yet see, and thousands of young men as hopeful now crowding to the barriers for the career do not yet see, that if the single man plant himself indomitably on his instincts, and there abide, the huge world will come round to him.

Patience,—patience; with the shades of all the good and great for company; and for solace the perspective of your own infinite life; and for work the study and the communication of principles, the making those instincts prevalent, the conversion of the world. Is it not the chief disgrace in the world, not to be an unit; not to be reckoned one character; not to yield that peculiar fruit which each man was created to bear, but to be reckoned in the gross, in the hundred, or the thousand, of the party, the section, to which we belong; and our opinion predicted geographically, as the north, or the south? Not so, brothers and friends,—please God, ours shall not be so. We will walk on our own feet; we will work with our own hands; we will speak our own minds. Then shall man be no longer a name for pity, for doubt, and for sensual indulgence. The dread of man and the love of man shall be a wall of defense and a wreath of joy around all. A nation of men will for the first time exist, because each believes himself inspired by the Divine Soul which also inspires all men.

COMPENSATION[93]

The wings of Time are black and white,
Pied with morning and with night.
Mountain tall and ocean deep
Trembling balance duly keep.
In changing moon, in tidal wave,
Glows the feud of Want and Have.
Gauge of more and less through
space Electric star and pencil plays.
The lonely Earth amid the balls
That hurry through the eternal halls,
A makeweight flying to the void,
Supplemental asteroid,
Or compensatory spark,
Shoots across the neutral Dark.

Man's the elm, and Wealth the vine,
Stanch and strong the tendrils twine;
Through the frail ringlets thee deceive,
None from its stock that vine can reave.
Fear not, then, thou child infirm,
There's no god dare wrong a worm.
Laurel crowns cleave to deserts,
And power to him who power exerts;
Hast not thy share? On winged feet,
Lo! it rushes thee to meet;
And all that Nature made thy own,
Floating in air or pent in stone,
Will rive the hills and swim the sea,
And, like thy shadow, follow thee.

Ever since I was a boy, I have wished to write a discourse on
Compensation: for it seemed to me when very young, that on this subject
life was ahead of theology, and the people knew more than the preachers
taught. The documents,[94] too, from which the doctrine is to be drawn,
charmed my fancy by their endless variety, and lay always before me,

even in sleep; for they are the tools in our hands, the bread in our basket, the transactions of the street, the farm, and the dwelling-house, greetings, relations, debts and credits, the influence of character, the nature and endowment of all men. It seemed to me, also, that in it might be shown men a ray of divinity, the present action of the soul of this world, clean from all vestige of tradition, and so the heart of man might be bathed by an inundation of eternal love, conversing with that which he knows was always and always must be, because it really is now. It appeared, moreover, that if this doctrine could be stated in terms with any resemblance to those bright intuitions in which this truth is sometimes revealed to us, it would be a star in many dark hours and crooked passages in our journey that would not suffer us to lose our way.

I was lately confirmed in these desires by hearing a sermon at church. The preacher, a man esteemed for his orthodoxy, unfolded in the ordinary manner the doctrine of the Last Judgment. He assumed that judgment is not executed in this world; that the wicked are successful; that the good are miserable;[95] and then urged from reason and from Scripture a compensation to be made to both parties in the next life. No offense appeared to be taken by the congregation at this doctrine. As far as I could observe, when the meeting broke up, they separated without remark on the sermon.

Yet what was the import of this teaching? What did the preacher mean by saying that the good are miserable in the present life? Was it that houses and lands, offices, wine, horses, dress, luxury, are had by unprincipled men, whilst the saints are poor and despised; and that a compensation is to be made to these last hereafter, by giving them the like gratifications another day,—bank stock and doubloons,[96] venison and champagne? This must be the compensation intended; for what else? Is it that they are to have leave to pray and praise? to love and serve men? Why, that they can do now. The legitimate inference the disciple would draw was: "We are to have *such* a good time as the sinners have now"; or, to push it to its extreme import: "You sin now; we shall sin by and by; we would sin now, if we could; not being successful, we expect our revenue to-morrow."

The fallacy lay in the immense concession that the bad are successful; that justice is not done now. The blindness of the preacher consisted in deferring to the base estimate of the market of what constitutes a manly success, instead of confronting and convicting the world from the truth; announcing the presence of the soul; the omnipotence of the will: and so establishing the standard of good and ill, of success and falsehood.

I find a similar base tone in the popular religious works of the day, and the same doctrines assumed by the literary men when occasionally they treat the related topics. I think that our popular theology has gained in decorum, and not in principle, over the superstitions it has displaced. But men are better than this theology. Their daily life gives it the lie. Every ingenuous and aspiring soul leaves the doctrine behind him in his own experience; and all men feel sometimes the falsehood which they cannot demonstrate. For men are wiser than they know. That which they hear in schools and pulpits without afterthought, if said in conversation, would probably be questioned in silence. If a man dogmatize in a mixed company on Providence and the divine laws, he is answered by a silence which conveys well enough to an observer the dissatisfaction of the hearer, but his incapacity to make his own statement.

I shall attempt in this and the following chapter to record some facts that indicate the path of the law of Compensation; happy beyond my expectation, if I shall truly draw the smallest arc of this circle.

Polarity,[97] or action and reaction, we meet in every part of nature; in darkness and light; in heat and cold; in the ebb and flow of waters; in male and female; in the inspiration and expiration of plants and animals; in the equation of quantity and quality in the fluids of the animal body; in the systole and diastole[98] of the heart; in the undulations of fluids, and of sound; in the centrifugal and centripetal gravity; in electricity, galvanism, and chemical affinity. Superinduce magnetism at one end of a needle; the opposite magnetism takes place at the other end. If the south attracts, the north repels. To empty here, you must condense there. An inevitable dualism bisects nature, so that each thing is a half, and suggests another thing to make it whole; as, spirit, matter; man, woman; odd, even; subjective, objective; in, out; upper, under; motion, rest; yea, nay.

Whilst the world is thus dual, so is everyone of its parts. The entire system of things gets represented in every particle. There is somewhat that resembles the ebb and flow of the sea, day and night, man and woman, in a single needle of the pine, in a kernel of corn, in each individual of every animal tribe. The reaction, so grand in the elements, is repeated within these small boundaries. For example, in the animal kingdom the physiologist has observed that no creatures are favorites, but a certain compensation balances every gift and every defect. A surplusage given to one part is paid out of a reduction from another part of the same creature. If the head and neck are enlarged, the trunk and extremities are cut short.

The theory of the mechanic forces is another example. What we gain in power is lost in time; and the converse. The periodic or compensating errors of the planets is another instance. The influences of climate and soil in political history is another. The cold climate invigorates. The barren soil does not breed fevers, crocodiles, tigers, or scorpions.

The same dualism underlies the nature and condition of man. Every excess causes a defect; every defect an excess. Every sweet hath its sour; every evil its good. Every faculty which is a receiver of pleasure has an equal penalty put on its abuse. It is to answer for its moderation with its life. For every grain of wit there is a grain of folly. For everything you have missed, you have gained something else; and for everything you gain, you lose something. If riches increase, they are increased[99] that use them. If the gatherer gathers too much, nature takes out of the man what she puts into his chest, swells the estate, but kills the owner. Nature hates monopolies and exceptions. The waves of the sea do not more speedily seek a level from their loftiest tossing, than the varieties of condition tend to equalize themselves. There is always some leveling circumstance that puts down the overbearing, the strong, the rich, the fortunate, substantially on the same ground with all others. Is a man too strong and fierce for society, and by temper and position a bad citizen,—a morose ruffian, with a dash of the pirate in him;—nature sends him a troop of pretty sons and daughters, who are getting along in the dame's classes at the village school, and love and fear for them smooths his grim scowl to courtesy. Thus she contrives to intenerate[100] the granite and felspar, takes the boar out and puts the lamb in, and keeps her balance true.

The farmer imagines power and place are fine things. But the President has paid dear for his White House.[101] It has commonly cost him all his peace, and the best of his many attributes. To preserve for a short time so conspicuous an appearance before the world, he is content to eat dust[102] before the real masters who stand erect behind the throne. Or, do men desire the more substantial and permanent grandeur of genius? Neither has this an immunity. He who by force of will or of thought, is great, and overlooks[103] thousands, has the charges of that eminence. With every influx of light comes new danger. Has he light? he must bear witness to the light, and always outrun that sympathy which gives him such keen satisfaction, by his fidelity to new revelations of the incessant soul. He must hate father and mother, wife and child. Has he all that the world loves and admires and covets?—he must cast behind him their admiration, and afflict them by faithfulness to his truth, and become a by-word and a hissing.

This law writes the laws of cities and nations. It is in vain to build or plot or combine against it. Things refuse to be mismanaged long. *Res nolunt diu male administrari.* [104] Though no checks to a new evil appear, the checks exist, and will appear. If the government is cruel, the governor's life is not safe. If you tax too high, the revenue will yield nothing. If you make the criminal code sanguinary, juries will not convict. If the law is too mild, private vengeance comes in. If the government is a terrific democracy, the pressure is resisted by an overcharge of energy in the citizen, and life glows with a fiercer flame. The true life and satisfactions of man seem to elude the utmost rigors or felicities of condition, and to establish themselves with great indifferency under all varieties of circumstances. Under all governments the influence of character remains the same, — in Turkey and in New England about alike. Under the primeval despots of Egypt, history honestly confesses that man must have been as free as culture could make him.

These appearances indicate the fact that the universe is represented in everyone of its particles. Everything in nature contains all the powers of nature. Everything is made of one hidden stuff; as the naturalist sees one type under every metamorphosis, and regards a horse as a running man, a fish as a swimming man, a bird as a flying man, a tree as a rooted man. Each new form repeats not only the main character of the type, but part for part all the details, all the aims, furtherances, hindrances, energies, and whole system of every other. Every occupation, trade, art, transaction, is a compend of the world and a correlative of every other. Each one is an entire emblem of human life; of its good and ill, its trials, its enemies, its course and its end. And each one must somehow accommodate the whole man, and recite all his destiny.

The world globes itself in a drop of dew.[105] The microscope cannot find the animalcule which is less perfect for being little.[106] Eyes, ears, taste, smell, motion, resistance, appetite, and organs of reproduction that take hold on eternity, — all find room to consist in the small creature. So do we put our life into every act. The true doctrine of omnipresence is, that God reappears with all his parts in every moss and cobweb.[107] The value of the universe contrives to throw itself into every point. If the good is there, so is the evil; if the affinity, so the repulsion; if the force, so the limitation.

Thus is the universe alive. All things are moral. That soul, which within us is a sentiment, outside of us is a law. We feel its inspiration; out there in history we can see its fatal strength. "It is in the world, and the world was made by it." Justice is not postponed. A perfect equity adjusts its balance in all parts of life. Οἱ κύβοι Διὸς ἀεὶ εὐπίπτουσι ,[108] — the dice of God are always loaded. The world looks like a multiplication table, or a mathematical equation, which, turn it how you will, balances itself. Take what figure you will, its exact value, nor more nor less, still returns to you. Every secret is told, every crime is punished, every virtue rewarded, every wrong redressed, in silence and certainty. What we call retribution is the universal necessity by which the whole appears wherever a part appears. If you see smoke, there must be fire. If you see a hand or limb, you know that the trunk to which it belongs is there behind.

Every act rewards itself, or, in other words, integrates itself, in a twofold manner; first, in the thing, or in real nature; and secondly, in the circumstance, or in apparent nature. Men call the circumstance the retribution. The causal retribution is in the thing, and is seen by the soul. The retribution in the circumstance is seen by the understanding; it is inseparable from the thing, but is often spread over a long time, and so does not become distinct until after many years. The specific stripes may follow late after the offense, but they follow because they accompany it. Crime and punishment grow out of one stem. Punishment is a fruit that unsuspected ripens within the flower of the pleasure which concealed it. Cause and effect, means and ends, seed and fruit, cannot be severed; for the effect already blooms in the cause, the end preëxists in the means, the fruit in the seed.

Whilst thus the world will be whole, and refuses to be disparted, we seek to act partially, to sunder, to appropriate; for example, — to gratify the senses, we sever the pleasure of the senses from the needs of the character. The ingenuity of man has always been dedicated to the solution of one problem, — how to detach the sensual sweet, the sensual strong, the sensual bright, etc., from the moral sweet, the moral deep, the moral fair; that is, again, to contrive to cut clean off this upper surface so thin as to leave it bottomless; to get a *one end*, without an *other end*. The soul says, Eat; the body would feast. The soul says, The man and woman shall be one flesh and one soul; the body would join the flesh only. The soul says, Have dominion over all things to the ends of virtue; the body would have the power over things to its own ends.

The soul strives amain[109] to live and work through all things. It would be the only fact. All things shall be added unto it, — power, pleasure, knowledge, beauty. The particular man aims to be somebody; to set up for himself; to truck and higgle for a private good; and, in particulars, to ride, that he may ride; to dress, that he may be dressed; to eat, that he may eat; and to govern, that he may be seen. Men seek to be great; they would have offices, wealth, power, and fame. They think that to be great is to possess one side of nature, — the sweet, without the other side, — the bitter.

This dividing and detaching is steadily counteracted. Up to this day, it must be owned, no projector has had the smallest success. The parted water reunites behind our hand. Pleasure is taken out of pleasant things, profit out of profitable things, power out of strong things, as soon as we seek to separate them from the whole. We can no more have things and get the sensual good, by itself, than we can get an inside that shall have no outside, or a light without a shadow. "Drive out nature with a fork, she comes running back."[110]

Life invests itself with inevitable conditions, which the unwise seek to dodge, which one and another brags that he does not know; that they do not touch him;—but the brag is on his lips, the conditions are in his soul. If he escapes them in one part, they attack him in another more vital part. If he has escaped them in form, and in the appearance, it is because he has resisted his life, and fled from himself, and the retribution is so much death. So signal is the failure of all attempts to make this separation of the good from the tax, that the experiment would not be tried,—since to try it is to be mad,—but for the circumstance, that when the disease began in the will, of rebellion and separation, the intellect is at once infected, so that the man ceases to see God whole in each object, but is able to see the sensual allurement of an object, and not see the sensual hurt; he sees the mermaid's head, but not the dragon's tail; and thinks he can cut off that which he would have, from that which he would not have. "How secret art thou who dwellest in the highest heavens in silence, O thou only great God, sprinkling with an unwearied Providence certain penal blindnesses upon such as have unbridled desires!"[111]

The human soul is true to these facts in the painting of fable, of history, of law, of proverbs, of conversation. It finds a tongue in literature unawares. Thus the Greeks called Jupiter,[112] Supreme Mind; but having traditionally ascribed to him many base actions, they involuntarily made amends to reason, by tying up the hands[113] of so bad a god. He is made as helpless as a king of England.[114] Prometheus[115] knows one secret which Jove must bargain for; Minerva,[116] another. He cannot get his own thunders; Minerva keeps the key of them.

"Of all the gods, I only know the keys
That ope the solid doors within whose
vaults His thunders sleep."

A plain confession of the in-working of the All, and of its moral aim. The Indian mythology ends in the same ethics; and it would seem impossible for any fable to be invented to get any currency which was not moral. Aurora[117] forgot to ask youth for her lover, and though Tithonus is immortal, he is old, Achilles[118] is not quite invulnerable; the sacred waters did not wash the heel by which Thetis held him. Siegfried,[119] in the Niebelungen, is not quite immortal, for a leaf fell on his back whilst he was bathing in the dragon's blood, and that spot which it covered is mortal. And so it must be. There is a crack in everything God has made. It would seem, there is always this vindictive circumstance stealing in at unawares, even into the wild poesy in which the human fancy attempted to make bold holiday, and to shake itself free of the old laws,—this back-stroke, this kick of the gun, certifying that the law is fatal; that in nature nothing can be given, all things are sold.

This is that ancient doctrine of Nemesis,[120] who keeps watch in the universe, and lets no offense go unchastised. The Furies,[121] they said, are attendants on justice, and if the sun in heaven should transgress his path, they would punish him. The poets related that stone walls, and iron swords, and leathern thongs had an occult sympathy with the wrongs of their owners; that the belt which Ajax gave Hector[122] dragged the Trojan hero over the field at the wheels of the car of Achilles, and the sword which Hector gave Ajax was that on whose point Ajax fell. They recorded, that when the Thasians[123] erected a statue to Theagenes, a victor in the games, one of his rivals went to it by night, and endeavored to throw it down by repeated blows, until at last he moved it from its pedestal, and was crushed to death beneath its fall.

This voice of fable has in it somewhat divine. It came from thought above the will of the writer. That is the best part of each writer, which has nothing private in it;[124] that which he does not know, that which flowed out of his constitution, and not from his too active invention; that which in the study of a single artist you might not easily find, but in the study of many, you would abstract as the spirit of them all. Phidias it is not, but the work of man in that early Hellenic[125] world, that I would know. The name and circumstance of Phidias, however convenient for history, embarrass when we come to the highest criticism. We are to see that which man was tending to do in a given period, and was hindered, or, if you will, modified in doing, by the interfering volitions of Phidias, of Dante, of Shakespeare, the organ whereby man at the moment wrought.

Still more striking is the expression of this fact in the proverbs of all nations, which are always the literature of reason, or the statements of an absolute truth, without qualification. Proverbs, like the sacred books of each nation, are the sanctuary of the intuitions. That which the droning world, chained to appearances, will not allow the realist to say in his own words, it will suffer him to say in proverbs without contradiction. And this law of laws which the pulpit, the senate, and the college deny, is hourly preached in all markets and workshops by flights of proverbs, whose teaching is as true and as omnipresent as that of birds and flies.

All things are double, one against another.—Tit for tat;[126] an eye for an eye; a tooth for a tooth; blood for blood; measure for measure; love for love.—Give and it shall be given you.—He that watereth shall be watered himself.—What will you have? quoth God; pay for it and take it.—Nothing venture, nothing have.—Thou shalt be paid exactly for what thou hast done, no more, no less.—Who doth not work shall not eat.—Harm watch, harm catch.—Curses always recoil on the head of him who imprecates them.— If you put a chain around the neck of a slave, the other end fastens itself around your own.—Bad counsel confounds the adviser.—The Devil is an ass.

It is thus written, because it is thus in life. Our action is overmastered and characterized above our will by the law of nature. We aim at a petty end quite aside from the public good, but our act arranges itself by irresistible magnetism in a line with the poles of the world.

A man cannot speak but he judges himself. With his will, or against his will, he draws his portrait to the eye of his companions by every word. Every opinion reacts on him who utters it. It is a thread-ball thrown at a mark, but the other end remains in the thrower's bag. Or, rather, it is a harpoon hurled at the whale, unwinding, as it flies, a coil of cord in the boat, and if the harpoon is not good, or not well thrown, it will go nigh to cut the steersman in twain, or to sink the boat.

You cannot do wrong without suffering wrong. "No man had ever a point of pride that was not injurious to him," said Burke.[127] The exclusive in fashionable life does not see that he excludes himself from enjoyment in the attempt to appropriate it. The exclusionist in religion does not see that he shuts the door of heaven on himself, in striving to shut out others. Treat men as pawns[128] and ninepins, and you shall suffer as well as they. If you leave out their heart, you shall lose your own. The senses would make things of all persons; of women, of children, of the poor. The vulgar proverb, "I will get it from his purse or get it from his skin," is sound philosophy.

All infractions of love and equity in our social relations are speedily punished. They are punished by fear. Whilst I stand in simple relations to my fellow-man, I have no displeasure in meeting him. We meet as water meets water, or as two currents of air mix, with perfect diffusion and interpenetration of nature. But as soon as there is any departure from simplicity, and attempt at halfness, or good for me that is not good for him, my neighbor feels the wrong; he shrinks from me as far as I have shrunk from him; his eyes no longer seek mine; there is war between us; there is hate in him and fear in me.

All the old abuses in society, universal and particular, all unjust accumulations of property and power, are avenged in the same manner. Fear is an instructor of great sagacity, and the herald of all revolutions. One thing he teaches, that there is rottenness where he appears. He is a carrion crow, and though you see not well what he hovers for, there is death somewhere. Our property is timid, our laws are timid, our cultivated classes are timid. Fear for ages has boded and mowed and gibbered over government and property. That obscene[129] bird is not there for nothing. He indicates great wrongs which must be revised.

Of the like nature is that expectation of change which instantly follows the suspension of our voluntary activity. The terror of cloudless noon, the emerald of Polycrates,[130] the awe of prosperity, the instinct which leads every generous soul to impose on itself tasks of a noble asceticism and vicarious virtue, are the tremblings of the balance of justice through the heart and mind of man.

Experienced men of the world know very well that it is best to pay scot and lot[131] as they go along, and that a man often pays dear for a small frugality. The borrower runs in his own debt. Has a man gained anything who has received a hundred favors and rendered none? Has he gained by borrowing, through indolence or cunning, his neighbor's wares, or horses, or money? There arises on the deed the instant acknowledgment of benefit on the one part, and of debt on the other; that is, of superiority and inferiority. The transaction remains in the memory of himself and his neighbor; and every new transaction alters, according to its nature, their relation to each other. He may soon come to see that he had better have broken his own bones than to have ridden in his neighbor's coach, and that "the highest price he can pay for a thing is to ask for it."

A wise man will extend this lesson to all parts of life, and know that it is the part of prudence to face every claimant, and pay every just demand on your time, your talents, or your heart. Always pay; for, first or last, you must pay your entire debt. Persons and events may stand for a time between you and justice, but it is only a postponement. You must pay at last your own debt. If you are wise, you will dread a prosperity which only loads you with more. Benefit is the end of nature. But for every benefit which you receive, a tax is levied. He is great who confers the most benefits. He is base—and that is the one base thing in the universe—to receive favors and render none. In the order of nature we cannot render benefits to those from whom we receive them, or only seldom.[132] But the benefit we receive must be rendered again, line for line, deed for deed, cent for cent, to somebody. Beware of too much good staying in your hand. It will fast corrupt and worm worms.[133] Pay it away quickly in some sort.

Labor is watched over by the same pitiless laws. Cheapest, say the prudent, is the dearest labor. What we buy in a broom, a mat, a wagon, a knife, is some application of good sense to a common want. It is best to pay in your land a skillful gardener, or to buy good sense applied to gardening; in your sailor, good sense applied to navigation; in the house, good sense applied to cooking, sewing, serving; in your agent, good sense applied to accounts and affairs. So do you multiply your presence, or spread yourself throughout your estate. But because of the dual constitution of things, in labor as in life there can be no cheating. The thief steals from himself. The swindler swindles himself. For the real price of labor is knowledge and virtue, whereof wealth and credit are signs. These signs, like paper money, may be counterfeited or stolen, but that which they represent, namely, knowledge and virtue, cannot be counterfeited or stolen. These ends of labor cannot be answered but by real exertions of the mind, and in obedience to pure motives. The cheat, the defaulter, the gambler, cannot extort the knowledge of material and moral nature which his honest care and pains yield to the operative. The law of nature is, Do the thing, and you shall have the power: but they who do not the thing have not the power.

Human labor, through all its forms, from the sharpening of a stake to the construction of a city or an epic, is one immense illustration of the perfect compensation of the universe. The absolute balance of Give and Take, the doctrine that everything has its price,—and if that price is not paid, not that thing but something else is obtained, and that it is impossible to get anything without its price,—is not less sublime in the columns of a ledger than in the budgets of states, in the laws of light and darkness, in all the action and reaction of nature. I cannot doubt that the high laws which each man sees implicated in those processes with which he is conversant, the stern ethics which sparkle on his chisel edge, which are measured out by his plumb and foot rule, which stand as manifest in the footing of the shop bill as in the history of a state,—do recommend to him his trade, and though seldom named, exalt his business to his imagination.

The league between virtue and nature engages all things to assume a hostile front to vice. The beautiful laws and substances of the world persecute and whip the traitor. He finds that things are arranged for truth and benefit, but there is no den in the wide world to hide a rogue. Commit a crime,[134] and the earth is made of glass. Commit a crime, and it seems as if a coat of snow fell on the ground, such as reveals in the woods the track of every partridge and fox and squirrel and mole. You cannot recall the spoken word,[135] you cannot wipe out the foot-track, you cannot draw up the ladder, so as to leave no inlet or clew. Some damning circumstance always transpires. The laws and substances of nature—water, snow, wind, gravitation—become penalties to the thief.

On the other hand, the law holds with equal sureness for all right action. Love, and you shall be loved. All love is mathematically just, as much as the two sides of an algebraic equation. The good man has absolute good, which like fire turns everything to its own nature, so that you cannot do him any harm; but as the royal armies sent against Napoleon, when he approached, cast down their colors and from enemies became friends, so disasters of all kinds, as sickness, offense, poverty, prove benefactors:—

"Winds blow and waters roll
Strength to the brave, and power and deity,
Yet in themselves are nothing."

The good are befriended even by weakness and defect. As no man had ever a point of pride that was not injurious to him, so no man had ever a defect that was not somewhere made useful to him. The stag in the fable[136] admired his horns and blamed his feet, but when the hunter came, his feet saved him, and afterwards, caught in the thicket, his horns destroyed him. Every man in his lifetime needs to thank his faults. As no man thoroughly understands a truth until he has contended against it, so no man has a thorough acquaintance with the hindrances or talents of men, until he has suffered from the one, and seen the triumph of the other over his own want of the same. Has he a defect of temper that unfits him to live in society? Thereby he is driven to entertain himself alone, and acquire habits of self-help; and thus, like the wounded oyster, he mends his shell with pearl.

Our strength grows out of our weakness. The indignation which arms itself with secret forces does not awaken until we are pricked and stung and sorely assailed. A great man is always willing to be little. Whilst he sits on the cushion of advantages, he goes to sleep. When he is punished, tormented, defeated, he has a chance to learn something; he has been put on his wits, on his manhood; he has gained facts; learns his ignorance; is cured of the insanity of conceit; has got moderation and real skill. The wise man throws himself on the side of his assailants. It is more his interest than it is theirs to find his weak point. The wound cicatrizes and falls off from him like a dead skin, and when they would triumph, lo! he has passed on invulnerable. Blame is safer than praise. I hate to be defended in a newspaper. As long as all that is said is said against me, I feel a certain assurance of success. But as soon as honeyed words of praise are spoken for me, I feel as one that lies unprotected before his enemies. In general, every evil to which we do not succumb is a benefactor. As the Sandwich Islander believes that the strength and valor of the enemy he kills passes into himself, so we gain the strength of the temptation we resist.

The same guards which protect us from disaster, defect, and enmity, defend us, if we will, from selfishness and fraud. Bolts and bars are not the best of our institutions, nor is shrewdness in trade a mark of wisdom.

Men suffer all their life long, under the foolish superstition that they can be cheated. But it is as impossible for a man to be cheated by anyone but himself,[137] as for a thing to be and not to be at the same time. There is a third silent party to all our bargains. The nature and soul of things takes on itself the guaranty of the fulfillment of every contract, so that honest service cannot come to loss. If you serve an ungrateful master, serve him the more. Put God in your debt. Every stroke shall be repaid. The longer the payment is withholden,[138] the better for you; for compound interest on compound interest is the rate and usage of this exchequer.

The history of persecution is a history of endeavors to cheat nature, to make water run up hill, to twist a rope of sand. It makes no difference whether the actors be many or one, a tyrant or a mob. A mob[139] is a society of bodies voluntarily bereaving themselves of reason, and traversing its work. The mob is man voluntarily descending to the nature of the beast. Its fit hour of activity is night. Its actions are insane like its whole constitution; it persecutes a principle; it would whip a right; it would tar and feather justice, by inflicting fire and outrage upon the houses and persons of those who have these. It resembles the prank of boys, who run with fire engines to put out the ruddy aurora streaming to the stars. The inviolate spirit turns their spite against the wrongdoers. The martyr cannot be dishonored. Every lash inflicted is a tongue of fame; every prison, a more illustrious abode; every burned book or house enlightens the world; every suppressed or expunged word reverberates through the earth from side to side. Hours of sanity and consideration are always arriving to communities, as to individuals, when the truth is seen, and the martyrs are justified.

Thus do all things preach the indifferency of circumstances. The man is all. Everything has two sides, a good and an evil. Every advantage has its tax. I learn to be content. But the doctrine of compensation is not the doctrine of indifferency. The thoughtless say, on hearing these representations, What boots it to do well? there is one event to good and evil; if I gain any good, I must pay for it; if I lose any good, I gain some other; all actions are indifferent.

There is a deeper fact in the soul than compensation, to wit, its own nature. The soul is not a compensation, but a life. The soul *is*. Under all this running sea of circumstance, whose waters ebb and flow with perfect balance, lies the aboriginal abyss of real Being. Essence, or God, is not a relation, or a part, but the whole. Being is the vast affirmative, excluding negation, self-balanced, and swallowing up all relations, parts, and times within itself. Nature, truth, virtue, are the influx from thence. Vice is the absence or departure of the same. Nothing, Falsehood, may indeed stand as the great Night or shade, on which, as a background, the living universe paints itself forth, but no fact is begotten by it; it cannot work, for it is not. It cannot work any good; it cannot work any harm. It is harm inasmuch as it is worse not to be than to be.

We feel defrauded of the retribution due to evil acts, because the criminal adheres to his vice and contumacy, and does not come to a crisis or judgment anywhere in visible nature. There is no stunning confutation of his nonsense before men and angels. Has he therefore outwitted the law? Inasmuch as he carries the malignity and the lie with him, he so far deceases from nature. In some manner there will be a demonstration of the wrong to the understanding also; but should we not see it, this deadly deduction makes square the eternal account.

Neither can it be said, on the other hand, that the gain of rectitude must be bought by any loss. There is no penalty to virtue; no penalty to wisdom; they are proper additions of being. In a virtuous action, I properly *am*; in a virtuous act, I add to the world; I plant into deserts conquered from Chaos and Nothing, and see the darkness receding on the limits of the horizon. There can be no excess to love; none to knowledge; none to beauty, when these attributes are considered in the purest sense. The soul refuses limits, and always affirms an Optimism,[140] never a Pessimism.

Man's life is a progress, and not a station. His instinct is trust. Our instinct uses "more" and "less" in application to man, of the *presence of the soul*, and not of its absence; the brave man is greater than the coward; the true, the benevolent, the wise, is more a man, and not less, than the fool and knave. There is no tax on the good of virtue; for that is the incoming of God himself, or absolute existence without any comparative. Material good has its tax, and if it came without desert or sweat, has no root in me, and the next wind will blow it away. But all the good of nature is the soul's, and may be had, if paid for in nature's lawful coin, that is, by labor which the heart and the head allow. I no longer wish to meet a good I do not earn; for example, to find a pot of buried gold, knowing that it brings with it new burdens. I do not wish more external goods,—neither possessions, nor honors, nor powers, nor persons. The gain is apparent; the tax is certain. But there is no tax on the knowledge that the compensation exists, and that it is not desirable to dig up treasure. Herein I rejoice with a serene eternal peace. I contract the boundaries of possible mischief. I learn the wisdom of St. Bernard,[141]—"Nothing can, work me damage except myself; the harm, that I sustain I carry about with me, and never am a real sufferer but by my own fault."

In the nature of the soul is the compensation for the inequalities of condition. The radical tragedy of nature seems to be the distinction of More and Less. How can Less not feel the pain; how not feel indignation or malevolence towards More? Look at those who have less faculty, and one feels sad, and knows not well what to make of it. He almost shuns their eye; he fears they will upbraid God. What should they do? It seems a great injustice. But see the facts nearly, and these mountainous inequalities vanish. Love reduces them, as the sun melts the iceberg in the sea. The heart and soul of all men being one, this bitterness of *His* and *Mine* ceases. His is mine. I am my brother, and my brother is me. If I feel overshadowed and outdone by great neighbors, I can yet love; I can still receive; and he that loveth maketh his own the grandeur he loves. Thereby I make the discovery that my brother is my guardian, acting for me with the friendliest designs, and the estate I so admired and envied is my own. It is the nature of the soul to appropriate all things. Jesus[142] and Shakespeare are fragments of the soul, and by love I conquer and incorporate them in my own conscious domain. His[143] virtue,—is not that mine? His wit,—if it cannot be made mine, it is not wit.

Such, also, is the natural history of calamity. The changes which break up at short intervals the prosperity of men are advertisements of a nature whose law is growth. Every soul is by this intrinsic necessity quitting its whole system of things, its friends, and home, and laws, and faith, as the shellfish crawls out of its beautiful but stony case, because it no longer admits of its growth, and slowly forms a new house. In proportion to the vigor of the individual, these revolutions are frequent, until in some happier mind they are incessant, and all worldly relations hang very loosely about him, becoming, as it were, a transparent fluid membrane through which the living form is seen, and not, as in most men, an indurated heterogeneous fabric of many dates, and of no settled character, in which the man is imprisoned. Then there can be enlargement, and the man of to-day scarcely recognizes the man of yesterday. And such should be the outward biography of man in time, a putting off of dead circumstances day by day, as he renews his raiment day by day. But to us, in our lapsed estate, resting, not advancing, resisting, not coöperating with the divine expansion, this growth comes by shocks.

We cannot part with our friend. We cannot let our angels go. We do not see that they only go out, that archangels may come in. We are idolaters of the old. We do not believe in the riches of the soul, in its proper eternity and omnipresence. We do not believe there is any force in to-day to rival or recreate that beautiful yesterday. We linger in the ruins of the old tent, where once we had bread and shelter and organs, nor believe that the spirit can feed, cover, and nerve us again. We cannot again find aught so dear, so sweet, so graceful. But we sit and weep in vain. The voice of the Almighty saith, "Up and onward forevermore!" We cannot stay amid the ruins. Neither will we rely on the new; and so we walk ever with reverted eyes, like those monsters who look backwards.

And yet the compensations of calamity are made apparent to the understanding also, after long intervals of time. A fever, a mutilation, a cruel disappointment, a loss of wealth, a loss of friends, seems at the moment unpaid loss, and unpayable. But the sure years reveal the deep remedial force that underlies all facts. The death of a dear friend, wife, brother, lover, which seemed nothing but privation, somewhat later assumes the aspect of a guide or genius; for it commonly operates revolutions in our way of life, terminates an epoch of infancy or of youth which was waiting to be closed, breaks up a wonted occupation, or a household, or style of living, and allows the formation of new ones more friendly to the growth of character. It permits or constrains the formation of new acquaintances, and the reception of new influences that prove of the first importance to the next years; and the man or woman who would have remained a sunny garden flower, with no room for its roots and too much sunshine for its head, by the falling of the walls and the neglect of the gardener, is made the banyan[144] of the forest, yielding shade and fruit to wide neighborhoods of men.

SELF-RELIANCE

"Ne te quæsiveris extra."[145]

"Man is his own star; and the soul that can
Render an honest and a perfect man,
Commands all light, all influence, all fate;
Nothing to him falls early or too late.
Our acts our angels are, or good or ill,
Our fatal shadows that walk by us still."[146]

Cast the bantling on the rocks,
Suckle him with the she-wolf's teat;
Wintered with the hawk and fox,
Power and speed be hands and feet.[147]

I read the other day some verses written by an eminent painter which were original and not conventional. The soul always hears an admonition in such lines, let the subject be what it may. The sentiment they instill is of more value than any thought they may contain. To believe your own thought, to believe that what is true for you in your private heart is true for all men,—that is genius.[148] Speak your latent conviction, and it shall be the universal sense;[149] for the inmost in due time becomes the outmost,— and our first thought is rendered back to us by the trumpets of the Last Judgment. Familiar as the voice of the mind is to each, the highest merit we ascribe to Moses, Plato,[150] and Milton[151] is, that they set at naught books and traditions, and spoke not what men, but what they thought. A man should learn to detect and watch that gleam of light which flashes across his mind from within, more than the luster of the firmament of bards and sages. Yet he dismisses without notice his thought, because it is his. In every work of genius we recognize our own rejected thoughts:[152] they come back to us with a certain alienated majesty. Great works of art have no more affecting lesson for us than this. They teach us to abide by our spontaneous impression with good-humored inflexibility then most when[153] the whole cry of voices is on the other side. Else, to-morrow a stranger will say with masterly good sense precisely what we have thought and felt all the time, and we shall be forced to take with shame our own opinion from another.

There is a time in every man's education when he arrives at the conviction that envy is ignorance; that imitation is suicide;[154] that he must take himself for better, for worse, as his portion; that though the wide universe is full of good, no kernel of nourishing corn can come to him but through his toil bestowed on that plot of ground which is given to him to till. The power which resides in him is new in nature, and none but he knows what that is which he can do, nor does he know until he has tried. Not for nothing one face, one character, one fact, makes much impression on him, and another none. This sculpture in the memory is not without preëstablished harmony. The eye was placed where one ray should fall, that it might testify of that particular ray. We but half express ourselves,[155] and are ashamed of that divine idea which each of us represents. It may be safely trusted as proportionate and of good issues, so it be faithfully imparted, but God will not have his work made manifest by cowards. A man is relieved and gay when he has put his heart into his work and done his best; but what he has said or done otherwise shall give him no peace. It is a deliverance which does not deliver. In the attempt his genius deserts him; no muse befriends; no invention, no hope.

Trust thyself:[156] every heart vibrates to that iron string. Accept the place the divine providence has found for you, the society of your contemporaries, the connection of events. Great men have always done so, and confided themselves childlike to the genius of their age, betraying their perception that the absolutely trustworthy was seated at their heart, working through their hands, predominating in all their being. And we are now men, and must accept in the highest mind the same transcendent destiny; and not minors and invalids in a protected corner, not cowards fleeing before a revolution, but guides, redeemers, and benefactors, obeying the Almighty effort, and advancing on Chaos[157] and the Dark.

What pretty oracles nature yields us on this text, in the face and behavior of children, babes, and even brutes! That divided and rebel mind, that distrust of a sentiment because our arithmetic has computed the strength and means opposed to our purpose, these[158] have not. Their mind being whole, their eye is as yet unconquered, and when we look in their faces we are disconcerted. Infancy conforms to nobody: all conform to it, so that one babe commonly makes four or five[159] out of the adults who prattle and play to it. So God has armed youth and puberty and manhood no less with its own piquancy and charm, and made it enviable and gracious and its claims not to be put by, if it will stand by itself. Do not think the youth has no force, because he cannot speak to you and me. Hark! in the next room his voice is sufficiently clear and emphatic. It seems he knows how to speak to his contemporaries. Bashful or bold, then, he will know how to make us seniors very unnecessary.

The nonchalance[160] of boys who are sure of a dinner, and would disdain as much as a lord to do or say aught to conciliate one, is the healthy attitude of human nature. A boy is in the parlor what the pit is in the playhouse;[161] independent, irresponsible, looking out from his corner on such people and facts as pass by, he tries and sentences them on their merits, in the swift, summary way of boys, as good, bad, interesting, silly, eloquent, troublesome. He cumbers himself never about consequences about interests; he gives an independent, genuine verdict. You must court him: he does not court you. But the man is, as it were, clapped into jail by his consciousness. As soon as he has once acted or spoken with *éclat* [162] he is a committed person, watched by the sympathy or the hatred of hundreds, whose affections must now enter into his account. There is no Lethe[163] for this. Ah, that he could pass again into his neutrality! Who[164] can thus avoid all pledges, and having observed, observe again from the same unaffected, unbiased, unbribable, unaffrighted innocence, must always be formidable. He would utter opinions on all passing affairs, which being seen to be not private, but necessary, would sink like darts into the ear of men, and put them in fear.

These are the voices which we hear in solitude, but they grow faint and inaudible as we enter into the world. Society everywhere is in conspiracy against the manhood of everyone of its members. Society is a joint-stock company, in which the members agree, for the better securing of his bread to each shareholder, to surrender the liberty and culture of the eater. The virtue in most request is conformity. Self-reliance is its aversion. It loves not realities and creators, but names and customs.

Whoso would be a man must be a nonconformist.[165] He who would gather immortal palms must not be hindered by the name of goodness, but must explore if it be goodness.[166] Nothing is at last sacred but the integrity of your own mind. Absolve you to yourself, and you shall have the suffrage[167] of the world. I remember an answer which when quite young I was prompted to make to a valued adviser, who was wont to importune me with the dear old doctrines of the church. On my saying, What have I to do with the sacredness of traditions, if I live wholly from within? my friend suggested: "But these impulses may be from below, not from above." I replied: "They do not seem to me to be such; but if I am the Devil's child, I will live then from the Devil." No law can be sacred to me but that of my nature. Good and bad are but names very readily transferable to that or this;[168] the only right is what is after my constitution, the only wrong what is against it. A man is to carry himself in the presence of all opposition, as if everything were titular and ephemeral but he. I am ashamed to think how easily we capitulate to badges and names, to large societies and dead institutions. Every decent and well-spoken individual affects and sways me more than is right. I ought to go upright and vital, and speak the rude truth in all ways. If malice and vanity wear the coat of philanthropy, shall that pass? If an angry bigot assumes this bountiful cause of Abolition, and comes to me with his last news from Barbadoes,[169] why should I not say to him: "Go love thy infant; love thy wood-chopper: be good-natured and modest: have that grace; and never varnish your hard, uncharitable ambition with this incredible tenderness for black folk a thousand miles off. Thy love afar is spite at home." Rough and graceless would be such greeting, but truth is handsomer than the affectation of love. Your goodness must have some edge to it,—else it is none. The doctrine of hatred must be preached as the counteraction of the doctrine of love when that pules and whines. I shun father and mother and wife and brother, when my genius calls me. I would write on the lintels of the door-post, *Whim*.[170] I hope it is somewhat better than whim at last, but we cannot spend the day in explanation. Expect me not to show cause why I seek or why I exclude company. Then, again, do not tell me, as a good man did to-day, of my obligation to put all poor men in good situations. Are they *my* poor? I tell thee, thou foolish philanthropist, that I grudge the dollar, the dime, the cent, I give to such men as do not belong to me and to whom I do not belong. There is a class of persons to whom by all spiritual affinity I am bought and sold; for them I will go to prison, if need be; but your miscellaneous popular charities; the education at college of fools; the building of meeting-houses to the vain end to which many now stand; alms to sots; and the thousand-fold Relief Societies;— though I confess with shame I sometimes succumb and give the dollar, it is a wicked dollar which by and by I shall have the manhood to withhold.

Virtues are, in the popular estimate, rather the exception than the rule. There is the man *and* his virtues. Men do what is called a good action, as some piece of courage or charity, much as they would pay a fine in expiation of daily non-appearance on parade. Their works are done as an apology or extenuation of their living in the world,—as invalids and the insane pay a high board. Their virtues are penances. I do not wish to expiate, but to live. My life is for itself and not for a spectacle. I much prefer that it should be of a lower strain, so it be genuine and equal, than that it should be glittering and unsteady. I wish it to be sound and sweet, and not to need diet and bleeding. [171] I ask primary evidence that you are a man, and refuse this appeal from the man to his actions. I know that for myself it makes no difference whether I do or forbear those actions which are reckoned excellent. I cannot consent to pay for a privilege where I have intrinsic right. Few and mean as my gifts may be, I actually am, and do not need for my own assurance or the assurance of my fellows any secondary testimony.

What I must do is all that concerns me, not what the people think. This rule, equally arduous in actual and in intellectual life, may serve for the whole distinction between greatness and meanness. It is the harder, because you will always find those who think they know what is your duty better than you know it. It is easy in the world to live after the world's opinion; it is easy in solitude to live after our own; but the great man is he who in the midst of the crowd keeps with perfect sweetness the independence of solitude.[172]

The objection to conforming to usages that have become dead to you is, that it scatters your force. It loses your time and blurs the impression of your character. If you maintain a dead church, contribute to a dead Bible-society, vote with a great party either for the government or against it, spread your table like base housekeepers,—under all these screens I have difficulty to detect the precise[173] man you are. And, of course, so much force is withdrawn from your proper life. But do your work, and I shall know you.[174] Do your work, and you shall reinforce yourself. A man must consider what a blindman's-buff is this game of conformity. If I know your sect, I anticipate your argument. I hear a preacher announce for his text and topic the expediency of one of the institutions of his church. Do I not know beforehand that not possibly can he say a new and spontaneous word? Do I not know that, with[175] all this ostentation of examining the grounds of the institution, he will do no such thing? Do I not know that he is pledged to himself not to look but at one side,—the permitted side, not as a man, but as a parish minister? He is a retained attorney, and these airs of the bench[176] are the emptiest affectation. Well, most men have bound their eyes with one or another handkerchief,[177] and attached themselves to some one of these communities of opinion.[178] This conformity makes them not false in a few particulars, authors of a few lies, but false in all particulars. Their every truth is not quite true. Their two is not the real two, their four not the real four; so that every word they say chagrins us, and we know not where to begin to set them right. Meantime nature is not slow to equip us in the prison-uniform of the party to which we adhere. We come to wear one cut of face and figure, and acquire by degrees the gentlest asinine expression. There is a mortifying experience in particular which does not fail to wreak itself also in the general history; I mean "the foolish face of praise," the forced smile which we put on in company where we do not feel at ease in answer to conversation which does not interest us. The muscles, not spontaneously moved, but moved by a low usurping willfulness, grow tight about the outline of the face with the most disagreeable sensation.

For nonconformity the world whips you with its displeasure.[179] And therefore a man must know how to estimate a sour face. The bystanders look askance on him in the public street or in the friend's parlor. If this aversation had its origin in contempt and resistance like his own, he might well go home with a sad countenance; but the sour faces of the multitude, like their sweet faces, have no deep cause, but are put on and off as the wind blows and a newspaper directs.[180] Yet is the discontent of the multitude more formidable than that of the senate and the college. It is easy enough for a firm man who knows the world to brook the rage of the cultivated classes. Their rage is decorous and prudent, for they are timid as being very vulnerable themselves. But when to their feminine rage the indignation of the people is added, when the ignorant and the poor are aroused, when the unintelligent brute force that lies at the bottom of society is made to growl and mow, it needs the habit of magnanimity and religion to treat it godlike as a trifle of no concernment.

The other terror[181] that scares us from self-trust is our consistency;[182] a reverence for our past act or word, because the eyes of others have no other data for computing our orbit[183] than our past acts, and we are loth to disappoint them.

But why should you keep your head over your shoulder? Why drag about this corpse of your memory, lest you contradict somewhat[184] you have stated in this or that public place? Suppose you should contradict yourself; what then? It seems to be a rule of wisdom never to rely on your memory alone, scarcely even in acts of pure memory, but to bring the past for judgment into the thousand-eyed present, and live ever in a new day. In your metaphysics you have denied personality to the Deity; yet when the devout motions of the soul come, yield to them heart and life, though they should clothe God with shape and color. Leave your theory, as Joseph his coat in the hand of the harlot, and flee.[185]

A foolish consistency is the hobgoblin of little minds, adored by little statesmen and philosophers and divines. With consistency a great soul has simply nothing to do. He may as well concern himself with the shadow on the wall. Speak what you think now in hard words, and to-morrow speak what to-morrow thinks in hard words again, though it contradict everything you said to-day.—"Ah, so you shall be sure to be misunderstood."—Is it so bad, then, to be misunderstood? Pythagoras[186] was misunderstood, and Socrates,[187] and Jesus, and Luther,[188] and Copernicus,[189] and

Galileo,[190] and Newton,[191] and every pure and wise spirit that ever took flesh. To be great is to be misunderstood.

I suppose no man can violate his nature. All the sallies of his will are rounded in by the law of his being, as the inequalities of Andes[192] and Himmaleh[193] are insignificant in the curve of the sphere. Nor does it matter how you gauge and try him. A character is like an acrostic or Alexandrian stanza;[194]—read it forward, backward, or across, it still spells the same thing. In this pleasing, contrite wood-life which God allows me, let me record day by day my honest thought without prospect or retrospect, and, I cannot doubt, it will be found symmetrical, though I mean it not, and see it not. My book should smell of pines and resound with the hum of insects. The swallow over my window should interweave that thread or straw he carries in his bill into my web also. We pass for what we are. Character teaches above our wills. Men imagine that they communicate their virtue or vice only by overt actions, and do not see that virtue or vice emit a breath every moment.

There will be an agreement in whatever variety of actions, so they be each honest and natural in their hour. For of one will, the actions will be harmonious, however unlike they seem. These varieties are lost sight of at a little distance, at a little height of thought. One tendency unites them all. The voyage of the best ship is a zigzag line of a hundred tacks.[195] See the line from a sufficient distance, and it straightens itself to the average tendency. Your genuine action will explain itself, and will explain your other genuine actions. Your conformity explains nothing. Act singly, and what you have already done singly will justify you now. Greatness appeals to the future. If I can be firm enough to-day to do right, and scorn eyes,[196] I must have done so much right before as to defend me now. Be it how it will, do right now. Always scorn appearances, and you always may. The force of character is cumulative. All the foregone days of virtue work their health into this. What makes the majesty of the heroes of the senate and the field, which so fills the imagination? The consciousness of a train of great days and victories behind. They shed an united light on the advancing actor. He is attended as by a visible escort of angels. That is it which throws thunder into Chatham's[197] voice, and dignity into Washington's port, and America into Adams's[198] eye. Honor is venerable to us because it is no ephemeris. It is always ancient virtue. We worship it to-day because it is not of to-day. We love it and pay it homage, because it is not a trap for our love and homage, but is self-dependent, self-derived, and therefore of an old immaculate pedigree, even if shown in a young person.

I hope in these days we have heard the last of conformity and consistency. Let the words be gazetted and ridiculous henceforward. Instead of the gong for dinner, let us hear a whistle from the Spartan[199] fife. Let us never bow and apologize more. A great man is coming to eat at my house. I do not wish to please him; I wish that he should wish to please me. I will stand here for humanity, and though I would make it kind, I would make it true. Let us affront and reprimand the smooth mediocrity and squalid contentment of the times, and hurl in the face of custom, and trade, and office, the fact which is the upshot of all history, that there is a great responsible Thinker and Actor working wherever a man works; that a true man belongs to no other time or place, but is the center of things. Where he is, there is nature. He measures you, and all men, and all events. Ordinarily, everybody in society reminds us of somewhat else, or of some other person. Character, reality, reminds you of nothing else; it takes place of the whole creation. The man must be so much, that he must make all circumstances indifferent. Every true man is a cause, a country, and an age; requires infinite spaces and numbers and time fully to accomplish his design;—and posterity seem to follow his steps as a train of clients. A man Cæsar[200] is born, and for ages after we have a Roman Empire. Christ is born, and millions of minds so grow and cleave to his genius, that he is confounded with virtue and the possible of man. An institution is the lengthened shadow of one man; as Monachism, of the hermit Antony;[201] the Reformation, of Luther; Quakerism, of Fox;[202] Methodism, of Wesley;[203] Abolition, of Clarkson.[204] Scipio,[205] Milton called "the height of Rome"; and all history resolves itself very easily into the biography of a few stout and earnest persons.

Let a man then know his worth, and keep things under his feet. Let him not peep or steal, or skulk up and down with the air of a charity-boy, a bastard, or an interloper, in the world which exists for him. But the man in the street, finding no worth in himself which corresponds to the force which built a tower or sculptured a marble god, feels poor when he looks on these. To him a palace, a statue, a costly book, have an alien and forbidding air, much like a gay equipage, and seem to say like that, "Who are you, Sir?" Yet they all are his, suitors for his notice, petitioners to his faculties that they will come out and take possession. The picture waits for my verdict: it is not to command me, but I am to settle its claims to praise. That popular fable of the sot who was picked up dead drunk in the street, carried to the duke's house, washed and dressed and laid in the duke's bed, and, on his waking, treated with all obsequious ceremony like the duke, and assured that he had been insane,[206] owes its popularity to the fact that it symbolizes so well the state of man, who is in the world a sort of sot, but now and then wakes up, exercises his reason, and finds himself a true prince.

Our reading is mendicant and sycophantic. In history, our imagination plays us false. Kingdom and lordship, power and estate, are a gaudier vocabulary than private John and Edward in a small house and common day's work; but the things of life are the same to both; the sum total of both is the same. Why all this deference to Alfred,[207] and Scanderbeg,[208] and Gustavus?[209] Suppose they were virtuous; did they wear out virtue? As great a stake depends on your private act to-day, as followed their public and renowned steps. When private men shall act with original views, the luster will be transferred from the actions of kings to those of gentlemen.

The world has been instructed by its kings, who have so magnetized the eyes of nations. It has been taught by this colossal symbol the mutual reverence that is due from man to man. The joyful loyalty with which men have everywhere suffered the king, the noble, or the great proprietor to walk among them by a law of his own, make his own scale of men and things, and reverse theirs, pay for benefits not with money but with honor, and represent the law in his person, was the hieroglyphic[210] by which they obscurely signified their consciousness of their own right and comeliness, the right of every man.

The magnetism which all original action exerts is explained when we inquire the reason of self-trust. Who is the Trustee? What is the aboriginal Self, on which a universal reliance may be grounded? What is the nature and power of that science-baffling star, without parallax,[211] without calculable elements, which shoots a ray of beauty even into trivial and impure actions, if the least mark of independence appear? The inquiry leads us to that source, at once the essence of genius, of virtue, and of life, which we call Spontaneity or Instinct. We denote this primary wisdom as Intuition, whilst all later teachings are tuitions. In that deep force, the last fact behind which analysis cannot go, all things find their common origin. For the sense of being which in calm hours rises, we know not how, in the soul, is not diverse from things, from space, from light, from time, from man, but one with them, and proceeds obviously from the same source whence their life and being also proceed. We first share the life by which things exist, and afterwards see them as appearances in nature, and forget that we have shared their cause. Here is the fountain of action and of thought. Here are the lungs of that inspiration which giveth man wisdom, and which cannot be denied without impiety and atheism. We lie in the lap of immense intelligence, which makes us receivers of its truth and organs of its activity. When we discern justice, when we discern truth, we do nothing of ourselves, but allow a passage to its beams. If we ask whence this comes, if we seek to pry into the soul that causes, all philosophy is at fault. Its presence or its absence is all we can affirm. Every man discriminates between the voluntary acts of his mind, and his involuntary perceptions, and knows that to his involuntary perceptions a perfect faith is due. He may err in the expression of them, but he knows that these things are so, like day and night, not to be disputed. My willful actions and acquisitions are but roving;—the idlest reverie, the faintest native emotion, command my curiosity and respect. Thoughtless people contradict as readily the statement of perceptions as of opinions, or rather much more readily; for, they do not distinguish between perception and notion. They fancy that I choose to see this or that thing. But perception is not whimsical, it is fatal. If I see a trait, my children will see it after me, and in course of time, all mankind,—although it may chance that no one has seen it before me. For my perception of it is as much a fact as the sun.

The relations of the soul to the divine spirit are so pure, that it is profane to seek to interpose helps. It must be that when God speaketh he should communicate, not one thing, but all things; should fill the world with his voice; should scatter forth light, nature, time, souls, from the center of the present thought; and new date and new create the whole. Whenever a mind is simple, and receives a divine wisdom, old things pass away,—means, teachers, texts, temples, fall; it lives now, and absorbs past and future into the present hour. All things are made sacred by relation to it,—one as much as another. All things are dissolved to their center by their cause, and, in the universal miracle, petty and particular miracles disappear. If, therefore, a man claims to know and speak of God, and carries you backward to the phraseology of some old moldered nation in another country, in another world, believe him not. Is the acorn better than the oak which is its fullness and completion? Is the parent better than the child into whom he has cast his ripened being?[212] Whence, then, this worship of the past?[213] The centuries are conspirators against the sanity and authority of the soul. Time and space are but physiological colors which the eye makes, but the soul is light; where it is, is day; where it was, is night; and history is an impertinence and an injury, if it be anything more than a cheerful apologue or parable of my being and becoming.

Man is timid and apologetic; he is no longer upright; he dares not say "I think," "I am," but quotes some saint or sage. He is ashamed before the blade of grass or the blowing rose. These roses under my window make no reference to former roses or to better ones; they are for what they are; they exist with God to-day. There is no time to them. There is simply the rose; it is perfect in every moment of its existence. Before a leaf-bud has burst, its whole life acts; in the full-blown flower there is no more; in the leafless root there is no less. Its nature is satisfied, and it satisfies nature, in all moments alike. But man postpones, or remembers; he does not live in the present, but with a reverted eye laments the past, or, heedless of the riches that surround him, stands on tiptoe to foresee the future. He cannot be happy and strong until he too lives with nature in the present, above time.

This should be plain enough. Yet see what strong intellects dare not yet hear God himself, unless he speak the phraseology of I know not what David, or Jeremiah, or Paul. We shall not always set so great a price on a few texts, on a few lives.[214] We are like children who repeat by rote the sentences of grandames and tutors, and, as they grow older, of the men and talents and characters they chance to see,—painfully recollecting the exact words they spoke; afterwards, when they come into the point of view which those had who uttered those saying, they understand them, and are willing to let the words go; for, at any time, they can use words as good when occasion comes. If we live truly, we shall see truly. It is as easy for the strong man to be strong, as it is for the weak to be weak. When we have new perception, we shall gladly disburden the memory of its hoarded treasures as old rubbish. When a man lives with God, his voice shall be as sweet as the murmur of the brook and the rustle of the corn.

And now at last the highest truth on this subject remains unsaid; probably cannot be said; for all that we say is the far-off remembering of the intuition. That thought, by what I can now nearest approach to say it, is this. When good is near you, when you have life in yourself, it is not by any known or accustomed way; you shall not discern the footprints of any other; you shall not see the face of man; you shall not hear any name;—the way, the thought, the good, shall be wholly strange and new. It shall exclude example and experience. You take the way from man, not to man. All persons that ever existed are its forgotten ministers. Fear and hope are alike beneath it. There is somewhat low even in hope. In the hour of vision, there is nothing that can be called gratitude, nor properly joy. The soul raised over passion beholds identity and eternal causation, perceives the self-existence of Truth and Right, and calms itself with knowing that all things go well. Vast spaces of nature, the Atlantic Ocean, the South Sea,—long intervals of time, years, centuries,—are of no account. This which I think and feel underlay every former state of life and circumstances, as it does underlie my present, and what is called life, and what is called death.

Life only avails, not the having lived. Power ceases in the instant of repose; it resides in the moment of transition from a past to a new state, in the shooting of the gulf, in the darting to an aim. This one fact the world hates, that the soul *becomes*; for that forever degrades the past, turns all riches to poverty, all reputation to shame, confounds the saint with the rogue, shoves Jesus and Judas[215] equally aside. Why, then, do we prate of self-reliance? Inasmuch as the soul is present, there will be power not confident but agent.[216] To talk of reliance is a poor external way of speaking. Speak rather of that which relies, because it works and is. Who has more obedience than I masters me, though he should not raise his finger. Round him I must revolve by the gravitation of spirits. We fancy it rhetoric, when we speak of eminent virtue. We do not yet see that virtue is Height, and that a man or a company of men, plastic and permeable to principles, by the law of nature must overpower and ride all cities, nations, kings, rich men, poets, who are not.

This is the ultimate fact which we so quickly reach on this, as on every topic, the resolution of all into the ever-blessed One. Self-existence is the attribute of the Supreme Cause, and it constitutes the measure of good by the degree in which it enters into all lower forms. All things real are so by so much virtue as they contain. Commerce, husbandry, hunting, whaling, war eloquence, personal weight, are somewhat, and engage my respect as examples of its presence and impure action. I see the same law working in nature for conservation and growth. Power is in nature the essential measure of right. Nature suffers nothing to remain in her kingdoms which cannot help itself. The genesis and maturation of a planet, its poise and orbit, the bended tree recovering itself from the strong wind, the vital resources of every animal and vegetable, are demonstrations of the self-sufficing, and therefore self-relying soul.

Thus all concentrates: let us not rove; let us sit at home with the cause. Let us stun and astonish the intruding rabble of men and books and institutions, by a simple declaration of the divine fact. Bid the invaders take the shoes from off their feet, for God is here within.[217] Let our simplicity judge them, and our docility to our own law demonstrate the poverty of nature and fortune beside our native riches.

But now we are a mob. Man does not stand in awe of man, nor is his genius admonished to stay at home to put itself in communication with the internal ocean, but it goes abroad to beg a cup of water of the urns of other men. We must go alone. I like the silent church before the service begins, better than any preaching. How far off, how cool, how chaste the persons look, begirt each one with a precinct or sanctuary! So let us always sit. Why should we assume the faults of our friend, or wife, or father, or child, because they sit around our hearth, or are said to have the same blood? All men have my blood, and I have all men's.[218] Not for that will I adopt their petulance or folly, even to the extent of being ashamed of it. But your isolation must not be mechanical, but spiritual, that is, must be elevation. At times the whole world seems to be in conspiracy to importune you with emphatic trifles. Friend, client, child, sickness, fear, want, charity, all knock at once at thy closet door, and say, "Come out unto us." But keep thy state; come not into their confusion. The power men possess to annoy men, I give them by a weak curiosity. No man can come near me but through my act.

"What we love that we have, but by desire we bereave ourselves of the love."

If we cannot at once rise to the sanctities of obedience and faith, let us at least resist our temptations; let us enter into the state of war, and wake Thor and Woden,[219] courage and constancy, in our Saxon breasts. This is to be done in our smooth times by speaking the truth. Check this lying hospitality and lying affection. Live no longer to the expectation of these deceived and deceiving people with whom we converse. Say to them, O father, O mother, O wife, O brother, O friend, I have lived with you after appearances hitherto. Henceforward I am the truth's. Be it known unto you that henceforward I obey no law less than the eternal law. I will have no covenants but proximities.[220] I shall endeavor to nourish my parents, to support my family, to be the chaste husband of one wife,—but these relations I must fill after a new and unprecedented way. I appeal from your customs. I must be myself. I cannot break myself any longer for you, or you.[221] If you can love me for what I am, we shall be the happier. If you cannot, I will still seek to deserve that you should. I will not hide my tastes or aversions. I will so trust that what is deep is holy, that I will do strongly before the sun and moon whatever inly rejoices me, and the heart appoints. If you are noble, I will love you; if you are not, I will not hurt you and myself by hypocritical attentions. If you are true, but not in the same truth with me, cleave to your companions; I will seek my own. I do this not selfishly, but humbly and truly. It is alike your interest, and mine, and all men's however long we have dwelt in lies, to live in truth. Does this sound harsh to-day? You will soon love what is dictated by your nature as well as mine, and, if we follow the truth, it will bring us out safe at last.[222] But so may you give these friends pain. Yes, but I cannot sell my liberty and my power, to save their sensibility. Besides, all persons have their moments of reason, when they look out into the region of absolute truth; then will they justify me, and do the same thing.

The populace think that your rejection of popular standards is a rejection of all standard, and mere antinomianism;[223] and the bold sensualist will use the name of philosophy to gild his crimes. But the law of consciousness abides. There are two confessionals, in one or the other of which we must be shriven. You may fulfill your round of duties by clearing yourself in the *direct*, or in the *reflex* way. Consider whether you have satisfied your relations to father, mother, cousin, neighbor, town, cat, and dog; whether any of these can upbraid you. But I may also neglect this reflex standard, and absolve me to myself. I have my own stern claims and perfect circle. It denies the name of duty to many offices that are called duties. But if I can discharge its debts, it enables me to dispense with the popular code. If any one imagines that this law is lax, let him keep its commandment one day.

And truly it demands something godlike in him who has cast off the common motives of humanity, and has ventured to trust himself for a taskmaster. High be his heart, faithful his will, clear his sight, that he may in good earnest be doctrine, society, law, to himself, that a simple purpose may be to him as strong as iron necessity is to others!

If any man consider the present aspects of what is called by distinction *society*, he will see the need of these ethics. The sinew and heart of man seem to be drawn out, and we are become timorous, desponding whimperers. We are afraid of truth, afraid of fortune, afraid of death, and afraid of each other. Our age yields no great and perfect persons. We want men and women who shall renovate life and our social state, but we see that most natures are insolvent, cannot satisfy their own wants, have an ambition out of all proportion to their practical force,[224] and do lean and beg day and night continually. Our housekeeping is mendicant, our arts, our occupations, our marriages, our religion, we have not chosen, but society has chosen for us. We are parlor soldiers. We shun the rugged battle of fate, where strength is born.

If our young men miscarry in their first enterprises, they lose all heart. If the young merchant fails, men say he is *ruined*. If the finest genius studies at one of our colleges, and is not installed in an office within one year afterwards in the cities or suburbs of Boston or New York, it seems to his friends and to himself that he is right in being disheartened, and in complaining the rest of his life. A sturdy lad from New Hampshire or Vermont, who in turn tries all the professions, who *teams it, farms it*,[225] *peddles*, keeps a school, preaches, edits a newspaper, goes to Congress, buys a township, and so forth, in successive years, and always, like a cat, falls on his feet, is worth a hundred of these city dolls. He walks abreast with his days, and feels no shame in not "studying a profession," for he does not postpone his life, but lives already. He has not one chance, but a hundred chances. Let a Stoic[226] open the resources of man, and tell men they are not leaning willows, but can and must detach themselves; that with the exercise of self-trust, new powers shall appear; that a man is the word made flesh,[227] born to shed healing to the nations,[228] that he should be ashamed of our compassion, and that the moment he acts from himself, tossing the laws, the books, idolatries and customs out of the window, we pity him no more, but thank and revere him,—and that teacher shall restore the life of man to splendor, and make his name dear to all history.

It is easy to see that a greater self-reliance must work a revolution in all the offices and relations of men; in their religion; in their education; in their pursuits; their modes of living; their association; in their property; in their speculative views.

1. In what prayers do men allow themselves![229] That which they call a holy office is not so much as brave and manly. Prayer looks abroad and asks for some foreign addition to come through some foreign virtue, and loses itself in endless mazes of natural and supernatural, and mediatorial and miraculous. Prayer that craves a particular commodity,—anything less than all good,—is vicious. Prayer is the contemplation of the facts of life from the highest point of view. It is the soliloquy of a beholding and jubilant soul.[230] It is the spirit of God pronouncing his works good. But prayer as a means to effect a private end is meanness and theft. It supposes dualism and not unity in nature and consciousness. As soon as the man is at one with God, he will not beg. He will then see prayer in all action. The prayer of the farmer kneeling in his field to weed it, the prayer of the rower kneeling with the stroke of his oar, are true prayers heard throughout nature, though for cheap ends. Caratach,[231] in Fletcher's Bonduca, when admonished to inquire the mind of the god Audate, replies,—

"His hidden meaning lies in our endeavors;
Our valors are our best gods."

Another sort of false prayers are our regrets. Discontent is the want of self-reliance; it is infirmity of will. Regret calamities, if you can thereby help the sufferer; if not, attend your own work, and already the evil begins to be repaired. Our sympathy is just as base. We come to them who weep foolishly, and sit down and cry for company, instead of imparting to them truth and health in rough electric shocks, putting them once more in communication with their own reason. The secret of fortune is joy in our hands. Welcome evermore to gods and men is the self-helping man. For him all doors are flung wide: him all tongues greet, all honors crown, all eyes follow with desire. Our love goes out to him and embraces him, because he did not need it. We solicitously and apologetically caress and celebrate him, because he held on his way and scorned our disapprobation. The gods love him because men hated him. "To the persevering mortal," said Zoroaster,[232] "the blessed Immortals are swift."

As men's prayers are a disease of the will, so are their creeds a disease of the intellect. They say with those foolish Israelites, "Let not God speak to us, lest we die. Speak thou, speak any man with us, and we will obey."[233] Everywhere I am hindered of meeting God in my brother, because he has shut his own temple doors, and recites fables merely of his brother's, or his brother's brother's God. Every new mind is a new classification. If it prove a mind of uncommon activity and power, a Locke,[234] a Lavoisier,[235] a Hutton,[236] a Betham,[237] a Fourier,[238] it imposes its classification on other men, and lo! a new system. In proportion to the depth of the thought, and so to the number of the objects it touches and brings within reach of the pupil, is his complacency. But chiefly is this apparent in creeds and churches, which are also classifications of some powerful mind acting on the elemental thought of duty, and man's relation to the Highest. Such is Calvinism,[239] Quakerism,[240] Swedenborgism.[241] The pupil takes the same delight in subordinating everything to the new terminology, as a girl who has just learned botany in seeing a new earth and new seasons thereby. It will happen for a time, that the pupil will find his intellectual power has grown by the study of his master's mind. But in all unbalanced minds, the classification is idolized, passes for the end, and not for a speedily exhaustible means, so that the walls of the system blend to their eye in the remote horizon with the walls of the universe; the luminaries of heaven seem to them hung on the arch their master built. They cannot imagine how you aliens have any right to see,—how you can see; "It must be somehow that you stole the light from us." They do not yet perceive that light, unsystematic, indomitable, will break into any cabin, even into theirs. Let them chirp awhile and call it their own. If they are honest and do well, presently their neat new pinfold will be too strait and low, will crack, will lean, will rot and vanish, and the immortal light, all young and joyful, million-orbed, million-colored, will beam over the universe as on the first morning.

2. It is for want of self-culture that the superstition of Traveling, whose idols are Italy, England, Egypt, retains its fascination for all educated Americans. They who made England, Italy, or Greece venerable in the imagination did so by sticking fast where they were, like an axis of the earth. In manly hours, we feel that duty is our place. The soul is no traveler; the wise man stays at home, and when his necessities, his duties, on any occasion call him from his house, or into foreign lands, he is at home still; and shall make men sensible by the expression of his countenance, that he goes the missionary of wisdom and virtue, and visits cities and men like a sovereign, and not like an interloper or a valet.

I have no churlish objection to the circumnavigation of the globe, for the purposes of art, of study, and benevolence, so that the man is first domesticated, or does not go abroad with the hope of finding somewhat greater than he knows. He who travels to be amused, or to get somewhat which he does not carry,[242] travels away from himself, and grows old even in youth among old things. In Thebes,[243] in Palmyra,[244] his will and mind have become old and dilapidated as they. He carries ruins to ruins.

Traveling is a fool's paradise. Our first journeys discover to us the indifference of places. At home I dream that at Naples, at Rome, I can be intoxicated with beauty, and lose my sadness. I pack my trunk, embrace my friends, embark on the sea, and at last wake up in Naples, and there beside me is the stern fact, the sad self, unrelenting, identical, that I fled from.[245] I seek the Vatican,[246] and the palaces. I affect to be intoxicated with sights and suggestions, but I am not intoxicated. My giant goes with me wherever I go.

3. But the rage of traveling is a symptom of a deeper unsoundness affecting the whole intellectual action. The intellect is vagabond, and our system of education fosters restlessness. Our minds travel when our bodies are forced to stay at home. We imitate; and what is imitation but the traveling of the mind? Our houses are built with foreign taste; our shelves are garnished with foreign ornaments; our opinions, our tastes, our faculties, lean, and follow the Past and the Distant. The soul created the arts wherever they have flourished. It was in his own mind that the artist sought his model. It was an application of his own thought to the thing to be done and the conditions to be observed. And why need we copy the Doric[247] or the Gothic[248] model? Beauty, convenience, grandeur of thought, and quaint expression are as near to us as to any, and if the American artist will study with hope and love the precise thing to be done by him considering the climate, the soil, the length of the day, the wants of the people, the habit and form of the government, he will create a house in which all these will find themselves fitted, and taste and sentiment will be satisfied also.

Insist on yourself; never imitate.[249] Your own gift you can present every moment with the cumulative force of a whole life's cultivation; but of the adopted talent of another, you have only an extemporaneous, half possession. That which each can do best, none but his Maker can teach him. No man yet knows what it is, nor can, till that person has exhibited it. Where is the master who could have taught Shakespeare?[250] Where is the master who could have instructed Franklin,[251] or Washington, or Bacon,[252] or Newton?[253] Every great man is a unique. The Scipionism of Scipio[254] is precisely that part he could not borrow. Shakespeare will never be made by the study of Shakespeare. Do that which is assigned to you, and you cannot hope too much or dare too much. There is at this moment for you an utterance brave and grand as that of the colossal chisel of Phidias,[255] or trowel of the Egyptians,[256] or the pen of Moses,[257] or Dante,[258] but different from all these. Not possibly will the soul all rich, all eloquent, with thousand-cloven tongue, deign to repeat itself; but if you can hear what these patriarchs say, surely you can reply to them in the same pitch of voice; for the ear and the tongue are two organs of one nature. Abide in the simple and noble regions of thy life, obey thy heart, and thou shalt reproduce the Foreworld[259] again.

4. As our Religion, our Education, our Art look abroad, so does our spirit of society. All men plume themselves on the improvement of society, and no man improves.

Society never advances. It recedes as fast on one side as it gains on the other. It undergoes continual changes; it is barbarous, it is civilized, it is Christianized, it is rich, it is scientific; but this change is not amelioration. For everything that is given, something is taken. Society acquires new arts, and loses old instincts. What a contrast between the well-clad, reading, writing, thinking American, with a watch, a pencil, and a bill of exchange in his pocket, and the naked New Zealander,[260] whose property is a club, a spear, a mat, and an undivided twentieth of a shed to sleep under! But compare the health of the two men, and you shall see that the white man has lost his aboriginal strength. If the traveler tell us truly, strike the savage with a broad ax, and in a day or two the flesh shall unite and heal as if you struck the blow into soft pitch, and the same blow shall send the white to his grave.

The civilized man has built a coach, but has lost the use of his feet. He is supported on crutches, but lacks so much support of muscle. He has a fine Geneva[261] watch, but he fails of the skill to tell the hour by the sun. A Greenwich nautical almanac[262] he has, and so being sure of the information when he wants it, the man in the street does not know a star in the sky. The solstice[263] he does not observe; the equinox he knows as little; and the whole bright calendar of the year is without a dial in his mind. His notebooks impair his memory; his libraries overload his wit; the insurance office increases the number of accidents; and it may be a question whether machinery does not encumber; whether we have not lost by refinement some energy, by a Christianity entrenched in establishments and forms, some vigor of wild virtue. For every Stoic was a Stoic; but in Christendom where is the Christian?

There is no more deviation in the moral standard than in the standard of height or bulk. No greater men are now than ever were. A singular equality may be observed between great men of the first and of the last ages; nor can all the science, art, religion, and philosophy of the nineteenth century avail to educate greater men than Plutarch's[264] heroes, three or four and twenty centuries ago. Not in time is the race progressive. Phocion,[265] Socrates, Anaxagoras,[266] Diogenes,[267] are great men, but they leave no class. He who is really of their class will not be called by their name, but will be his own man, and, in his turn, the founder of a sect. The arts and inventions of each period are only its costume, and do not invigorate men. The harm of the improved machinery may compensate its good. Hudson[268] and Bering[269] accomplished so much in their fishing boats, as to astonish Parry[270] and Franklin,[271] whose equipment exhausted the resources of science and art. Galileo, with an opera-glass, discovered a more splendid series of celestial phenomena than any one since. Columbus[272] found the New World in an undecked boat. It is curious to see the periodical disuse and perishing of means and machinery, which were introduced with loud laudation a few years or centuries before. The great genius returns to essential man. We reckoned the improvements of the art of war among the triumphs of science, and yet Napoleon[273] conquered Europe by the bivouac, which consisted of falling back on naked valor, and disencumbering it of all aids. The Emperor held it impossible to make a perfect army, says Las Casas,[274] "without abolishing our arms, magazines, commissaries, and carriages, until, in imitation of the Roman custom, the soldier should receive his supply of corn, grind it in his handmill, and bake his bread himself."

Society is a wave. The wave moves onward, but the water of which it is composed does not. The same particle does not rise from the valley to the ridge. Its unity is only phenomenal. The persons who make up a nation to-day, next year die, and their experience with them.

And so the reliance on Property, including the reliance on governments which protect it, is the want of self-reliance. Men have looked away from themselves and at things so long, that they have come to esteem the religious, learned, and civil institutions as guards of property, and they deprecate assaults on these, because they feel them to be assaults on property. They measure their esteem of each other by what each has, and not by what each is. But a cultivated man becomes ashamed of his property, out of new respect for his nature. Especially he hates what he has, if he see that it is accidental,—came to him by inheritance, or gift, or crime; then he feels that it is not having; it does not belong to him, has no root in him, and merely lies there, because no revolution or no robber takes it away. But that which a man is, does always by necessity acquire, and what the man acquires is living property, which does not wait the beck of rulers, or mobs, or revolutions, or fire, or storm, or bankruptcies, but perpetually renews itself wherever the man breathes. "Thy lot or portion of life," said the Caliph Ali,[275] "is seeking after thee; therefore be at rest from seeking after it." Our dependence on these foreign goods leads us to our slavish respect for numbers. The political parties meet in numerous conventions; the greater the concourse, and with each new uproar of announcement, The delegation from Essex![276] The Democrats from New Hampshire! The Whigs of Maine!

the young patriot feels himself stronger than before by a new thousand of eyes and arms. In like manner the reformers summon conventions, and vote and resolve in multitude. Not so, O friends! will the god deign to enter and inhabit you, but by a method precisely the reverse. It is only as a man puts off all foreign support, and stands alone, that I see him to be strong and to prevail. He is weaker by every recruit to his banner. Is not a man better than a town? Ask nothing of men, and in the endless mutation, thou only firm column must presently appear the upholder of all that surrounds thee. He who knows that power is inborn, that he is weak because he has looked for good out of him and elsewhere, and so perceiving, throws himself unhesitatingly on his thought, instantly rights himself, stands in the erect position, commands his limbs, works miracles; just as a man who stands on his feet is stronger than a man who stands on his head.

So use all that is called Fortune.[277] Most men gamble with her, and gain all, and lose all, as her wheel rolls. But do thou leave as unlawful these winnings, and deal with Cause and Effect, the chancelors of God. In the Will work and acquire, and thou hast chained the wheel of Chance, and shalt sit hereafter out of fear from her rotations. A political victory, a rise of rents, the recovery of your sick, or the return of your absent friend, or some other favorable event, raises your spirits, and you think good days are preparing for you. Do not believe it. Nothing can bring you peace but yourself. Nothing can bring you peace but the triumph of principles.

FRIENDSHIP[278]

1. We have a great deal more kindness than is ever spoken. Barring all the selfishness that chills like east winds the world, the whole human family is bathed with an element of love like a fine ether. How many persons we meet in houses, whom we scarcely speak to, whom yet we honor, and who honor us! How many we see in the street, or sit with in church, whom, though silently, we warmly rejoice to be with! Read the language of these wandering eyebeams. The heart knoweth.

2. The effect of the indulgence of this human affection is a certain cordial exhilaration. In poetry, and in common speech, the emotions of benevolence and complacency which are felt toward others, are likened to the material effects of fire; so swift, or much more swift, more active, more cheering are these fine inward irradiations. From the highest degree of passionate love, to the lowest degree of good will, they make the sweetness of life.

3. Our intellectual and active powers increase with our affection. The scholar sits down to write, and all his years of meditation do not furnish him with one good thought or happy expression; but it is necessary to write a letter to a friend, and, forthwith, troops of gentle thoughts invest themselves, on every hand, with chosen words. See in any house where virtue and self-respect abide, the palpitation which the approach of a stranger causes. A commended stranger is expected and announced, and an uneasiness between pleasure and pain invades all the hearts of a household. His arrival almost brings fear to the good hearts that would welcome him. The house is dusted, all things fly into their places, the old coat is exchanged for the new, and they must get up a dinner if they can. Of a commended stranger, only the good report is told by others, only the good and new is heard by us. He stands to us for humanity. He is, what we wish. Having imagined and invested him, we ask how we should stand related in conversation and action with such a man, and are uneasy with fear. The same idea exalts conversation with him. We talk better than we are wont. We have the nimblest fancy, a richer memory, and our dumb devil has taken leave for the time. For long hours we can continue a series of sincere, graceful, rich communications, drawn from the oldest, secretest experience, so that they who sit by, of our own kinsfolk and acquaintance, shall feel a lively surprise at our unusual powers. But as soon as the stranger begins to

intrude his partialities, his definitions, his defects, into the conversation, it is all over. He has heard the first, the last and best, he will ever hear from us. He is no stranger now. Vulgarity, ignorance, misapprehension, are old acquaintances. Now, when he comes, he may get the order, the dress, and the dinner, but the throbbing of the heart, and the communications of the soul, no more.

4. What is so pleasant as these jets of affection which relume[279] a young world for me again? What is so delicious as a just and firm encounter of two, in a thought, in a feeling? How beautiful, on their approach to this beating heart, the steps and forms of the gifted and the true! The moment we indulge our affections, the earth is metamorphosed; there is no winter, and no night; all tragedies, all ennuis vanish; all duties even; nothing fills the proceeding eternity but the forms all radiant of beloved persons. Let the soul be assured that somewhere in the universe it should rejoin its friend, and it would be content and cheerful alone for a thousand years.

5. I awoke this morning with devout thanksgiving for my friends, the old and the new. Shall I not call God, the Beautiful, who daily showeth himself so to me in his gifts? I chide society, I embrace solitude, and yet I am not so ungrateful as not to see the wise, the lovely, and the noble-minded, as from time to time they pass my gate.[280] Who hears me, who understands me, becomes mine,—a possession for all time. Nor is nature so poor, but she gives me this joy several times, and thus we weave social threads of our own, a new web of relations; and, as many thoughts in succession substantiate themselves, we shall by-and-by stand in a new world of our own creation, and no longer strangers and pilgrims is a traditionary globe. My friends have come[281] to me unsought. The great God gave them to me. By oldest right, by the divine affinity of virtue with itself, I find them, or rather, not I, but the Deity in me and in them, both deride and cancel the thick walls of individual character, relation, age, sex and circumstance, at which he usually connives, and now makes many one. High thanks I owe you, excellent lovers, who carry out the world for me to new and noble depths, and enlarge the meaning of all my thoughts. These are new poetry of the first Bard[282]—poetry without stop—hymn, ode and epic,[283] poetry still flowing, Apollo[284] and the Muses[285] chanting still. Will these two separate themselves from me again, or some of them? I know not, but I fear it not; for my relation to them is so pure, that we hold by simple affinity, and the Genius[286] of my life being thus social, the same affinity will exert its energy on whomsoever is as noble as these men and women, wherever I may be.

6. I confess to an extreme tenderness of nature on this point. It is almost dangerous to me to "crush the sweet poison,[287] of misused wine" of

the affections. A new person is to me a great event, and hinders me from sleep. I have had such fine fancies lately about two or three persons, as have given me delicious hours, but the joy ends in the day: it yields no fruit. Thought is not born of it; my action is very little modified. I must feel pride in my friend's accomplishments as if they were mine, and a property in his virtues. I feel as warmly when he is praised, as the lover when he hears applause of his engaged maiden. We over-estimate the conscience of our friend. His goodness seems better than our goodness, his nature finer, his temptations less. Everything that is his,—his name, his form, his dress, books and instruments,—fancy enhances. Our own thought sounds new and larger from his mouth.

7. Yet the systole and diastole[288] of the heart are not without their analogy in the ebb and flow of love. Friendship, like the immortality[289] of the soul, is too good to be believed. The lover, beholding his maiden, half knows that she is not verily that which he worships; and in the golden hour of friendship, we are surprised with shades of suspicion and unbelief. We doubt that we bestow on our hero the virtues in which he shines, and afterward worship the form to which we have ascribed this divine inhabitation. In strictness, the soul does not respect men as it respects itself. In strict science, all persons underlie the same condition of an infinite remoteness. Shall we fear to cool our love by mining for the metaphysical foundation of this Elysian temple?[290] Shall I not be as real as the things I see? If I am, I shall not fear to know them for what they are. Their essence is not less beautiful than their appearance, though it needs finer organs for its apprehension. The root of the plant is not unsightly to science, though for chaplets and festoons we cut the stem short. And I must hazard the production of the bald fact amid these pleasing reveries, though it should prove an Egyptian skull at our banquet.[291] A man who stands united with his thought, conceives magnificently to himself. He is conscious of a universal success,[292] even though bought by uniform particular failures. No advantages, no powers, no gold or force can be any match for him. I cannot choose but rely on my own poverty, more than on your wealth. I cannot make your consciousness tantamount to mine. Only the star dazzles; the planet has a faint, moon-like ray. I hear what you say of the admirable parts and tried temper of the party you praise, but I see well that for all his purple cloaks I shall not like him, unless he is at least a poor Greek like me. I cannot deny it, O friend, that the vast shadow of the Phenomenal includes thee, also, in its pied and painted immensity,—thee, also, compared with whom all else is shadow. Thou art not Being, as Truth is, as Justice is,—thou art not my soul, but a picture and effigy of that. Thou hast come to me lately, and already thou art seizing thy hat and cloak. It is not that the

soul puts forth friends, as the tree puts forth leaves, and presently, by the germination of new buds, extrudes the old leaf?[293] The law of nature is alternation forevermore. Each electrical state superinduces the opposite. The soul environs itself with friends, that it may enter into a grander self-acquaintance or solitude; and it goes alone, for a season, that it may exalt its conversation or society. This method betrays itself along the whole history of our personal relations. The instinct of affection revives the hope of union with our mates, and the returning sense of insulation recalls us from the chase. Thus every man passes his life in the search after friendship, and if he should record his true sentiment, he might write a letter like this, to each new candidate for his love: —

Dear Friend: —

If I was sure of thee, sure of thy capacity, sure to match my mood with thine, I should never think again of trifles, in relation to thy comings and goings. I am not very wise; my moods are quite attainable; and I respect thy genius; it is to me as yet unfathomed; yet dare I not presume in thee a perfect intelligence of me, and so thou art to me a delicious torment. Thine ever, or never.

8. Yet these uneasy pleasures and fine pains are for curiosity, and not for life. They are not to be indulged. This is to weave cobweb, and not cloth. Our friendships hurry to short and poor conclusions, because we have made them a texture of wine and dreams,[294] instead of the tough fiber of the human heart. The laws of friendship are great, austere, and eternal, of one web with the laws of nature and of morals. But we have aimed at a swift and petty benefit, to suck a sudden sweetness. We snatch at the slowest fruit in the whole garden of God, which many summers and many winters must ripen. We seek our friend not sacredly but with an adulterate passion which would appropriate him to ourselves. In vain. We are armed all over with subtle antagonisms, which, as soon as we meet, begin to play, and translate all poetry into stale prose. Almost all people descend to meet. All association must be a compromise, and, what is worst, the very flower and aroma of the flower of each of the beautiful natures disappears as they approach each other. What a perpetual disappointment is actual society, even of the virtuous and gifted! After interviews have been compassed with long foresight, we must be tormented presently by baffled blows, by sudden, unseasonable apathies, by epilepsies of wit and of animal spirits, in the heyday of friendship and thought. Our faculties do not play us true, and both parties are relieved by solitude.

9. I ought to be equal to every relation. It makes no difference how many friends I have, and what content I can find in conversing with each, if there

be one to whom I am not equal. If I have shrunk unequal from one contest instantly, the joy I find in all the rest becomes mean and cowardly. I should hate myself, if then I made my other friends my asylum.

"The valiant warrior[295] famoused for fight,
After a hundred victories, once foiled,
Is from the book of honor razed quite,
And all the rest forgot for which he toiled."

10. Our impatience is thus sharply rebuked. Bashfulness and apathy are a tough husk in which a delicate organization is protected from premature ripening. It would be lost if it knew itself before any of the best souls were yet ripe enough to know and own it. Respect the *naturalangsamkeit* [296] which hardens the ruby in a million years, and works in duration, in which Alps and Andes come and go as rainbows. The good spirit of our life has no heaven which is the price of rashness. Love, which is the essence of God, is not for levity, but for the total worth of man. Let us not have this childish luxury in our regards, but the austerest worth; let us approach our friend with an audacious trust in the truth of his heart, in the breadth, impossible to be overturned, of his foundations.

11. The attractions of this subject are not to be resisted, and I leave, for the time, all account of subordinate social benefit, to speak of that select and sacred relation which is a kind of absolute, and which even leaves the language of love suspicious and common, so much is this purer, and nothing is so much divine.

12. I do not wish to treat friendships daintily, but with roughest courage. When they are real, they are not glass threads or frost-work, but the solidest thing we know. For now, after so many ages of experience, what do we know of nature, or of ourselves? Not one step has man taken toward the solution of the problem of his destiny. In one condemnation of folly stand the whole universe of men. But the sweet sincerity of joy and peace, which I draw from this alliance with my brother's soul, is the nut itself whereof all nature and all thought is but the husk and shell. Happy is the house that shelters a friend! It might well be built, like a festal bower or arch, to entertain him a single day. Happier, if he know the solemnity of that relation, and honor its law! He who offers himself a candidate for that covenant comes up, like an Olympian,[297] to the great games, where the first-born of the world are the competitors. He proposes himself for contest where Time, Want, Danger are in the lists, and he alone is victor who has truth enough in his constitution to preserve the delicacy of his beauty from the wear and tear of all these. The gifts of fortune may be present or absent, but all the hap in that contest depends on intrinsic nobleness, and the contempt of trifles.

There are two elements that go to the composition of friendship, each so sovereign, that I can detect no superiority in either, no reason why either should be first named. One is Truth. A friend is a person with whom I may be sincere. Before him, I may think aloud. I am arrived at last in the presence of a man so real and equal that I may drop even those undermost garments of dissimulation, courtesy, and second thought, which men never put off, and may deal with him with the simplicity and wholeness, with which one chemical atom meets another. Sincerity is the luxury allowed, but diadems and authority, only to the highest rank, *that* being permitted to speak truth as having none above it to court or conform unto. Every man alone is sincere. At the entrance of a second person, hypocrisy begins. We parry and fend the approach of our fellow-man by compliments, by gossip, by amusements, by affairs. We cover up our thought from him under a hundred folds. I knew a man who,[298] under a certain religious frenzy, cast off this drapery, and omitting all compliments and commonplace, spoke to the conscience of every person he encountered, and that with great insight and beauty. At first he was resisted, and all men agreed he was mad. But persisting, as indeed he could not help doing, for some time in this course, he attained to the advantage of bringing every man of his acquaintance into true relations with him. No man would think of speaking falsely with him, or of putting him off with any chat of markets or reading-rooms. But every man was constrained by so much sincerity to the like plain dealing and what love of nature, what poetry, what symbol of truth he had, he did certainly show him. But to most of us society shows not its face and eye, but its side and its back. To stand in true relations with men in a false age, is worth a fit of insanity, is it not? We can seldom go erect. Almost every man we meet requires some civility,—requires to be humored; he has some fame, some talent, some whim of religion or philanthropy in his head that is not to be questioned, and which spoils all conversation with him. But a friend is a sane man who exercises not my ingenuity, but me. My friend gives me entertainment without requiring any stipulation on my part. A friend, therefore, is a sort of paradox[299] in nature. I who alone am, I who see nothing in nature whose existence I can affirm with equal evidence to my own, behold now the semblance of my being in all its height, variety and curiosity, reiterated in a foreign form; so that a friend may well be reckoned the masterpiece of nature.

13. The other element of friendship is tenderness. We are holden to men by every sort of tie, by blood, by pride, by fear, by hope, by lucre, by lust, by hate, by admiration, by every circumstance and badge and trifle, but we can scarce believe that so much character can subsist in another as to draw us by love. Can another be so blessed, and we so pure, that we can offer him

tenderness? When a man becomes dear to me, I have touched the goal of fortune. I find very little written directly to the heart of this matter in books. And yet I have one text which I cannot choose but remember. My author says,[300]—"I offer myself faintly and bluntly to those whose I effectually am, and tender myself least to him to whom I am the most devoted." I wish that friendship should have feet, as well as eyes and eloquence. It must plant itself on the ground, before it vaults over the moon. I wish it to be a little of a citizen, before it is quite a cherub.[301] We chide the citizen because he makes love a commodity. It is an exchange of gifts, of useful loans; it is good neighborhood; it watches with the sick; it holds the pall at the funeral; and quite loses sight of the delicacies and nobility of the relation. But though we cannot find the god under this disguise of a sutler, yet, on the other hand, we cannot forgive the poet if he spins his thread too fine, and does not substantiate his romance by the municipal virtues of justice, punctuality, fidelity and pity. I hate the prostitution of the name of friendship to signify modish and worldly alliances. I much prefer the company of plow-boys and tin-peddlers, to the silken and perfumed amity which only celebrates its days of encounter by a frivolous display, by rides in a curricle,[302] and dinners at the best taverns. The end of friendship is a commerce the most strict and homely that can be joined; more strict than any of which we have experience. It is for aid and comfort through all the relations and passages of life and death. It is fit for serene days, and graceful gifts, and country rambles, but also for rough roads and hard fare, shipwreck, poverty, and persecution. It keeps company with the sallies of the wit and the trances of religion. We are to dignify to each other the daily needs and offices of man's life, and embellish it by courage, wisdom and unity. It should never fall into something usual and settled, but should be alert and inventive, and add rhyme and reason to what was drudgery.

14. Friendship may be said to require natures so rare and costly, each so well-tempered, and so happily adapted, and withal so circumstanced, (for even in that particular, a poet says, love demands that the parties be altogether paired,) that its satisfaction can very seldom be assured. It cannot subsist in its perfection, say some of those who are learned in this warm lore of the heart, betwixt more than two. I am not quite so strict in my terms, perhaps because I have never known so high a fellowship as others. I please my imagination more with a circle of godlike men and women variously related to each other, and between whom subsists a lofty intelligence. But I find this law of *one to one*,[303] peremptory for conversation, which is the practice and consummation of friendship. Do not mix waters too much. The best mix as ill as good and bad. You shall have very useful and cheering discourse at several times with two several men, but let all three of you come

together, and you shall not have one new and hearty word. Two may talk and one may hear, but three cannot take part in a conversation of the most sincere and searching sort. In good company there is never such discourse between two, across the table, as takes place when you leave them alone. In good company, the individuals at once merge their egotism into a social soul exactly co-extensive with the several consciousnesses there present. No partialities of friend to friend, no fondnesses of brother to sister, of wife to husband, are there pertinent, but quite otherwise. Only he may then speak who can sail on the common thought of the party, and not poorly limited to his own. Now this convention, which good sense demands, destroys the high freedom of great conversation, which requires an absolute running of two souls into one.

15. No two men but being left alone with each other, enter into simpler relations. Yet it is affinity that determines *which* two shall converse. Unrelated men give little joy to each other; will never suspect the latent powers of each. We talk sometimes of a great talent for conversation, as if it were a permanent property in some individuals. Conversation is an evanescent relation,—no more. A man is reputed to have thought and eloquence; he cannot, for all that, say a word to his cousin or his uncle. They accuse his silence with as much reason as they would blame the insignificance of a dial in the shade. In the sun it will mark the hour. Among those who enjoy his thought, he will regain his tongue.

16. Friendship requires that rare mean betwixt likeness and unlikeness, that piques each with the presence of power and of consent in the other party. Let me be alone to the end of the world, rather than that my friend should overstep by a word or a look his real sympathy. I am equally balked by antagonism and by compliance. Let him not cease an instant to be himself. The only joy I have in his being mine, is that the *not mine* is *mine*. I hate, where I looked for a manly furtherance, or at least a manly resistance, to find a mush of concession. Better be a nettle in the side of your friend, than his echo. The condition which high friendship demands is ability to do without it. That high office requires great and sublime parts. There must be very two before there can be very one. Let it be an alliance of two large formidable natures, mutually beheld, mutually feared, before yet they recognize the deep identity which beneath these disparities unites them.

17. He only is fit for this society who is magnanimous; who is sure that greatness and goodness are always economy; who is not swift to intermeddle with his fortunes. Let him not intermeddle with this. Leave to the diamond its ages to grow, nor expect to accelerate the births of the eternal. Friendship demands a religious treatment. We talk of choosing our

friends, but friends are self-elected. Reverence is a great part of it. Treat your friend as a spectacle. Of course he has merits that are not yours, and that you cannot honor, if you must needs hold him close to your person. Stand aside; give those merits room; let them mount and expand. Are you the friend of your friend's buttons, or of his thought? To a great heart he will still be a stranger in a thousand particulars, that he may come near in the holiest ground. Leave it to girls and boys to regard a friend as property, and to suck a short and all-confounding pleasure instead of the noblest benefits.

18. Let us buy our entrance to this guild by a long probation. Why should we desecrate noble and beautiful souls by intruding on them? Why insist on rash personal relations with your friend? Why go to his house, or know his mother and brother and sisters? Why be visited by him at your own? Are these things material to our covenant? Leave this touching and clawing. Let him be to me a spirit. A message, a thought, a sincerity, a glance from him I want, but not news, nor pottage. I can get politics, and chat, and neighborly conveniences, from cheaper companions. Should not the society of my friend be to me poetic, pure, universal, and great as nature itself? Ought I to feel that our tie is profane in comparison with yonder bar of cloud that sleeps on the horizon, or that clump of waving grass that divides the brook? Let us not vilify but raise it to that standard. That great defying eye, that scornful beauty of his mien and action, do not pique yourself on reducing, but rather fortify and enhance. Worship his superiorities; wish him not less by a thought, but hoard and tell them all. Guard him as thy counterpart. Let him be to thee forever a sort of beautiful enemy, untamable, devoutly revered, and not a trivial conveniency to be soon outgrown and cast aside. The hues of the opal, the light of the diamond, are not to be seen, if the eye is too near. To my friend I write a letter, and from him I receive a letter. That seems to you a little. It suffices me. It is a spiritual gift worthy of him to give and of me to receive. It profanes nobody. In these warm lines the heart will trust itself, as it will not to the tongue, and pour out the prophecy of a godlier existence than all the annals of heroism have yet made good.

19. Respect so far the holy laws of this fellowship as not to prejudice its perfect flower by your impatience for its opening. We must be our own before we can be another's. There is at least this satisfaction in crime, according to the Latin proverb;—you can speak to your accomplice on even terms. *Crimen quos [304]_ inquinat, æquat.* To those whom we admire and love, at first we cannot. Yet the least defect of self-possession vitiates, in my judgment, the entire relation. There can never be deep peace between two spirits, never mutual respect until, in their dialogue, each stands for the whole world.

20. What is so great as friendship, let us carry with what grandeur of spirit we can. Let us be silent,—so we may hear the whisper of the gods. Let us not interfere. Who set you to cast about what you should say to the select souls, or how to say anything to such? No matter how ingenious, no matter how graceful and bland. There are innumerable degrees of folly and wisdom, and for you to say aught is to be frivolous. Wait, and thy heart shall speak. Wait until the necessary and everlasting overpowers you, until day and night avail themselves of your lips. The only reward of virtue, is virtue; the only way to have a friend is to be one. You shall not come nearer a man by getting into his house. If unlike, his soul only flees the faster from you, and you shall catch never a true glance of his eye. We see the noble afar off, and they repel us; why should we intrude? Late,—very late,—we perceive that no arrangements, no introductions, no consuetudes or habits of society, would be of any avail to establish us in such relations with them as we desire,—but solely the uprise of nature in us to the same degree it is in them; then shall we meet as water with water; and if we should not meet them then, we shall not want them, for we are already they. In the last analysis, love is only the reflection of a man's own worthiness from other men. Men have sometimes exchanged names with their friends, as if they would signify that in their friend each loved his own soul.

21. The higher the style we demand of friendship, of course the less easy to establish it with flesh and blood. We walk alone in the world. Friends, such as we desire, are dreams and fables. But a sublime hope cheers ever the faithful heart, that elsewhere, in other regions of the universal power, souls are now acting, enduring and daring, which can love us, and which we can love. We may congratulate ourselves that the period of nonage,[305] of follies, of blunders, and of shame, is passed in solitude, and when we are finished men, we shall grasp heroic hands in heroic hands. Only be admonished by what you already see, not to strike leagues of friendship with cheap persons, where no friendship can be. Our impatience betrays us into rash and foolish alliances which no God attends. By persisting in your path, though you forfeit the little you gain the great. You demonstrate yourself, so as to put yourself out of the reach of false relations, and you draw to you the first-born of the world, those rare pilgrims whereof only one or two wander in nature at once, and before whom the vulgar great show as specters and shadows merely.

22. It is foolish to be afraid of making our ties too spiritual, as if so we could lose any genuine love. Whatever correction of our popular views we make from insight, nature will be sure to bear us out in, and though it seem

to rob us of some joy, will repay us with a greater. Let us feel, if we will, the absolute insulation of man. We are sure that we have all in us. We go to Europe, or we pursue persons, or we read books, in the instinctive faith that these will call it out and reveal us to ourselves. Beggars all. The persons are such as we; the Europe, an old faded garment of dead persons; the books, their ghosts. Let us drop this idolatry. Let us give over this mendicancy. Let us even bid our dearest friends farewell, and defy them, saying, "Who are you? Unhand me. I will be dependent no more." Ah! seest thou not, O brother, that thus we part only to meet again on a higher platform, and only be more each other's, because we are more our own? A friend is Janus-faced[306]: he looks to the past and the future. He is the child of all my foregoing hours, the prophet of those to come, and the harbinger[307] of a greater friend.

23. I do then with my friends as I do with my books. I would have them where I can find them, but I seldom use them. We must have society on our own terms, and admit or exclude it on the slightest cause. I cannot afford to speak much with my friend. If he is great, he makes me so great that I cannot descend to converse. In the great days, presentiments hover before me, far before me in the firmament. I ought then to dedicate myself to them. I go in that I may seize them, I go out that I may seize them. I fear only that I may lose them receding into the sky in which now they are only a patch of brighter light. Then, though I prize my friends, I cannot afford to talk with them and study their visions, lest I lose my own. It would indeed give me a certain household joy to quit this lofty seeking, this spiritual astronomy, or search of stars, and come down to warm sympathies with you; but then I know well I shall mourn always the vanishing of my mighty gods. It is true, next week I shall have languid moods, when I can well afford to occupy myself with foreign objects; then I shall regret the lost literature of your mind, and wish you were by my side again. But if you come, perhaps you will fill my mind only with new visions, not with yourself but with your lusters, and I shall not be able any more than now to converse with you. So I will owe to my friends this evanescent intercourse. I will receive from them, not what they have, but what they are. They shall give me that which properly they cannot give, but which emanates from them. But they shall not hold me by any relations less subtile and pure. We will meet as though we met not, and part as though we parted not.

24. It has seemed to me lately more possible than I knew, to carry a friendship greatly, on one side, without due correspondence on the other. Why should I cumber myself with regrets that the receiver is not capacious?

It never troubles the sun that some of his rays fall wide and vain into ungrateful space, and only a small part on the reflecting planet. Let your greatness educate the crude and cold companion. If he is unequal, he will presently pass away; but thou art enlarged by thy own shining, and no longer a mate for frogs and worms, dost soar and burn with the gods of the empyrean.[308] It is thought a disgrace to love unrequited. But the great will see that true love cannot be unrequited. True love transcends the unworthy object, and dwells and broods on the eternal, and when the poor interposed mask crumbles, it is not sad, but feels rid of so much earth, and feels its independency the surer. Yet these things may hardly be said without a sort of treachery to the relation. The essence of friendship is entireness, a total magnanimity and trust. It must not surmise or provide for infirmity. It treats its object as a god, that it may deify both.

HEROISM[309]

"Paradise is under the shadow of swords,"[310]
Mahomet.

1. In the elder English dramatists,[311] and mainly in the plays of Beaumont and Fletcher,[312] there is a constant recognition of gentility, as if a noble behavior were as easily marked in the society of their age, as color is in our American population. When any Rodrigo, Pedro, or Valerio[313] enters, though he be a stranger, the duke or governor exclaims, This is a gentleman,—and proffers civilities without end; but all the rest are slag and refuse. In harmony with this delight in personal advantages, there is in their plays a certain heroic cast of character and dialogue,—as in Bonduca, Sophocles, the Mad Lover, the Double Marriage,[314]—wherein the speaker is so earnest and cordial, and on such deep grounds of character, that the dialogue, on the slightest additional incident in the plot, rises naturally into poetry. Among many texts, take the following. The Roman Martius has conquered Athens—all but the invincible spirits of Sophocles, the duke of Athens, and Dorigen, his wife. The beauty of the latter inflames Martius, and he seeks to save her husband; but Sophocles will not ask his life, although assured, that a word will save him, and the execution of both proceeds.

"*Valerius.* Bid thy wife farewell.

Soph. No, I will take no leave. My Dorigen,
Yonder, above, 'bout Ariadne's crown.[315]
My spirit shall hover for thee. Prithee, haste.

Dor. Stay, Sophocles—with this, tie up my sight;
Let not soft nature so transformed be,
And lose her gentler sexed humanity,
To make me see my lord bleed. So, 'tis well;
Never one object underneath the sun
Will I behold before my Sophocles:
Farewell; now teach the Romans how to die.

Mar. Dost know what 'tis to die?

Soph. Thou dost not, Martius,
And therefore, not what 'tis to live; to die
Is to begin to live. It is to end
An old, stale, weary work, and to commence
A newer and a better. 'Tis to leave
Deceitful knaves for the society
Of gods and goodness. Thou, thyself, must part
At last, from all thy garlands, pleasures, triumphs,
And prove thy fortitude what then 'twill do.

Val. But art not grieved nor vexed to leave thy life thus?

Soph. Why should I grieve or vex for being sent
To them I ever loved best? Now, I'll kneel,
But with my back toward thee; 'tis the last duty
This trunk can do the gods.

Mar. Strike, strike, Valerius,
Or Martius' heart will leap out at his mouth:
This is a man, a woman! Kiss thy lord,
And live with all the freedom you were wont.
O love! thou doubly hast afflicted me
With virtue and with beauty. Treacherous heart,
My hand shall cast thee quick into my urn,
Ere thou transgress this knot of piety.

Val. What ails my brother?

Soph. Martius, oh Martius,
Thou now hast found a way to conquer me.

Dor. O star of Rome! what gratitude can speak
Fit words to follow such a deed as this?

Mar. This admirable duke, Valerius,
With his disdain of fortune and of death,
Captived himself, has captived me,
And though my arm hath ta'en his body here,
His soul hath subjugated Martius' soul.
By Romulus,[316] he is all soul, I think;

He hath no flesh, and spirit cannot be gyved;
Then we have vanquished nothing; he is free,
And Martius walks now in captivity."

2. I do not readily remember any poem, play, sermon, novel, or oration, that our press vents in the last few years, which goes to the same tune. We have a great many flutes and flageolets, but not often the sound of any fife. Yet, Wordsworth's Laodamia, and the ode of "Dion,"[317] and some sonnets, have a certain noble music; and Scott[318] will sometimes draw a stroke like the portrait of Lord Evandale, given by Balfour of Burley.[319] Thomas Carlyle,[320] with his natural taste for what is manly and daring in character, has suffered no heroic trait in his favorites to drop from his biographical and historical pictures. Earlier, Robert Burns[321] has given us a song or two. In the Harleian Miscellanies,[322] there is an account of the battle of Lutzen,[323] which deserves to be read. And Simon Ockley's[324] History of the Saracens recounts the prodigies of individual valor with admiration, all the more evident on the part of the narrator, that he seems to think that his place in Christian Oxford[325] requires of him some proper protestations of abhorrence. But if we explore the literature of Heroism, we shall quickly come to Plutarch,[326] who is its Doctor and historian. To him we owe the Brasidas,[327] the Dion,[328] the Epaminondas,[329] the Scipio[330] of old, and I must think we are more deeply indebted to him than to all the ancient writers. Each of his "Lives" is a refutation to the despondency and cowardice of our religious and political theorists. A wild courage, a Stoicism[331] not of the schools, but of the blood, shines in every anecdote, and has given that book its immense fame.

3. We need books of this tart cathartic virtue, more than books of political science, or of private economy. Life is a festival only to the wise. Seen from the nook and chimney-side of prudence, it wears a ragged and dangerous front. The violations of the laws of nature by our predecessors and our contemporaries are punished in us also. The disease and deformity around us certify the infraction of natural, intellectual, and moral laws, and often violation on violation to breed such compound misery. A lockjaw that bends a man's head back to his heels, hydrophobia that makes him bark at his wife and babes, insanity that makes him eat grass; war, plague, cholera, famine indicate a certain ferocity in nature, which, as it had its inlet by human crime, must have its outlet by human suffering. Unhappily, almost no man exists who has not in his own person become, to some amount, a stockholder in the sin, and so made himself liable to a share in the expiation.

4. Our culture, therefore, must not omit the arming of the man. Let him hear in season that he is born into the state of war, and that the commonwealth and his own well-being require that he should not go dancing in the weeds

of peace, but warned, self-collected, and neither defying nor dreading the thunder, let him take both reputation and life in his hand, and, with perfect urbanity, dare the gibbet and the mob by the absolute truth of his speech, and the rectitude of his behavior.

5. Toward all this external evil, the man within the breast assumes a warlike attitude, and affirms his ability to cope single-handed with the infinite army of enemies. To this military attitude of the soul we give the name of Heroism. Its rudest form is the contempt for safety and ease, which makes the attractiveness of war. It is a self-trust which slights the restraints of prudence, in the plenitude of its energy and power to repair the harms it may suffer. The hero is a mind of such balance that no disturbances can shake his will, but pleasantly, and, as it were, merrily, he advances to his own music, alike in frightful alarms, and in the tipsy mirth of universal dissoluteness. There is somewhat not philosophical in heroism; there is somewhat not holy in it; it seems not to know that other souls are of one texture with it; it has pride; it is the extreme of individual nature. Nevertheless, we must profoundly revere it. There is somewhat in great actions, which does not allow us to go behind them. Heroism feels and never reasons, and therefore is always right; and although a different breeding, different religion, and greater intellectual activity, would have modified or even reversed the particular action, yet for the hero, that thing he does is the highest deed, and is not open to the censure of philosophers or divines. It is the avowal of the unschooled man, that he finds a quality in him that is negligent of expense, of health, of life, of danger, of hatred, of reproach, and knows that his will is higher and more excellent than all actual and all possible antagonists.

6. Heroism works in contradiction to the voice of mankind, and in contradiction, for a time, to the voice of the great and good. Heroism is an obedience[332] to a secret impulse of an individual's character. Now to no other man can its wisdom appear as it does to him, for every man must be supposed to see a little further on his own proper path than any one else. Therefore, just and wise men take umbrage at his act, until after some little time be past: then they see it to be in unison with their acts. All prudent men see that the action is clean contrary to a sensual prosperity; for every heroic act measures itself by its contempt of some external good. But it finds its own success at last, and then the prudent also extol.

7. Self-trust is the essence of heroism. It is the state of the soul at war, and its ultimate objects are the last defiance of falsehood and wrong, and the power to bear all that can be inflicted by evil agents. It speaks the truth, and it is just, generous, hospitable, temperate, scornful of petty calculations, and scornful of being scorned. It persists; it is of an undaunted boldness, and of a fortitude not to be wearied out. Its jest is the littleness of common

life. That false prudence which dotes on health and wealth is the butt and merriment of heroism. Heroism, like Plotinus,[333] is almost ashamed of its body. What shall it say, then, to the sugar-plums, and cats'-cradles, to the toilet, compliments, quarrels, cards, and custard, which rack the wit of all human society. What joys has kind nature provided for us dear creatures! There seems to be no interval between greatness and meanness. When the spirit is not master of the world then it is its dupe. Yet the little man takes the great hoax so innocently, works in it so headlong and believing, is born red, and dies gray, arranging his toilet, attending on his own health, laying traps for sweet food and strong wine, setting his heart on a horse or a rifle, made happy with a little gossip or a little praise, that the great soul cannot choose but laugh at such earnest nonsense. "Indeed, these humble considerations[334] make me out of love with greatness. What a disgrace is it to me to take note how many pairs of silk stockings thou hast, namely, these and those that were the peach-colored ones; or to bear the inventory of thy shirts, as one for superfluity, and one other for use!"

8. Citizens, thinking after the laws of arithmetic, consider the inconvenience of receiving strangers at their fireside, reckon narrowly the loss of time and the unusual display: the soul of a better quality thrusts back the unreasonable economy into the vaults of life, and says, I will obey the God, and the sacrifice and the fire he will provide. Ibn Hankal,[335] the Arabian geographer, describes a heroic extreme in the hospitality of Sogd, in Bokhar,[336] "When I was in Sogd I saw a great building, like a palace, the gates of which were open and fixed back to the wall with large nails. I asked the reason, and was told that the house had not been shut, night or day, for a hundred years. Strangers may present themselves at any hour, and in whatever number; the master has amply provided for the reception of the men and their animals, and is never happier than when they tarry for some time. Nothing of the kind have I seen in any other country." The magnanimous know very well that they who give time, or money, or shelter, to the stranger—so it be done for love, and not for ostentation—do, as it were, put God under obligation to them, so perfect are the compensations of the universe. In some way the time they seem to lose is redeemed, and the pains they seem to take remunerate themselves. These men fan the flame of human love, and raise the standard of civil virtue among mankind. But hospitality must be for service, and not for show, or it pulls down the host. The brave soul rates itself too high to value itself by the splendor of its table and draperies. It gives what it hath, and all it hath, but its own majesty can lend a better grace to bannocks[337] and fair water than belong to city feasts.

9. The temperance of the hero proceeds from the same wish to do no dishonor to the worthiness he has. But he loves it for its elegancy, not for

its austerity. It seems not worth his while to be solemn, and denounce with bitterness flesh-eating or wine-drinking, the use of tobacco, or opium, or tea, or silk, or gold. A great man scarcely knows how he dines, how he dresses; but without railing or precision, his living is natural and poetic. John Eliot,[338] the Indian Apostle, drank water, and said of wine,—"It is a noble, generous liquor, and we should be humbly thankful for it, but, as I remember, water was made before it." Better still is the temperance of king David[339] who poured out on the ground unto the Lord the water which three of his warriors had brought him to drink, at the peril of their lives.

10. It is told of Brutus,[340] that when he fell on his sword, after the battle of Philippi,[341] he quoted a line of Euripides,[342]—"O virtue! I have followed thee through life, and I find thee at last but a shade." I doubt not the hero is slandered by this report. The heroic soul does not sell its justice and its nobleness. It does not ask to dine nicely, and to sleep warm. The essence of greatness is the perception that virtue is enough. Poverty is its ornament. It does not need plenty, and can very well abide its loss.

11. But that which takes my fancy most, in the heroic class, is the good humor and hilarity they exhibit. It is a height to which common duty can very well attain, to suffer and to dare with solemnity. But these rare souls set opinion, success, and life, at so cheap a rate, that they will not soothe their enemies by petitions, or the show of sorrow, but wear their own habitual greatness. Scipio,[343] charged with peculation, refuses to do himself so great a disgrace as to wait for justification, though he had the scroll of his accounts in his hands, but tears it to pieces before the tribunes. Socrates'[344] condemnation of himself to be maintained in all honor in the Prytaneum,[345] during his life, and Sir Thomas More's[346] playfulness at the scaffold, are of the same strain. In Beaumont and Fletcher's "Sea Voyage," Juletta tells the stout captain and his company,

Jul. Why, slaves, 'tis in our power to hang ye.

Master. Very likely,
'Tis in our powers, then, to be hanged, and scorn ye.

These replies are sound and whole. Sport is the bloom and glow of a perfect health. The great will not condescend to take anything seriously; all must be as gay as the song of a canary, though it were the building of cities, or the eradication of old and foolish churches and nations, which have cumbered the earth long thousands of years. Simple hearts put all the history and customs of this world behind them, and play their own play in innocent defiance of the Blue-Laws[347] of the world; and such would appear, could we see the human race assembled in vision, like little children frolicking together; though, to the eyes of mankind at large, they wear a stately and solemn garb of works and influences.

12. The interest these fine stories have for us, the power of a romance over the boy who grasps the forbidden book under his bench at school, our delight in the hero, is the main fact to our purpose. All these great and transcendent properties are ours. If we dilate in beholding the Greek energy, the Roman pride, it is that we are already domesticating the same sentiment. Let us find room for this great guest in our small houses. The first step of worthiness will be to disabuse us of our superstitious associations with places and times, with number and size. Why should these words, Athenian, Roman, Asia, and England, so tingle in the ear? Where the heart is, there the muses, there the gods sojourn, and not in any geography of fame. Massachusetts, Connecticut River, and Boston Bay, you think paltry places, and the ear loves names of foreign and classic topography. But here we are; and, if we will tarry a little, we may come to learn that here is best. See to it only that thyself is here;—and art and nature, hope and fate, friends, angels, and the Supreme Being, shall not be absent from the chamber where thou sittest. Epaminondas,[348] brave and affectionate, does not seem to us to need Olympus[349] to die upon, nor the Syrian sunshine. He lies very well where he is. The Jerseys[350] were handsome ground enough for Washington to tread, and London streets for the feet of Milton.[351] A great man makes his climate genial in the imagination of men, and its air the beloved element of all delicate spirits. That country is the fairest, which is inhabited by the noblest minds. The pictures which fill the imagination in reading the actions of Pericles,[352] Xenophon,[353] Columbus,[354] Bayard,[355] Sidney,[356] Hampden,[357] teach us how needlessly mean our life is, that we, by the depth of our living, should deck it with more than regal or national splendor, and act on principles that should interest man and nature in the length of our days.

13. We have seen or heard of many extraordinary young men, who never ripened, or whose performance in actual life was not extraordinary. When we see their air and mien, when we hear them speak of society, or books, or religion, we admire their superiority; they seem to throw contempt on our entire polity and social state; theirs is the tone of a youthful giant, who is sent to work revolutions. But they enter an active profession, and the forming Colossus[358] shrinks to the common size of man. The magic they used was the ideal tendencies, which always make the Actual ridiculous; but the tough world had its revenge the moment they put their horses of the sun to plow in its furrow. They found no example and no companion, and their heart fainted. What then? The lesson they gave in their first aspirations, is yet true; and a better valor and a purer truth shall one day

organize their belief. Or why should a woman liken herself to any historical woman, and think, because Sappho,[359] or Sévigné,[360] or De Staël,[361] or the cloistered souls who have had genius and cultivation, do not satisfy the imagination and the serene Themis,[362] none can,—certainly not she. Why not? She has a new and unattempted problem to solve, perchance that of the happiest nature that ever bloomed. Let the maiden, with erect soul, walk serenely on her way, accept the hint of each new experience, search, in turn, all the objects that solicit her eye, that she may learn the power and the charm of her new-born being which is the kindling of a new dawn in the recesses of space. The fair girl, who repels interference by a decided and proud choice of influences, so careless of pleasing, so wilful and lofty, inspires every beholder with somewhat of her own nobleness. The silent heart encourages her; O friend, never strike sail to a fear! Come into port greatly, or sail with God the seas. Not in vain you live, for every passing eye is cheered and refined by the vision.

14. The characteristic of a genuine heroism is its persistency. All men have wandering impulses, fits and starts of generosity. But when you have chosen your part, abide by it, and do not weakly try to reconcile yourself with the world. The heroic cannot be the common, nor the common the heroic. Yet we have the weakness to expect the sympathy of people in those actions whose excellence is that they outrun sympathy, and appeal to a tardy justice. If you would serve your brother, because it is fit for you to serve him, do not take back your words when you find that prudent people do not commend you. Adhere to your own act, and congratulate yourself if you have done something strange and extravagant, and broken the monotony of a decorous age. It was a high counsel[363] that I once heard given to a young person,—"Always do what you are afraid to do." A simple manly character need never make an apology, but should regard its past action with the calmness of Phocion,[364] when he admitted that the event of the battle was happy, yet did not regret his dissuasion from the battle.

15. There is no weakness or exposure for which we cannot find consolation in the thought,—this is a part of my constitution, part of my relation and office to my fellow-creature. Has nature covenanted with me that I should never appear to disadvantage, never make a ridiculous figure? Let us be generous of our dignity as well as of our money. Greatness once and forever has done with opinion. We tell our charities, not because we wish to be praised for them, not because we think they have great merit, but for our justification. It is a capital blunder; as you discover, when another man recites his charities.

16. To speak the truth, even with some austerity, to live with some rigor of temperance, or some extremes of generosity, seems to be an asceticism which common good-nature would appoint to those who are at ease and in plenty, in sign that they feel a brotherhood with the great multitude of suffering men. And not only need we breathe and exercise the soul by assuming the penalties of abstinence, of debt, of solitude, of unpopularity, but it behooves the wise man to look with a bold eye into those rarer dangers which sometimes invade men, and to familiarize himself with disgusting forms of disease, with sounds of execration, and the vision of violent death.

17. Times of heroism are generally times of terror, but the day never shines in which this element may not work. The circumstances of man, we say, are historically somewhat better in this country, and at this hour, than perhaps ever before. More freedom exists for culture. It will not now run against an ax at the first step out of the beaten track of opinion. But whoso is heroic will always find crises to try his edge. Human virtue demands her champions and martyrs, and the trial of persecution always proceeds. It is but the other day that the brave Lovejoy[365] gave his breast to the bullets of a mob, for the rights of free speech and opinion, and died when it was better not to live.

18. I see not any road to perfect peace which a man can walk, but to take counsel of his own bosom. Let him quit too much association, let him go home much, and establish himself in those courses he approves. The unremitting retention of simple and high sentiments in obscure duties is hardening the character to that temper which will work with honor, if need be, in the tumult, or on the scaffold. Whatever outrages have happened to men may befall a man again; and very easily in a republic, if there appear any signs of a decay of religion. Coarse slander, fire, tar and feathers, and the gibbet, the youth may freely bring home to his mind, and with what sweetness of temper he can, and inquire how fast he can fix his sense of duty, braving such penalties, whenever it may please the next newspaper and a sufficient number of his neighbors to pronounce his opinions incendiary.

19. It may calm the apprehension of calamity in the most susceptible heart to see how quick a bound nature has set to the utmost infliction of malice. We rapidly approach a brink over which no enemy can follow us.

"Let them rave:[366]
Thou art quiet in thy grave."

In the gloom of our ignorance of what shall be, in the hour when we are deaf to the higher voices, who does not envy them who have seen safely to an end their manful endeavor? Who that sees the meanness of our politics, but inly congratulates Washington that he is long already wrapped in his shroud, and forever safe; that he was laid sweet in his grave, the hope of humanity not yet subjugated in him? Who does not sometimes envy the good and brave, who are no more to suffer from the tumults of the natural world, and await with curious complacency the speedy term of his own conversation with finite nature? And yet the love that will be annihilated sooner than treacherous has already made death impossible, and affirms itself no mortal, but a native of the deeps of absolute and inextinguishable being.

MANNERS[367]

1. Half the world, it is said, knows not how the other half live. Our Exploring Expedition saw the Feejee Islanders[368] getting their dinner off human bones; and they are said to eat their own wives and children. The husbandry of the modern inhabitants of Gournou[369] (west of old Thebes) is philosophical to a fault. To set up their housekeeping, nothing is requisite but two or three earthen pots, a stone to grind meal, and a mat which is the bed. The house, namely, a tomb, is ready without rent or taxes. No rain can pass through the roof, and there is no door, for there is no want of one, as there is nothing to lose. If the house do not please them, they walk out and enter another, as there are several hundreds at their command. "It is somewhat singular," adds Berzoni, to whom we owe this account, "to talk of Happiness among people who live in sepulchers, among corpses and rags of an ancient nation which they knew nothing of." In the deserts of Borgoo[370] the rock-Tibboos still dwell in caves, like cliff-swallows, and the language of these negroes is compared by their neighbors to the shrieking of bats, and to the whistling of birds. Again, the Bornoos[371] have no proper names; individuals are called after their height, thickness, or other accidental quality, and have nick-names merely. But the salt, the dates, the ivory, and the gold, for which these horrible regions are visited, find their way into countries, where the purchaser and consumer can hardly be ranked in one race with these cannibals and man-stealers; countries where man serves himself with metals, wood, stone, glass, gum, cotton, silk and wool; honors himself with architecture;[372] writes laws, and contrives to execute his will through the hands of many nations; and, especially, establishes a select society, running through all the countries of intelligent men, a self-constituted aristocracy, or fraternity of the best, which, without written law, or exact usage of any kind, perpetuates itself, colonizes every new-planted island, and adopts and makes its own whatever personal beauty or extraordinary native endowment anywhere appears.

2. What fact more conspicuous in modern history, than the creation of the gentleman? Chivalry[373] is that, and loyalty is that, and, in English literature, half the drama, and all the novels, from Sir Philip Sidney[374] to Sir Walter Scott,[375] paint this figure. The word *gentleman*, which, like the word Christian, must hereafter characterize the present and the

few preceding centuries, by the importance attached to it, is a homage to personal and incommunicable properties. Frivolous and fantastic additions have got associated with the name, but the steady interest of mankind in it must be attributed to the valuable properties which it designates. An element which unites all the most forcible persons of every country; makes them intelligible and agreeable to each other, and is somewhat so precise, that it is at once felt if an individual lack the masonic sign,[376] cannot be any casual product, but must be an average result of the character and faculties universally found in men. It seems a certain permanent average; as the atmosphere is a permanent composition, whilst so many gases are combined only to be decompounded. *Comme il faut*, is the Frenchman's description of good society, *as we must be*. It is a spontaneous fruit of talents and feelings of precisely that class who have most vigor, who take the lead in the world of this hour, and, though far from pure, far from constituting the gladdest and highest tone of human feeling, is as good as the whole society permits it to be. It is made of the spirit, more than of the talent of men, and is a compound result, into which every great force enters as an ingredient, namely, virtue, wit, beauty, wealth, and power.

3. There is something equivocal in all the words in use to express the excellence of manners and social cultivation, because the qualities are fluxional, and the last effect is assumed by the senses as the cause. The word *gentleman* has not any correlative abstract[377] to express the quality. *Gentility* is mean, and *gentilesse* [378] is obsolete. But we must keep alive in the vernacular the distinction between *fashion*, a word of narrow and often sinister meaning, and the heroic character which the gentleman imports. The usual words, however, must be respected: they will be found to contain the root of the matter. The point of distinction in all this class of names, as courtesy, chivalry, fashion, and the like, is, that the flower and fruit, not the grain of the tree, are contemplated. It is beauty which is the aim this time, and not worth. The result is now in question, although our words intimate well enough the popular feeling, that the appearance supposes a substance. The gentleman is a man of truth, lord of his own actions, and expressing that lordship in his behavior, not in any manner dependent and servile either on persons, or opinions, or possessions. Beyond this fact of truth and real force, the word denotes good-nature and benevolence: manhood first, and then gentleness. The popular notion certainly adds a condition of ease and fortune; but that is a natural result of personal force and love, that they should possess and dispense the goods of the world. In times of violence, every eminent person must fall in with many opportunities to approve his stoutness and worth; therefore every man's name that emerged at all from the mass in the feudal ages,[379] rattles in our ear like a flourish of trumpets.

But personal force never goes out of fashion. That is still paramount to-day, and, in the moving crowd of good society, the men of valor and reality are known, and rise to their natural place. The competition is transferred from war to politics and trade, but the personal force appears readily enough in these new arenas.

4. Power first, or no leading class. In politics and in trade, bruisers and pirates are of better promise than talkers and clerks. God knows[380] that all sorts of gentlemen knock at the door; but whenever used in strictness, and with any emphasis, the name will be found to point at original energy. It describes a man standing in his own right, and working after untaught methods. In a good lord, there must first be a good animal, at least to the extent of yielding the incomparable advantage of animal spirits.[381] The ruling class must have more, but they must have these, giving in every company the sense of power,[382] which makes things easy to be done which daunt the wise. The society of the energetic class, in their friendly and festive meetings, is full of courage, and of attempts, which intimidate the pale scholar. The courage which girls exhibit is like a battle of Lundy's Lane,[383] or a sea-fight. The intellect relies on memory to make some supplies to face these extemporaneous squadrons. But memory is a base mendicant with basket and badge, in the presence of these sudden masters. The rulers of society must be up to the work of the world, and equal to their versatile office: men of the right Cæsarian pattern,[384] who have great range of affinity. I am far from believing the timid maxim[385] of Lord Falkland,[386] ("That for ceremony there must go two to it; since a bold fellow will go through the cunningest forms,") and am of opinion that the gentleman is the bold fellow whose forms are not to be broken through; and only that plenteous nature is rightful master, which is the complement of whatever person it converses with. My gentleman gives the law where he is; he will outpray saints in chapel, outgeneral veterans in the field, and outshine all courtesy in the hall. He is good company for pirates, and good with academicians; so that it is useless to fortify yourself against him; he has the private entrance to all minds, and I could as easily exclude myself as him. The famous gentlemen of Asia and Europe have been of this strong type: Saladin,[387] Sapor,[388] the Cid,[389] Julius Cæsar,[390] Scipio,[391] Alexander,[392] Pericles,[393] and the lordliest personages. They sat very carelessly in their chairs, and were too excellent themselves to value any condition at a high rate.

5. A plentiful fortune is reckoned necessary, in the popular judgment, to the completion of this man of the world: and it is a material deputy which walks through the dance which the first has led. Money is not essential, but this wide affinity is, which transcends the habits of clique and caste,

and makes itself felt by men of all classes. If the aristocrat is only valid in fashionable circles, and not with truckmen, he will never be a leader in fashion; and if the man of the people cannot speak on equal terms with the gentleman, so that the gentleman shall perceive that he is already really of his own order, he is not to be feared. Diogenes,[394] Socrates,[395] and Epaminondas[396] are gentlemen of the best blood, who have chosen the condition of poverty, when that of wealth was equally open to them. I use these old names, but the men I speak of are my contemporaries.[397] Fortune will not supply to every generation one of these well-appointed knights, but every collection of men furnishes some example of the class: and the politics of this country, and the trade of every town, are controlled by these hardy and irresponsible doers, who have invention to take the lead, and a broad sympathy which puts them in fellowship with crowds, and makes their action popular.

6. The manners of this class are observed and caught with devotion by men of taste. The association of these masters with each other, and with men intelligent of their merits, is mutually agreeable and stimulating. The good forms, the happiest expressions of each, are repeated and adopted. By swift consent, everything superfluous is dropped, everything graceful is renewed. Fine manners[398] show themselves formidable to the uncultivated man. They are a subtler science of defence to parry and intimidate; but once matched by the skill of the other party, they drop the point of the sword,—points and fences disappear, and the youth finds himself in a more transparent atmosphere, wherein life is a less troublesome game, and not a misunderstanding rises between the players. Manners aim to facilitate life, to get rid of impediments, and bring the man pure to energize. They aid our dealing and conversation, as a railway aids traveling, by getting rid of all avoidable obstructions of the road, and leaving nothing to be conquered but pure space. These forms very soon become fixed, and a fine sense of propriety is cultivated with more heed, that it becomes a badge of social and civil distinctions. Thus grows up Fashion, an equivocal semblance, the most puissant, the most fantastic and frivolous, the most feared and followed, and which morals and violence assault in vain.

7. There exists a strict relation between the class of power, and the exclusive and polished circles. The last are always filled or filling from the first. The strong men usually give some allowance even to the petulances of fashion, for that affinity they find in it. Napoleon,[399] child of the revolution, destroyer of the old noblesse,[400] never ceased to court the Faubourg St. Germain[401]: doubtless with the feeling, that fashion is a homage to men of his stamp. Fashion, though in a strange way, represents all manly virtue. It is a virtue gone to seed: it is a kind of posthumous honor.

It does not often caress the great, but the children of the great: it is a hall of the Past. It usually sets its face against the great of this hour. Great men are not commonly in its halls: they are absent in the field: they are working, not triumphing. Fashion is made up of their children; of those, who, through the value and virtue of somebody, have acquired lustre to their name, marks of distinction, means of cultivation and generosity, and, in their physical organization, a certain health and excellence, which secures to them, if not the highest power to work, yet high power to enjoy. The class of power, the working heroes, the Cortez,[402] the Nelson,[403] the Napoleon, see that this is the festivity and permanent celebration of such as they; that fashion is funded talent; is Mexico,[404] Marengo,[405] and Trafalgar[406] [407] beaten out thin; that the brilliant names of fashion run back to just such busy names as their own, fifty or sixty years ago. They are the sowers, their sons shall be the reapers, and *their* sons, in the ordinary course of things, must yield the possession of the harvest, to new competitors with keener eyes and stronger frames. The city is recruited from the country. In the year 1805, it is said, every legitimate monarch in Europe was imbecile. The city would have died out, rotted, and exploded, long ago, but that it was reinforced from the fields. It is only country which came to town day before yesterday, that is city and court to-day.

8. Aristocracy and fashion are certain inevitable results. These mutual selections are indestructible. If they provoke anger in the least favored class, and the excluded majority revenge themselves on the excluding minority, by the strong hand, and kill them, at once a new class finds itself at the top, as certainly as cream rises in a bowl of milk: and if the people should destroy class after class, until two men only were left, one of these would be the leader, and would be involuntarily served and copied by the other. You may keep this minority out of sight and out of mind, but it is tenacious of life, and is one of the estates of the realm.[408] I am the more struck with this tenacity, when I see its work. It respects the administration of such unimportant matters, that we should not look for any durability in its rule. We sometimes meet men under some strong moral influence, as a patriotic, a literary, a religious movement, and feel that the moral sentiment rules man and nature. We think all other distinctions and ties will be slight and fugitive, this of caste or fashion, for example; yet come from year to year, and see how permanent that is, in this Boston or New York life of man, where, too, it has not the lease countenance from the law of the land. Not in Egypt or in India a firmer or more impassable line. Here are associations whose ties go over, and under, and through it, a meeting of merchants, a military corps, a college-class, a fire-club, a professional association, a political, a religious convention;—the persons seem to draw inseparably near; yet

that assembly once dispersed, its members will not in the year meet again. Each returns to his degree in the scale of good society, porcelain remains porcelain, and earthen earthen. The objects of fashion may be frivolous, or fashion may be objectless, but the nature of this union and selection can be neither frivolous nor accidental. Each man's rank in that perfect graduation depends on some symmetry in his structure, or some agreement in his structure to the symmetry of society. Its doors unbar instantaneously to a natural claim of their own kind. A natural gentleman finds his way in, and will keep the oldest patrician out, who has lost his intrinsic rank. Fashion understands itself; good-breeding and personal superiority of whatever country readily fraternize with those of every other. The chiefs of savage tribes have distinguished themselves in London and Paris, by the purity of their tournure.[409]

9. To say what good of fashion we can,—it rests on reality, and hates nothing so much as pretenders;—to exclude and mystify pretenders, and send them into everlasting "Coventry,"[410] is its delight. We contemn, in turn, every other gift of men of the world; but the habit, even in little and the least matters, of not appealing to any but our own sense of propriety, constitutes the foundation of all chivalry. There is almost no kind of self-reliance, so it be sane and proportioned, which fashion does not occasionally adopt, and give it the freedom of its saloons. A sainted soul is always elegant, and, if it will, passes unchallenged into the most guarded ring. But so will Jock the teamster pass, in some crisis that brings him thither, and find favor, as long as his head is not giddy with the new circumstance, and the iron shoes do not wish to dance in waltzes and cotillions. For there is nothing settled in manners, but the laws of behavior yield to the energy of the individual. The maiden at her first ball, the countryman at a city dinner, believes that there is a ritual according to which every act and compliment must be performed, or the failing party must be cast out of this presence. Later, they learn that good sense and character make their own forms every moment, and speak or abstain, to take wine or refuse it, stay or go, sit in a chair or sprawl with children on the floor, or stand on their head, or what else soever, in a new and aboriginal way: and that strong will is always in fashion, let who will be unfashionable. All that fashion demands is composure, and self-content. A circle of men perfectly well-bred would be a company of sensible persons, in which every man's native manners and character appear. If the fashionist have not this quality, he is nothing. We are such lovers of self-reliance, that we excuse in man many sins, if he will show us a complete satisfaction in his position, which asks no leave to be of mine, or any man's good opinion. But any deference to some eminent man or woman of the world, forfeits all privilege of nobility. He is an underling: I

have nothing to do with him; I will speak with his master. A man should not go where he cannot carry his whole sphere or society with him, — not bodily, the whole circle of his friends, but atmospherically. He should preserve in a new company the same attitude of mind and reality of relation, which his daily associates draw him to, else he is shorn of his best beams, and will be an orphan in the merriest club. "If you could see Vich Ian Vohr with his tail on![411] — " But Vich Ian Vohr must always carry his belongings in some fashion, if not added as honor, then severed as disgrace.

10. There will always be in society certain persons who are mercuries[412] of its approbation, and whose glance will at any time determine for the curious their standing in the world. These are the chamberlains of the lesser gods. Accept their coldness as an omen of grace with the loftier deities, and allow them all their privilege. They are clear in their office, nor could they be thus formidable, without their own merits. But do not measure the importance of this class by their pretension, or imagine that a fop can be the dispenser of honor and shame. They pass also at their just rate; for how can they otherwise, in circles which exist as a sort of herald's office[413] for the sifting of character?

11. As the first thing man requires of man is reality, so that appears in all the forms of society. We pointedly, and by name, introduce the parties to each other. Know you before all heaven and earth, that this is Andrew, and this is Gregory; — they look each other in the eye; they grasp each other's hand, to identify and signalize each other. It is a great satisfaction. A gentleman never dodges; his eyes look straight forward, and he assures the other party, first of all, that he has been met. For what is it that we seek, in so many visits and hospitalities? Is it your draperies, pictures, and decorations? Or, do we not insatiably ask. Was a man in the house? I may easily go into a great household where there is much substance, excellent provision for comfort, luxury, and taste, and yet not encounter there any Amphitryon,[414] who shall subordinate these appendages. I may go into a cottage, and find a farmer who feels that he is the man I have come to see, and fronts me accordingly. It was therefore a very natural point of old feudal etiquette, that a gentleman who received a visit, though it were of his sovereign, should not leave his roof, but should wait his arrival at the door of his house. No house, though it were the Tuileries,[415] or the Escurial,[416] is good for anything without a master. And yet we are not often gratified by this hospitality. Everybody we know surrounds himself with a fine house, fine books, conservatory, gardens, equipage, and all manner of toys, as screens to interpose between himself and his guests. Does it not seem as if man was of a very sly, elusive nature, and dreaded nothing so much as a full rencounter front to front with his fellow? It were unmerciful, I know,

quite to abolish the use of these screens, which are of eminent convenience, whether the guest is too great, or too little. We call together many friends who keep each other in play, or by luxuries and ornaments we amuse the young people, and guard our retirement. Or if, perchance, a searching realist comes to our gate, before whose eyes we have no care to stand, then again we run to our curtain, and hide ourselves as Adam[417] at the voice of the Lord God in the garden. Cardinal Caprara,[418] the Pope's[419] legate at Paris, defended himself from the glances of Napoleon, by an immense pair of green spectacles. Napoleon remarked them, and speedily managed to rally them off: and yet Napoleon, in his turn, was not great enough, with eight hundred thousand troops at his back, to face a pair of free-born eyes, but fenced himself with etiquette, and within triple barriers of reserve: and, as all the world knows from Madame de Stael,[420] was wont, when he found himself observed, to discharge his face of all expression. But emperors and rich men are by no means the most skillful masters of good manners. No rent roll nor army-list can dignify skulking and dissimulations: and the first point of courtesy must always be truth, as really all forms of good-breeding point that way.

12. I have just been reading, in Mr. Hazlitt's[421] translation, Montaigne's[422] account of his journey into Italy, and am struck with nothing more agreeably than the self-respecting fashions of the time. His arrival in each place, the arrival of a gentleman of France, is an event of some consequence. Wherever he goes, he pays a visit to whatever prince or gentleman of note resides upon his road, as a duty to himself and to civilization. When he leaves any house in which he has lodged for a few weeks, he causes his arms to be painted and hung up as a perpetual sign to the house, as was the custom of gentlemen.

13. The complement of this graceful self-respect, and that of all the points of good breeding I most require and insist upon, is deference. I like that every chair should be a throne, and hold a king. I prefer a tendency to stateliness, to an excess of fellowship. Let the incommunicable objects of nature and the metaphysical isolation of man teach us independence. Let us not be too much acquainted. I would have a man enter his house through a hall filled with heroic and sacred sculptures, that he might not want the hint of tranquillity and self-poise.[423] We should meet each morning, as from foreign countries, and spending the day together, should depart at night, as into foreign countries. In all things I would have the island of a man inviolate. Let us sit apart as the gods, talking from peak to peak all round Olympus. No degree of affection need invade this religion. This is myrrh and rosemary to keep the other sweet. Lovers should guard their strangeness. If they forgive too much, all slides into confusion and meanness. It is easy to

push this deference to a Chinese etiquette;[424] but coolness and absence of heat and haste indicate fine qualities. A gentleman makes no noise: a lady is serene Proportionate is our disgust at those invaders who fill a studious house with blast and running, to secure some paltry convenience. Not less I dislike a low sympathy of each with his neighbors's needs. Must we have a good understanding with one another's palates? as foolish people who have lived long together, know when each wants salt or sugar. I pray my companion, if he wishes for bread, to ask me for bread, and if he wishes for sassafras or arsenic, to ask me for them, and not to hold out his plate, as if I knew already. Every natural function can be dignified by deliberation and privacy. Let us leave hurry to slaves. The compliments and ceremonies of our breeding should recall,[425] however remotely, the grandeur of our destiny.

14. The flower of courtesy does not very well bide handling, but if we dare to open another leaf, and explore what parts go to its conformation, we shall find also an intellectual quality. To the leaders of men, the brain as well as the flesh and the heart must furnish a proportion. Defect in manners is usually the defect of fine perceptions. Men are too coarsely made for the delicacy of beautiful carriage and customs. It is not quite sufficient to good breeding, a union of kindness and independence. We imperatively require a perception of, and a homage to, beauty in our companions. Other virtues are in request in the field and work yard, but a certain degree of taste is not to be spared in those we sit with. I could better eat with one who did not respect the truth or the laws, than with a sloven and unpresentable person. Moral qualities rule the world, but at short distances the senses are despotic. The same discrimination of fit and fair runs out, if with less rigor, into all parts of life. The average spirit of the energetic class is good sense, acting under certain limitations and to certain ends. It entertains every natural gift. Social in its nature, it respects everything which tends to unite men. It delights in measure.[426] The love of beauty is mainly the love of measure or proportion. The person who screams, or uses the superlative degree, or converses with heat, puts whole drawing-rooms to flight. If you wish to be loved, love measure. You must have genius, or a prodigious usefulness, if you will hide the want of measure. This perception comes in to polish and perfect the parts of the social instrument. Society will pardon much to genius and special gifts, but, being in its nature a convention, it loves what is conventional, or what belongs to coming together. That makes the good and bad of manners, namely, what helps or hinders fellowship. For, fashion is not good sense absolute, but relative; not good sense private, but good sense entertaining company. It hates corners and sharp points of character, hates quarrelsome, egotistical, solitary, and gloomy people; hates whatever can

interfere with total blending of parties; whilst it values all peculiarities as in the highest degree refreshing, which can consist with good fellowship. And besides the general infusion of wit to heighten civility, the direct splendor of intellectual power is ever welcome in fine society as the costliest addition to its rule and its credit.

15. The dry light must shine in to adorn our festival, but it must be tempered and shaded, or that will also offend. Accuracy is essential to beauty, and quick perceptions to politeness, but not too quick perceptions. One may be too punctual and too precise. He must leave the omniscience of business at the door, when he comes into the palace of beauty. Society loves creole natures,[427] and sleepy, languishing manners, so that they cover sense, grace, and good-will: the air of drowsy strength, which disarms criticism; perhaps, because such a person seems to reserve himself for the best of the game, and not spend himself on surfaces; an ignoring eye, which does not see the annoyances, shifts, and inconveniences, that cloud the brow and smother the voice of the sensitive.

16. Therefore, besides personal force and so much perception as constitutes unerring taste, society demands in its patrician class, another element already intimated, which it significantly terms good-nature, expressing all degrees of generosity, from the lowest willingness and faculty to oblige, up to the heights of magnanimity and love. Insight we must have, or we shall run against one another, and miss the way to our food; but intellect is selfish and barren. The secret of success in society, is a certain heartiness and sympathy. A man who is not happy in the company, cannot find any word in his memory that will fit the occasion. All his information is a little impertinent. A man who is happy there, finds in every turn of the conversation equally lucky occasions for the introduction of that which he has to say. The favorites of society, and what it calls *whole souls*, are able men, and of more spirit than wit, who have no uncomfortable egotism, but who exactly fill the hour and the company, contented and contenting, at a marriage or a funeral, a ball or a jury, a water-party or a shooting-match. England, which is rich in gentlemen, furnished, in the beginning of the present century, a good model of that genius which the world loves, in Mr. Fox,[428] who added to his great abilities the most social disposition, and real love of men. Parliamentary history has few better passages than the debate, in which Burke[429] and Fox separated in the House of Commons; when Fox urged on his old friend the claims of old friendship with such tenderness, that the house was moved to tears. Another anecdote is so close to my matter, that I must hazard the story. A tradesman who had long dunned him for a note of three hundred guineas, found him one day counting gold, and demanded payment. "No," said Fox, "I owe this money

to Sheridan[430]: it is a debt of honor: if an accident should happen to me, he has nothing to show." "Then," said the creditor, "I change my debt into a debt of honor," and tore the note in pieces. Fox thanked the man for his confidence, and paid him, saying, "his debt was of older standing, and Sheridan must wait." Lover of liberty, friend of the Hindoo, friend of the African slave, he possessed a great personal popularity; and Napoleon said of him on the occasion of his visit to Paris, in 1805, "Mr. Fox will always hold the first place in an assembly at the Tuileries."

17. We may easily seem ridiculous in our eulogy of courtesy, whenever we insist on benevolence as its foundation. The painted phantasm Fashion rises to cast a species of derision on what we say. But I will neither be driven from some allowance to Fashion as a symbolic institution, nor from the belief that love is the basis of courtesy. "We must obtain *that*, if we can; but by all means we must affirm *this*. Life owes much of its spirit to these sharp contrasts. Fashion which affects to be honor, is often, in all men's experience, only a ballroom code. Yet, so long as it is the highest circle, in the imagination of the best heads on the planet, there is something necessary and excellent in it; for it is not to be supposed that men have agreed to be the dupes of anything preposterous; and the respect which these mysteries inspire in the most rude and sylvan characters, and the curiosity with which details of high life are read, betray the universality of the love of cultivated manners. I know that a comic disparity would be felt, if we should enter the acknowledged 'first circles,' and apply these terrific standards of justice, beauty, and benefit, to the individuals actually found there. Monarchs and heroes, sages and lovers, these gallants are not. Fashion has many classes and many rules of probation and admission; and not the best alone. There is not only the right of conquest, which genius pretends,—the individual, demonstrating his natural aristocracy best of the best;—but less claims will pass for the time; for Fashion loves lions, and points, like Circe,[431] to her horned company. This gentleman is this afternoon arrived from Denmark; and that is my Lord Ride, who came yesterday from Bagdad; here is Captain Friese, from Cape Turnagain, and Captain Symmes,[432] from the interior of the earth; and Monsieur Jovaire, who came down this morning in a balloon; Mr. Hobnail, the reformer; and Reverend Jul Bat, who has converted the whole torrid zone in his Sunday school; and Signer Torre del Greco, who extinguished Vesuvius by pouring into it the Bay of Naples; Spahr, the Persian ambassador; and Tul Wil Shan, the exiled nabob of Nepaul, whose saddle is the new moon.—But these are monsters of one day, and to-morrow will be dismissed to their holes and dens; for, in these rooms every chair is waited for. The artist, the scholar, and, in general, the clerisy,[433] wins its way up into these places, and gets represented here,

somewhat on this footing of conquest. Another mode is to pass through all the degrees, spending a year and a day in St. Michael's Square,[434] being steeped in Cologne water,[435] and perfumed, and dined, and introduced, and properly grounded in all the biography, and politics, and anecdotes of the boudoirs.

18. Yet these fineries may have grace and wit. Let there be grotesque sculpture about the gates and offices of temples. Let the creed and commandments even have the saucy homage of parody. The forms of politeness universally express benevolence in superlative degrees. What if they are in the mouths of selfish men, and used as means of selfishness? What if the false gentleman almost bows the true out of the world? What if the false gentleman contrives so to address his companion, as civilly to exclude all others from his discourse, and also to make them feel excluded? Real service will not lose its nobleness. All generosity is not merely French and sentimental; nor is it to be concealed, that living blood and a passion of kindness does at last distinguish God's gentleman from Fashion's. The epitaph of Sir Jenkin Grout is not wholly unintelligible to the present age. "Here lies Sir Jenkin Grout, who loved his friend, and persuaded his enemy: what his mouth ate, his hand paid for: what his servants robbed, he restored: if a woman gave him pleasure, he supported her in pain: he never forgot his children: and whoso touched his finger, drew after it his whole body." Even the line of heroes is not utterly extinct. There is still ever some admirable person in plain clothes, standing on the wharf, who jumps in to rescue a drowning man; there is still some absurd inventor of charities; some guide and comforter of runaway slaves; some friend of Poland;[436] some Philhellene;[437] some fanatic who plants shade-trees for the second and third generation, and orchards when he is grown old; some well-concealed piety; some just man happy in an ill-fame; some youth ashamed of the favors of fortune, and impatiently casting them on other shoulders. And these are the centers of society, on which it returns for fresh impulses. These are the creators of Fashion, which is an attempt to organize beauty of behavior. The beautiful and the generous are in the theory, the doctors and apostles of this church: Scipio, and the Cid, and Sir Philip Sidney, and Washington, and every pure and valiant heart, who worshiped Beauty by word and by deed. The persons who constitute the natural aristocracy, are not found in the actual aristocracy, or only on its edge; as the chemical energy of the spectrum is found to be greatest just outside of the spectrum. Yet that is the infirmity of the seneschals, who do not know their sovereign, when he appears. The theory of society supposes the existence and sovereignty of these. It divines afar off their coming. It says with the elder gods, —

"As Heaven and Earth are fairer far[438]
Than Chaos and blank Darkness, though once chiefs;
And as we show beyond that Heaven and Earth,
In form and shape compact and beautiful;
So, on our heels a fresh perfection treads;
A power, more strong in beauty, born of us,
And fated to excel us, as we pass
In glory that old Darkness:
... for, 'tis the eternal law,
That first in beauty shall be first in might."

19. Therefore, within the ethnical circle of good society, there is a narrower and higher circle, concentration of its light, and flower of courtesy, to which there is always a tacit appeal of pride and reference, as to its inner and imperial court, the parliament of love and chivalry. And this is constituted of those persons in whom heroic dispositions are native, with the love of beauty, the delight in society, and the power to embellish the passing day. If the individuals who compose the purest circles of aristocracy in Europe, the guarded blood of centuries, should pass in review, in such manner as that we could, leisurely and critically, inspect their behavior, we might find no gentleman, and no lady; for although excellent specimens of courtesy and high-breeding would gratify us in the assemblage, in the particulars, we should detect offense. Because, elegance comes of no breeding, but of birth. There must be romance of character, or the most fastidious exclusion of impertinencies will not avail. It must be genius which takes that direction: it must be not courteous, but courtesy. High behavior is as rare in fiction as it is in fact. Scott is praised for the fidelity with which he painted the demeanor and conversation of the superior classes. Certainly, kings and queens, nobles and great ladies, had some right to complain of the absurdity that had been put in their mouths, before the days of Waverley;[439] but neither does Scott's dialogue bear criticism. His lords brave each other in smart epigrammatic speeches, but the dialogue is in costume, and does not please on the second reading; it is not warm with life. In Shakespeare alone, the speakers do not strut and bridle, the dialogue is easily great, and he adds to so many titles that of being the best-bred man in England, and in Christendom. Once or twice in a lifetime we are permitted to enjoy the charm of noble manners, in the presence of a man or woman who have no bar in their nature, but whose character emanates freely in their word and gesture. A beautiful form is better than a beautiful face: a beautiful behavior is better than a beautiful form: it gives a higher pleasure than statues or pictures; it is the finest of the fine arts. A man is but a little thing in the midst of the objects of nature, yet, by the moral quality radiating from his countenance,

he may abolish all considerations of magnitude, and in his manners equal the majesty of the world. I have seen an individual whose manners though wholly within the conventions of elegant society, were never learned there, but were original and commanding, and held out protection and prosperity; one who did not need the aid of a court-suit, but carried the holiday in his eye; who exhilarated the fancy by flinging wide the doors of new modes of existence; who shook off the captivity of etiquette, with happy, spirited bearing, good-natured and free as Robin Hood;[440] yet with the port of an emperor,—if need be, calm, serious, and fit to stand the gaze of millions.

20. The open air and the fields, the street and public chambers, are the places where Man executes his will; let him yield or divide the scepter at the door of the house. Woman, with her instinct of behavior, instantly detects in man a love of trifles, any coldness or imbecility, or, in short, any want of that large, flowing, and magnanimous deportment, which is indispensable as an exterior in the hall. Our American institutions have been friendly to her, and at this moment I esteem it a chief felicity of this country, that it excels in women. A certain awkward consciousness of inferiority in the men, may give rise to the new chivalry in behalf of Woman's Rights. Certainly, let her be as much better placed in the laws and in social forms, as the most zealous reformer can ask, but I confide so entirely in her inspiring and musical nature, that I believe only herself can show us how she shall be served. The wonderful generosity of her sentiments raises her at times into heroical and godlike regions, and verifies the pictures of Minerva,[441] Juno,[442] or Polymnia;[443] and, by the firmness with which she treads her upward path, she convinces the coarsest calculators that another road exists than that which their feet know. But besides those who make good in our imagination the place of muses and of Delphic Sibyls,[444] are there not women who fill our vase with wine and roses to the brim, so that the wine runs over and fills the house with perfume; who inspire us with courtesy; who unloose our tongues, and we speak; who anoint our eyes, and we see? We say things we never thought to have said; for once, our walls of habitual reserve vanished, and left us at large; we were children playing with children in a wide field of flowers. Steep us, we cried, in these influences, for days, for weeks, and we shall be sunny poets, and will write out in many-colored words the romance that you are. Was it Hafiz[445] or Firdousi[446] that said of his Persian Lilla, "She was an elemental force, and astonished me by her amount of life, when I saw her day after day radiating, every instant, redundant joy and grace on all around her.[447] She was a solvent powerful to reconcile all heterogeneous persons into one society; like air or water, an element of such a great range of affinities, that it combines readily with a thousand substances. Where she is present, all others will be more than they

are wont. She was a unit and whole, so that whatsoever she did, became her. She had too much sympathy and desire to please, than that you could say, her manners were marked with dignity, yet no princess could surpass her clear and erect demeanor on each occasion. She did not study the Persian grammar, nor the books of the seven poets, but all the poems of the seven seemed to be written upon her. For, though the bias of her nature was not to thought, but to sympathy, yet was she so perfect in her own nature, as to meet intellectual persons by the fullness of her heart, warming them by her sentiments; believing, as she did, that by dealing nobly with all, all would show themselves noble."

21. I know that this Byzantine[448] pile of chivalry of Fashion, which seems so fair and picturesque to those who look at the contemporary facts for science or for entertainment, is not equally pleasant to all spectators. The constitution of our society makes it a giant's castle to the ambitious youth who have not found their names enrolled in its Golden Book,[449] and whom it has excluded from its coveted honors and privileges. They have yet to learn that its seeming grandeur is shadowy and relative: it is great by their allowance: its proudest gates will fly open at the approach of their courage and virtue. For the present distress, however, of those who are predisposed to suffer from the tyrannies of this caprice, there are easy remedies. To remove your residence a couple of miles, or at most four, will commonly relieve the most extreme susceptibility. For, the advantages which fashion values are plants which thrive in very confined localities, in a few streets, namely. Out of this precinct, they go for nothing; are of no use in the farm, in the forest, in the market, in war, in the nuptial society, in the literary or scientific circle, at sea, in friendship, in the heaven of thought or virtue.

22. But we have lingered long enough in these painted courts. The worth of the thing signified must vindicate our taste for the emblem. Everything that is called fashion and courtesy humbles itself before the cause and fountain of honor, creator of titles and dignities, namely, the heart of love. This is the royal blood, this the fire, which, in all countries and contingencies, will work after its kind and conquer ind expand all that approaches it. This gives new meanings to every fact. This impoverishes the rich, suffering no grandeur but its own. What *is* rich? Are you rich enough to help anybody? to succor the unfashionable and the eccentric? rich enough to make the Canadian in his wagon, the itinerant with his consul's paper which commends him "To the charitable," the swarthy Italian with his few broken words of English, the lame pauper hunted by overseers from town to town, even the poor insane or besotted wreck of man or woman, feel the noble exception of your presence and your house, from the general bleakness and

stoniness; to make such feel that they were greeted with a voice which made them both remember and hope? What is vulgar, but to refuse the claim on acute and conclusive reasons? What is gentle, but to allow it, and give their heart and yours lone holiday from the national caution? Without the rich heart, wealth is an ugly beggar. The king of Schiraz[450] could not afford to be so bountiful as the poor Osman[451] who dwelt at his gate. Osman had a humanity so broad and deep, that although his speech was so bold and free with the Koran[452] as to disgust all the dervishes, yet was there never a poor outcast, eccentric, or insane man, some fool who had cut off his beard, or who had been mutilated under a vow, or had a pet madness in his brain, but fled at once to him, — that great heart lay there so sunny and hospitable in the center of the country, — that it seemed as if the instinct of all sufferers drew them to his side. And the madness which he harbored, he did not share. Is not this to be rich? this only to be rightly rich?

23. But I shall hear without pain, that I play the courtier very ill, and talk of that which I do not well understand. It is easy to see, that what is called by distinction society and fashion, has good laws as well as bad, has much that is necessary, and much that is absurd. Too good for banning, and too bad for blessing, it reminds us of a tradition of the pagan mythology, in any attempt to settle its character. "I overheard Jove,[453] one day," said Silenus,[454] "talking of destroying the earth; he said, it had failed; they were all rogues and vixens, who went from bad to worse, as fast as the days succeeded each other. Minerva said, she hoped not; they were only ridiculous little creatures, with this odd circumstance, that they had a blur, or indeterminate aspect, seen far or seen near; if you called them bad, they would appear so; if you called them good, they would appear so; and there was no one person or action among them, which would not puzzle her owl,[455] much more all Olympus, to know whether it was fundamentally bad or good."

GIFTS[456]

Gifts of one who loved me—'
Twas high time they came;
When he ceased to love me,
Time they stopped for shame.

1. It is said that the world is in a state of bankruptcy, that the world owes the world more than the world can pay, and ought to go into chancery,[457] and be sold. I do not think this general insolvency, which involves in some sort all the population, to be the reason of the difficulty experienced at Christmas and New Year, and other times, in bestowing gifts; since it is always so pleasant to be generous, though very vexatious to pay debts. But the impediment lies in the choosing. If, at any time, it comes into my head that a present is due from me to somebody, I am puzzled what to give, until the opportunity is gone. Flowers and fruits are always fit presents; flowers, because they are a proud assertion that a ray of beauty outvalues all the utilities of the world. These gay natures contrast with the somewhat stern countenance of ordinary nature: they are like music heard out of a work-house. Nature does not cocker us:[458] we are children, not pets: she is not fond: everything is dealt to us without fear or favor, after severe universal laws. Yet these delicate flowers look like the frolic and interference of love and beauty. Men use to tell us that we love flattery, even though we are not deceived by it, because it shows that we are of importance enough to be courted. Something like that pleasure, the flowers give us: what am I to whom these sweet hints are addressed? Fruits are acceptable gifts,[459] because they are the flower of commodities, and admit of fantastic values being attached to them. If a man should send to me to come a hundred miles to visit him, and should set before me a basket of fine summer-fruit, I should think there was some proportion between the labor and the reward.

2. For common gifts, necessity makes pertinences and beauty every day, and one is glad when an imperative leaves him no option, since if the man at the door have no shoes, you have not to consider whether you could procure him a paint-box. And as it is always pleasing to see a man eat bread or drink water, in the house or out of doors, so it is always a great satisfaction to supply these first wants. Necessity does everything well. In our condition of universal dependence, it seems heroic to let the petitioner[460] be the judge of his necessity, and to give all that is asked, though at great inconvenience.

If it be a fantastic desire, it is better to leave to others the office of punishing him. I can think of many parts I should prefer playing to that of the Furies. [461] Next to things of necessity, the rule for a gift, which one of my friends prescribed, is that we might convey to some person that which properly belonged to his character, and was easily associated with him in thought. But our tokens of compliment and love are for the most part barbarous. Rings and other jewels are not gifts, but apologies for gifts. The only gift is a portion of thyself. Thou must bleed for me. Therefore the poet brings his poem; the shepherd, his lamb; the farmer, corn; the miner, a gem; the sailor, coral and shells; the painter, his picture; the girl, a handkerchief of her own sewing. This is right and pleasing, for it restores society in so far to its primary basis, when a man's biography[462] is conveyed in his gift, and every man's wealth is an index of his merit. But it is a cold lifeless business when you go to the shops to buy me something which does not represent your life and talent, but a goldsmith's. That is fit for kings, and rich men who represent kings, and a false state of property, to make presents of gold and silver stuffs, as a kind of symbolical sin-offering,[463] or payment of blackmail.[464]

3. The law of benefits is a difficult channel, which requires careful sailing, or rude boats. It is not the office of a man to receive gifts. How dare you give them? We wish to be self-sustained. We do not quite forgive a forgiver. The hand that feeds us is in some danger of being bitten. We can receive anything from love, for that is a way of receiving it from ourselves; but not from any one who assumes to bestow. We sometimes hate the meat which we eat, because there seems something of degrading dependence in living by it.

"Brother, if Jove[465] to thee a present make,
Take heed that from his hands thou nothing take."

We ask the whole. Nothing less will content us. We arraign society, if it do not give us besides earth, and fire, and water, opportunity, love, reverence, and objects of veneration.

4. He is a good man, who can receive a gift well. We are either glad or sorry at a gift, and both emotions are unbecoming. Some violence, I think, is done, some degradation borne, when I rejoice or grieve at a gift. I am sorry when my independence is invaded, or when a gift comes from such as do not know my spirit, and so the act is not supported; and if the gift pleases me overmuch, then I should be ashamed that the donor should read my heart, and see that I love his commodity, and not him. The gift, to be true, must be the flowing of the giver unto me, correspondent to my flowing unto him. When the waters are at level, then my goods pass to him, and his to me. All his are mine, all mine his. I say to him, How can you give me this

pot of oil, or this flagon of wine, when all your oil and wine is mine, which belief of mine this gift seems to deny? Hence the fitness of beautiful, not useful things for gifts. This giving is flat usurpation, and therefore when the beneficiary is ungrateful, as all beneficiaries hate all Timons,[466] not at all considering the value of the gift, but looking back to the greater store it was taken from, I rather sympathize with the beneficiary, than with the anger of my lord, Timon. For, the expectation of gratitude is mean, and is continually punished by the total insensibility of the obliged person. It is a great happiness to get off without injury and heart-burning, from one who has had the ill luck to be served by you. It is a very onerous business,[467] this of being served, and the debtor naturally wishes to give you a slap. A golden text for these gentlemen is that which I admire in the Buddhist,[468] who never thanks, and who says, "Do not flatter your benefactors."

5. The reason of these discords I conceive to be, that there is no commensurability between a man and any gift. You cannot give anything to a magnanimous person. After you have served him, he at once puts you in debt by his magnanimity. The service a man renders his friend is trivial and selfish, compared with the service he knows his friend stood in readiness to yield him, alike before he had begun to serve his friend, and now also. Compared with that good-will I bear my friend, the benefit it is in my power to render him seems small. Besides, our action on each other, good as well as evil, is so incidental and at random, that we can seldom hear the acknowledgments of any person who would thank us for a benefit, without some shame and humiliation. We can rarely strike a direct stroke, but must be content with an oblique one; we seldom have the satisfaction of yielding a direct benefit, which is directly received. But rectitude scatters favors on every side without knowing it, and receives with wonder the thanks of all people.

6. I fear to breathe any treason against the majesty of love, which is the genius and god of gifts, and to whom we must not affect to prescribe. Let him give kingdoms or flower-leaves indifferently. There are persons from whom we always expect fairy tokens; let us not cease to expect them. This is prerogative, and not to be limited by our municipal rules. For the rest, I like to see that we cannot be bought and sold. The best of hospitality and of generosity is also not in the will, but in fate. I find that I am not much to you; you do not need me; you do not feel me; then am I thrust out of doors, though you proffer me house and lands. No services are of any value, but only likeness. When I have attempted to join myself to others by services, it proved an intellectual trick—no more. They eat your service like apples, and leave you out. But love them, and they feel for you, and delight in you all the time.

NATURE[469]

The rounded world is fair to see,
Nine times folded in mystery:
Though baffled seers cannot impart
The secret of its laboring heart,
Throb thine with Nature's throbbing breast,
And all is clear from east to west.
Spirit that lurks each form within
Beckons to spirit of its kin;
Self-kindled every atom glows,
And hints the future which it owes.

1. There are days[470] which occur in this climate, at almost any season of the year, wherein the world reaches its perfection, when the air, the heavenly bodies, and the earth, make a harmony, as if nature would indulge her offspring; when, in these bleak upper sides of the planet, nothing is to desire that we have heard of the happiest latitudes, and we bask in the shining hours of Florida and Cuba; when everything that has life gives sign of satisfaction, and the cattle that lie on the ground seem to have great and tranquil thoughts. These halcyons[471] may be looked for with a little more assurance in that pure October weather, which we distinguish by the name of Indian Summer.[472] The day, immeasurably long, sleeps over the broad hills and warm wide fields. To have lived through all its sunny hours, seems longevity enough. The solitary places do not seem quite lonely. At the gates of the forest, the surprised man of the world is forced to leave his city estimates of great and small, wise and foolish. The knapsack of custom falls off his back with the first step he makes into these precincts. Here is sanctity which shames our religions, and reality which discredits our heroes. Here we find nature to be the circumstance which dwarfs every other circumstance, and judges like a god all men that come to her. We have crept out of our close and crowded houses into the night and morning, and we see what majestic beauties daily wrap us in their bosom. How willingly we would escape the barriers which render them comparatively impotent, escape the sophistication and second thought, and suffer nature to entrance us. The tempered light of the woods is like a perpetual morning, and is stimulating and heroic. The anciently reported spells of these places creep

on us. The stems of pines, hemlocks, and oaks, almost gleam like iron on the excited eye. The incommunicable trees begin to persuade us to live with them, and quit our life of solemn trifles. Here no history, or church, or state, is interpolated on the divine sky and the immortal year. How easily we might walk onward into opening landscape, absorbed by new pictures, and by thoughts fast succeeding each other, until by degrees the recollection of home was crowded out of the mind, all memory obliterated by the tyranny of the present, and we were led in triumph by nature.

2. These enchantments are medicinal, they sober and heal us. These are plain pleasures, kindly and native to us. We come to our own, and make friends with matter, which the ambitious chatter of the schools would persuade us to despise. We never can part with it; the mind loves its old home: as water to our thirst, so is the rock, the ground, to our eyes, and hands, and feet. It is firm water: it is cold flame: what health, what affinity! Ever an old friend, ever like a dear friend and brother, when we chat affectedly with strangers, comes in this honest face, and takes a grave liberty with us, and shames us out of our nonsense. Cities give not the human senses room enough. We go out daily and nightly to feed the eyes on the horizon, and require so much scope, just as we need water for our bath. There are all degrees of natural influence, from these quarantine powers of nature, up to her dearest and gravest ministrations to the imagination and the soul. There is the bucket of cold water from the spring, the wood-fire to which the chilled traveler rushes for safety,—and there is the sublime moral of autumn and of noon. We nestle in nature, and draw our living as parasites from her roots and grains, and we receive glances from the heavenly bodies, which call us to solitude, and foretell the remotest future. The blue zenith is the point in which romance and reality meet. I think, if we should be rapt away into all that we dream of heaven, and should converse with Gabriel[473] and Uriel,[474] the upper sky would be all that would remain of our furniture.

3. It seems as if the day was not wholly profane, in which we have given heed to some natural object. The fall of snowflakes in a still air, preserving to each crystal its perfect form; the blowing of sleet over a wide sheet of water, and over plains; the waving rye-fields; the mimic waving of acres of houstonia, whose innumerable florets whiten and ripple before the eye; the reflections of trees and flowers in glassy lakes; the musical steaming odorous south wind, which converts all trees to wind-harps;[475] the crackling and spurting of hemlock in the flames; or of pine-logs, which yield glory to the walls and faces in the sitting-room,—these are the music and pictures of the most ancient religion. My house stands in low land, with limited outlook, and on the skirt of the village.[476] But I go with my friend[477] to the shore of our little river,[478] and with one stroke of the

paddle, I leave the village politics and personalities, yes, and the world of villages and personalities behind, and pass into a delicate realm of sunset and moonlight, too bright almost for spotted man to enter without novitiate and probation.[479] We penetrate bodily this incredible beauty: we dip our hands in this painted element: our eyes are bathed in these lights and forms. A holiday, a villeggiatura,[480] a royal revel, the proudest, most heart-rejoicing festival that valor and beauty, power and taste, ever decked and enjoyed, establishes itself on the instant. These sunset clouds, these delicately emerging stars, with their private and ineffable glances, signify it and proffer it. I am taught the poorness of our invention, the ugliness of towns and palaces. Art and luxury have early learned that they must work as enhancement and sequel to this original beauty. I am overinstructed for my return. Henceforth I shall be hard to please. I cannot go back to toys. I am grown expensive and sophisticated. I can no longer live without elegance: but a countryman shall be my master of revels. He who knows the most, he who knows what sweets and virtues are in the ground, the waters, the plants, the heavens, and how to come at these enchantments, is the rich and royal man. Only as far as masters of the world have called in nature to their aid, can they reach the height of magnificence. This is the meaning of their hanging-gardens,[481] villas, garden-houses, islands, parks, and preserves, to back their faulty personality with these strong accessories. I do not wonder that the landed interest should be invincible in the state with these dangerous auxiliaries. These bribe and invite; not kings, not palaces, not men, not women, but these tender and poetic stars, eloquent of secret promises. We heard what the rich man said, we knew of his villa, his grove, his wine, and his company, but the provocation and point of the invitation came out of these beguiling stars. In their soft glances, I see what men strove to realize in some Versailles,[482] or Paphos,[483] or Ctesiphon. [484] Indeed, it is the magical lights of the horizon, and the blue sky for the background, which save all our works of art, which were otherwise baubles. When the rich tax the poor with servility and obsequiousness, they should consider the effect of man reputed to be the possessors of nature, on imaginative minds. Ah! if the rich were rich as the poor fancy riches! A boy hears a military band play on the field at night, and he has kings and queens, and famous chivalry palpably before him. He hears the echoes of a horn in a hill country, in the Notch Mountains,[485] for example, which converts the mountains into an Æolian harp,[486] and this supernatural *tiralira* restores to him the Dorian[487] mythology, Apollo,[488] Diana,[489] and all divine hunters and huntresses. Can a musical note be so lofty, so haughtily beautiful! To the poor young poet, thus fabulous is his picture of society; he is loyal; he respects the rich; they are rich for the sake of his imagination; how poor his fancy would be, if they were not rich! That they have some high-fenced grove, which they call a park; that they live in larger and better-garnished saloons than he has visited, and go in coaches, keeping only the society of the elegant, to watering-places, and to distant cities, are the groundwork from which he has delineated estates of romance, compared with which their actual possessions are shanties and paddocks. The muse herself betrays her son, and enhances the gift of wealthy and well-born beauty, by a radiation out of the air, and clouds, and forests that skirt the road, — a certain haughty favor, as if from patrician genii to patricians, a kind of aristocracy in nature, a prince of the power of the air.

4. The moral sensibility which makes Edens[490] and Tempes[491] so easily, may not be always found, but the material landscape is never far off. We can find these enchantments without visiting the Como Lake,[492] or the Madeira Islands.[493] We exaggerate the praises of local scenery. In every landscape, the point of astonishment is the meeting of the sky and the earth, and that is seen from the first hillock as well as from the top of the Alleghanies. The stars at night stoop down over the brownest, homeliest common,[494] with all the spiritual magnificence which they shed on the Campagna,[495] or on the marble deserts of Egypt. The uprolled clouds and the colors of morning and evening, will transfigure maples and alders. The difference between landscape and landscape is small, but there is great difference in the beholders. There is nothing so wonderful in any particular landscape, as the necessity of being beautiful under which every landscape lies. Nature cannot be surprised in undress. Beauty breaks in everywhere.

5. But it is very easy to outrun the sympathy of readers on this topic, which school-men called *natura naturata*, or nature passive. One can hardly speak directly of it without excess. It is as easy to broach in mixed companies what is called "the subject of religion." A susceptible person does not like to indulge his tastes in this kind, without the apology of some trivial necessity: he goes to see a wood-lot, or to look at the crops, or to fetch a plant or a mineral from a remote locality, or he carries a fowling-piece, or a fishing-rod. I suppose this shame must have a good reason. A dilettantism[496] in nature is barren and unworthy. The fop of fields is no better than his brother of Broadway. Men are naturally hunters and inquisitive of woodcraft and I suppose that such a gazetteer as wood-cutters and Indians should furnish facts for would take place in the most sumptuous drawing-rooms of all the "Wreaths" and "Flora's chaplets"[497] of the book-shops; yet ordinarily, whether we are too clumsy for so subtle a topic, or from whatever cause, as soon as men begin to write on nature, they fall into euphuism. Frivolity is a most unfit tribute to Pan,[498] who ought to be represented in the mythology as the most continent of gods. I would not be frivolous before the admirable reserve and prudence of time, yet I cannot renounce the right

of returning often to this old topic. The multitude of false churches[499] accredits the true religion. Literature, poetry, science, are the homage of man to this unfathomed secret, concerning which no sane man can affect an indifference or incuriosity. Nature is loved by what is best in us. It is loved as the city of God, although, or rather because there is no citizen. The sunset is unlike anything that is underneath it: it wants men. And the beauty of nature must always seem unreal and mocking, until the landscape has human figures, that are as good as itself. If there were good men, there would never be this rapture in nature. If the king is in the palace nobody looks at the walls. It is when he is gone, and the house is filled with grooms and gazers, that we turn from the people, to find relief in the majestic men that are suggested by the pictures and architecture. The critics who complain of the sickly separation of the beauty of nature from the thing to be done, must consider that our hunting of the picturesque is inseparable from our protest against false society. Man is fallen; nature is erect, and serves as a differential thermometer, detecting the presence or absence of the divine sentiment in man. By fault of our dulness and selfishness, we are looking up to nature, but when we are convalescent, nature will look up to us. We see the foaming brook with compunction; if our own life flowed with the right energy, we should shame the brook. The stream of zeal sparkles with real fire, and not with reflex rays of sun and moon. Nature may be as selfishly studied as trade. Astronomy to the selfish becomes astrology; psychology, mesmerism (with intent to show where our spoons are gone); and anatomy and physiology become phrenology and palmistry.

6. But taking timely warning, and leaving many things unsaid on this topic, but not longer omit our homage to the Efficient Nature, *natura naturans*, the quick cause, before which all forms flee as the driven snows, itself secret, its works driven before it in flocks and multitudes, (as the ancient represented nature by Proteus,[500] a shepherd), and in undescribable variety. It publishes itself in creatures, reaching from particles and spicula, through transformation on transformation to the highest symmetries, arriving at consummate results without a shock or a leap. A little heat, that is, a little motion, is all that differences the bald, dazzling white, and deadly cold poles of the earth from the prolific tropical climates. All changes pass without violence, by reason of the two cardinal conditions of boundless space and boundless time. Geology has initiated us into the secularity of nature, and taught us to disuse our dame-school measures, and exchange our Mosaic[501] and Ptolemaic schemes[502] for her large style. We know nothing rightly, for want of perspective. Now we learn what patient periods must round themselves before the rock is formed, then before the rock is broken, and the first lichen race has disintegrated the thinnest external

plate into soil, and opened the door for the remote Flora,[503] Fauna,[504] Ceres,[505] and Pomona,[506] to come in. How far off yet is the trilobite! how far the quadruped! how inconceivably remote is man! All duly arrive,[507] and then race after race of men. It is a long way from granite to the oyster; farther yet to Plato,[508] and the preaching of the immortality of the soul. Yet all must come, as surely as the first atom has two sides.

7. Motion or change, and identity or rest, are the first and second secrets of nature: Motion and Rest. The whole code of her laws may be written on the thumb-nail, or the signet of a ring. The whirling bubble on the surface of a brook, admits us to the secret of the mechanics of the sky. Every shell on the beach is a key to it. A little water made to rotate in a cup explains the formation of the simpler shells; the addition of matter from year to year, arrives at last at the most complex forms; and yet so poor is nature with all her craft, that, from the beginning to the end of the universe, she has but one stuff,—but one stuff with its two ends, to serve up all her dream-like variety. Compound it how she will, star, sand, fire, water, tree, man, it is still one stuff, and betrays the same properties.

8. Nature is always consistent, though she feigns to contravene her own laws. She keeps her laws, and seems to transcend them. She arms and equips an animal to find its place and living in the earth, and, at the same time, she arms and equips another animal to destroy it. Space exists to divide creatures; but by clothing the sides of a bird with a few feathers, she gives him a petty omnipresence. The direction is forever onward, but the artist still goes back for materials, and begins again with the first elements on the most advanced stage: otherwise, all goes to ruin. If we look at her work, we seem to catch a glance of a system in transition. Plants are the young of the world, vessels of health and vigor; but they grope ever upward toward consciousness; the trees are imperfect men, and seem to bemoan their imprisonment, rooted in the ground. The animal is the novice and probationer of a more advanced order. The men, though young, having tasted the first drop from the cup of thought, are already dissipated: the maples and ferns are still uncorrupt; yet no doubt, when they come to consciousness, they too will curse and swear. Flowers so strictly belong to youth, that we adult men soon come to feel, that their beautiful generations concern not us: we have had our day; now let the children have theirs. The flowers jilt us, and we are old bachelors with our ridiculous tenderness.

9. Things are so strictly related, that according to the skill of the eye, from any one object the parts and properties of any other may be predicted. If we had eyes to see it, a bit of stone from the city wall would certify us of the necessity that man must exist, as readily as the city. That identity makes us all one, and reduces to nothing great intervals on our customary

scale. We talk of deviations from natural life, as if artificial life were not also natural. The smoothest curled courtier in the boudoirs of a palace has an animal nature, rude and aboriginal as a white bear, omnipotent to its own ends, and is directly related, there amid essences and billets-doux, to Himalaya mountain-chains[509] and the axis of the globe. If we consider how much we are nature's, we need not be superstitious about towns, as if that terrific or benefic force did not find us there also, and fashion cities. Nature, who made the mason, made the house. We may easily hear too much of rural influences. The cool, disengaged air of natural objects, makes them enviable to us, chafed and irritable creatures with red faces, and we think we shall be as grand as they, if we camp out and eat roots, but let us be men instead of wood-chucks, and the oak and the elm shall gladly serve us, though we sit in chairs of ivory on carpets of silk.

10. This guiding identity runs through all the surprises and contrasts of the piece, and characterizes every law. Man carries the world in his head, the whole astronomy and chemistry suspended in a thought. Because the history of nature is charactered in his brain, therefore is he the prophet and discoverer of her secrets. Every known fact in natural science was divined by the presentiment of somebody, before it was actually verified. A man does not tie his shoe without recognizing laws which bind the farthest regions of nature: moon, plant, gas, crystal, are concrete geometry and numbers. Common sense knows its own, and recognizes the fact at first sight in chemical experiment. The common sense of Franklin,[510] Dalton,[511] Davy[512] and Black,[513] is the same common sense which made the arrangements which now it discovers.

11. If the identity expresses organized rest, the counter action runs also into organization. The astronomers said,[514] "Give us matter, and a little motion, and we will construct the universe. It is not enough that we should have matter, we must also have a single impulse, one shove to launch the mass, and generate the harmony of the centrifugal and centripetal[515] forces. Once heave the ball from the hand, and we can show how all this mighty order grew." "A very unreasonable postulate," said the metaphysicians, "and a plain begging of the question. Could you not prevail to know the genesis of projection, as well as the continuation of it?" Nature, meanwhile, had not waited for the discussion, but, right or wrong, bestowed the impulse, and the balls rolled. It was no great affair, a mere push, but the astronomers were right in making much of it, for there is no end of the consequences of the act. That famous aboriginal push propagates itself through all the balls of the system, and through every atom of every ball, through all the races of creatures, and through the history and performances of every individual. Exaggeration is in the course of things. Nature sends no creature, no man

into the world, without adding a small excess of his proper quality. Given the planet, it is still necessary to add the impulse; so, to every creature nature added a little violence of direction in its proper path, a shove to put it on its way; in every instance, a slight generosity, a drop too much. Without electricity the air would rot, and without this violence of direction which men and women have, without a spice of bigot and fanatic, no excitement, no efficiency. We aim above the mark, to hit the mark. Every act hath some falsehood of exaggeration in it. And when now and then comes along some sad, sharp-eyed man, who sees how paltry a game is played, and refuses to play, but blabs the secret;—how then? is the bird flown? O no, the wary Nature sends a new troop of fairer forms, of lordlier youths, with a little more excess of direction to hold them fast to their several aims; makes them a little wrongheaded in that direction in which they are rightest, and on goes the game again with new whirl, for a generation or two more. The child with his sweet pranks, the fool of his senses, commanded by every sight and sound, without any power to compare and rank his sensations, abandoned to a whistle or a painted chip, to a lead dragoon, or a ginger-bread dog, individualizing everything, generalizing nothing, delighted with every new thing, lies down at night overpowered by the fatigue, which this day of continual petty madness has incurred. But Nature has answered her purpose with the curly, dimpled lunatic. She has tasked every faculty, and has secured the symmetrical growth of the bodily frame, by all these attitudes and exertions,—an end of the first importance, which could not be trusted to any care less perfect than her own. This glitter, this opaline luster plays round the top of every toy to his eye, to insure his fidelity, and he is deceived to his good. We are made alive and kept alive by the same arts. Let the Stoics[516] say what they please, we do not eat for the good of living, but because the meat is savory and the appetite is keen. The vegetable life does not content itself with casting from the flower or the tree a single seed, but it fills the air and earth with a prodigality of seeds, that if thousands perish, thousands may plant themselves, that hundreds may come up, that tens may live to maturity, that, at least, one may replace the parent. All things betray the same calculated profusion. The excess of fear with which the animal frame is hedged round, shrinking from cold, starting at sight of a snake, or a sudden noise, protects us, through a multitude of groundless alarms, from some one real danger at last. The lover seeks in marriage his private felicity and perfection, with no prospective end; and nature hides in his happiness her own end, namely, progeny, or the perpetuity of the race.

12. But the craft with which the world is made runs also into the mind and character of men. No man is quite sane; each has a vein of folly in his composition, a slight determination of blood to the head, to make sure of

holding him hard to some one point which nature had taken to heart. Great causes are never tried on their merits; but the cause is reduced to particulars to suit the size of the partisans, and the contention is ever hottest on minor matters. Not less remarkable is the overfaith of each man in the importance of what he has to do or say. The poet, the prophet, has a higher value for what he utters than any hearer, and therefore it gets spoken. The strong, self-complacent Luther[517] declares with an emphasis, not to be mistaken, that "God himself cannot do without wise men." Jacob Behmen[518] and George Fox[519] betray their egotism in the pertinacity of their controversial tracts, and James Naylor[520] once suffered himself to be worshiped as the Christ. Each prophet comes presently to identify himself with his thought, and to esteem his hat and shoes sacred. However this may discredit such persons with the judicious, it helps them with the people, as it gives heat, pungency, and publicity to their words. A similar experience is not infrequent in private life. Each young and ardent person writes a diary, in which, when the hours of prayer and penitence arrive, he inscribes his soul. The pages thus written are, to him, burning and fragrant: he reads them on his knees by midnight and by the morning star; he wets them with his tears: they are sacred; too good for the world, and hardly yet to be shown to the dearest friend. This is the man-child that is born to the soul, and her life still circulates in the babe. The umbilical cord has not yet been cut. After some time has elapsed, he begins to wish to admit his friend to this hallowed experience, and with hesitation, yet with firmness, exposes the pages to his eye. Will they not burn his eyes? The friend coldly turns them over, and passes from the writing to conversation, with easy transition, which strikes the other party with astonishment and vexation. He cannot suspect the writing itself. Days and nights of fervid life, of communion with angels of darkness and of light, have engraved their shadowy characters on that tear-stained book. He suspects the intelligence or the heart of his friend. Is there then no friend? He cannot yet credit that one may have impressive experience, and yet may not know how to put his private fact into literature; and perhaps the discovery that wisdom has other tongues and ministers than we, that though we should hold our peace, the truth would not the less be spoken, might check injuriously the flames of our zeal. A man can only speak, so long as he does not feel his speech to be partial and inadequate. It is partial, but he does not see it to be so, whilst he utters it. As soon as he is released from the instinctive and particular, and sees its partiality, he shuts his mouth in disgust. For, no man can write anything, who does not think that what he writes is for the time the history of the world; or do anything well, who does not esteem his work to be of importance. My work may be of none, but I must not think it is of none, or I shall not do it with impunity.

13. In like manner, there is throughout nature something mocking, something that leads us on and on, but arrives nowhere, keeps no faith with us. All promise outruns the performance. We live in a system of approximations. Every end is prospective of some other end, which is also temporary; a round and final success nowhere. We are encamped in nature, not domesticated. Hunger and thirst lead us on to eat and to drink; but bread and wine, mix and cook them how you will, leave us hungry and thirsty, after the stomach is full. It is the same with all our arts and performances. Our music, our poetry, our language itself are not satisfactions, but suggestions. The hunger for wealth, which reduces the planet to a garden, fools the eager pursuer. What is the end sought? Plainly to secure the ends of good sense and beauty, from the intrusion of deformity or vulgarity of any kind. But what an operose[521] method! What a train of means to secure a little conversation! This palace of brick and stone, these servants, this kitchen, these stables, horses and equipage, this bank-stock, and file of mortgages; trade to all the world, country-house and cottage by the water-side, all for a little conversation, high, clear, and spiritual! Could it not be had as well by beggars on the highway? No, all these things came from successive efforts of these beggars to remove friction from the wheels of life, and give opportunity. Conversation, character, were the avowed ends; wealth was good as it appeased the animal cravings, cured the smoky chimney, silenced the creaking door, brought friends together in a warm and quiet room, and kept the children and the dinner-table in a different apartment. Thought, virtue, beauty, were the ends; but it was known that men of thought and virtue sometimes had the headache, or wet feet, or could lose good time, whilst the room was getting warm in winter days. Unluckily, in the exertions necessary to remove these inconveniences, the main attention has been diverted to this object; the old aims have been lost sight of, and to remove friction has come to be the end. That is the ridicule of rich men, and Boston, London, Vienna, and now the governments generally of the world, are cities and governments of the rich, and the masses are not men, but *poor men*, that is, men who would be rich; this is the ridicule of the class, that they arrive with pains and sweat and fury nowhere; when all is done, it is for nothing. They are like one who has interrupted the conversation of a company to make his speech, and now has forgotten what he went to say. The appearance strikes the eye everywhere of an aimless society, of aimless nations. Were the ends of nature so great and cogent, as to exact this immense sacrifice of men?

14. Quite analogous to the deceits in life, there is, as might be expected, a similar effect on the eye from the face of external nature. There is in woods and waters a certain enticement and flattery, together with a failure to yield

a present satisfaction. This disappointment is felt in every landscape. I have seen the softness and beauty of the summer clouds floating feathery overhead, enjoying, as it seemed, their height and privilege of motion, whilst yet they appeared not so much the drapery of this place and hour, as fore-looking to such pavilions and gardens of festivity beyond. It is an odd jealousy; but the poet finds himself not near enough to this object. The pine tree, the river, the bank of flowers before him, does not seem to be nature. Nature is still elsewhere. This or this is but outskirt and far-off reflection[522] and echo of the triumph that has passed by, and is now at its glancing splendor and heyday, perchance in the neighboring fields, or, if you stand in the field, then in the adjacent woods. The present object shall give you this sense of stillness that follows a pageant which has just gone by. What splendid distance, what recesses of ineffable pomp and loveliness in the sunset! But who can go where they are, or lay his hand or plant his foot thereon? Off they fall from the round world forever and ever. It is the same among men and women as among the silent trees; always a referred existence, an absence, never a presence and satisfaction. Is it, that beauty can never be grasped? in persons and in landscapes is equally inaccessible? The accepted and betrothed lover has lost the wildest charm of his maiden in her acceptance of him. She was heaven whilst he pursued her as a star: she cannot be heaven, if she stoops to such a one as he.

15. What shall we say of this omnipresent appearance of that first projectile impulse, of this flattery and balking of so many well-meaning creatures? Must we not suppose somewhere in the universe a slight treachery and derision? Are we not engaged to a serious resentment of this use that is made of us? Are we tickled trout, and fools of nature? One looks at the face of heaven and earth lays all petulance at rest, and soothes us to wiser convictions. To the intelligent, nature converts itself into a vast promise, and will not be rashly explained. Her secret is untold. Many and many an Oedipus[523] arrives: he has the whole mystery teeming in his brain. Alas! the same sorcery has spoiled his skill; no syllable can he shape on his lips. Her mighty orbit vaults like the fresh rainbow into the deep, but no archangel's wing was yet strong enough to follow it, and report of the return of the curve. But it also appears, that our actions are seconded and disposed to greater conclusions than we designed. We are escorted on every hand through life by spiritual agents, and a beneficent purpose lies in wait for us. We cannot bandy words with nature, or deal with her as we deal with persons. If we measure our individual forces against hers, we may easily feel as if we were the sport of an insuperable destiny. But if, instead of identifying ourselves with the work, we feel that the soul of the workman streams through us, we shall find the peace of the morning dwelling first in

our hearts, and the fathomless powers of gravity and chemistry, and, over them, of life preëxisting within us in their highest form.

16. The uneasiness which the thought of our helplessness in the chain of causes occasions us, results from looking too much at one condition of nature, namely, Motion. But the drag is never taken from the wheel. Wherever the impulse exceeds the Rest or Identity insinuates its compensation. All over the wide fields of earth grows the prunella[524] or self-heal. After every foolish day we sleep off the fumes and furies of its hours; and though we are always engaged with particulars, and often enslaved to them, we bring with us to every experiment the innate universal laws. These, while they exist in the mind as ideas, stand around us in nature forever embodied, a present sanity to expose and cure the insanity of men. Our servitude to particulars betrays us into a hundred foolish expectations. We anticipate a new era from the invention of a locomotive, or a balloon; the new engine brings with it the old checks. They say that by electro-magnetism, your salad shall be grown from the seed whilst your fowl is roasting for dinner: it is a symbol of our modern aims and endeavors, — of our condensation and acceleration of objects: but nothing is gained: nature cannot be cheated: man's life is but seventy salads long, grow they swift or grow they slow. In these checks and impossibilities, however, we find our advantage, not less than in impulses. Let the victory fall where it will, we are on that side. And the knowledge that we traverse the whole scale of being, from the center to the poles of nature, and have some stake in every possibility, lends that sublime luster to death, which philosophy and religion have too outwardly and literally striven to express in the popular doctrine of the immortality of the soul. The reality is more excellent than the report. Here is no ruin, no discontinuity, no spent ball. The divine circulations never rest nor linger. Nature is the incarnation of a thought, and turns to a thought again, as ice becomes water and gas. The world is mind precipitated, and the volatile essence is forever escaping again into the state of free thought. Hence the virtue and pungency of the influence on the mind, of natural objects, whether inorganic or organized. Man imprisoned, man crystallized, man vegetative, speaks to man impersonated. That power which does not respect quantity, which makes the whole and the particle its equal channel, delegates its smile to the morning, and distills its essence into every drop of rain. Every moment instructs and every object: for wisdom is infused into every form. It has been poured into us as blood; it convulsed us as pain; it slid into us as pleasure; it enveloped us in dull, melancholy days, or in days of cheerful labor; we did not guess its essence, until after a long time.

SHAKSPEARE;[525]OR, THE POET

1. Great men are more distinguished by range and extent, than by originality. If we require the originality which consists in weaving, like a spider, their web from their own bowels; in finding clay, and making bricks, and building the house; no great men are original. Nor does valuable originality consist in unlikeness to other men. The hero is in the press of knights, and the thick of events; and, seeing what men want, and sharing their desire, he adds the needful length of sight and of arm, to come to the desired point. The greatest genius is the most indebted man. A poet is no rattlebrain, saying what comes uppermost and, because he says everything, saying, at last, something good; but a heart in unison with his time and country. There is nothing whimsical and fantastic in his production, but sweet and sad earnest, freighted with the weightiest convictions, and pointed with the most determined aim which any man or class knows of in his times.

2. The Genius[526] of our life is jealous of individuals and will not have any individual great, except through the general. There is no choice to genius. A great man does not wake up on some fine morning, and say, "I am full of life, I will go to sea, and find an Antarctic continent: to-day I will square the circle: I will ransack botany, and find a new food for man: I have a new architecture in my mind: I foresee a new mechanic power:" no, but he finds himself in the river of the thoughts and events, forced onward by the ideas and necessities of his contemporaries. He stands where all the eyes of men look one way, and their hands all point in the direction in which he should go. The church has reared him amidst rites and pomps, and he carries out the advice which her music gave him, and builds a cathedral needed by her chants and processions. He finds a war raging: it educates him, by trumpet, in barracks, and he betters the instruction. He finds two counties groping to bring coal, or flour, or fish, from the place of production to the place of consumption, and he hits on a railroad. Every master has found his materials collected, and his power lay in his sympathy with his people, and in his love of the materials he wrought in. What an economy of power! and what a compensation for the shortness of life! All is done to his hand. The world has brought him thus far on his way. The human race has gone out before him, sunk the hills, filled the hollows, and bridged

the rivers. Men, nations, poets, artisans, women, all have worked for him, and he enters into their labors. Choose any other thing, out of the line of tendency, out of the national feeling and history, and he would have all to do for himself: his powers would be expended in the first preparations. Great genial power, one would almost say, consists in not being original at all; in being altogether receptive; in letting the world do all, and suffering the spirit of the hour to pass unobstructed through the mind.

3. Shakspeare's youth[527] fell in a time when the English people were importunate for dramatic entertainments. The court took offense easily at political allusions, and attempted to suppress them. The Puritans,[528] a growing and energetic party and the religious among the Anglican Church,[529] would suppress them. But the people wanted them. Inn-yards, houses without roofs, and extemporaneous inclosures at country fairs, were the ready theaters of strolling players. The people had tasted this new joy; and, as we could not hope to suppress newspapers now,—no, not by the strongest party,—neither then could king, prelate, or puritan,—alone or united, suppress an organ, which was ballad, epic, newspaper, caucus, lecture, Punch,[530] and library, at the same time. Probably king, prelate, and puritan, all found their own account in it. It had become, by all causes, a national interest,—by no means conspicuous, so that some great scholar would have thought of treating it in an English history,—but not a whit less considerable, because it was cheap, and of no account, like a baker's shop. The best proof of its vitality is the crowd of writers which suddenly broke into this field; Kyd, Marlow, Greene,[531] Jonson, Chapman, Dekker, Webster, Heywood, Middleton, Peele, Ford, Massinger, Beaumont, and Fletcher.

4. The secure possession, by the stage, of the public mind, is of the first importance to the poet who works for it. He loses no time in idle experiments. Here is audience and expectation prepared. In the case of Shakspeare there is much more. At the time when[532] he left Stratford, and went up to London, a great body of stage-plays, of all dates and writers, existed in manuscript, and were in turn produced on the boards. Here is the Tale of Troy,[533] which the audience will bear hearing some part of, every week; the Death of Julius Cæsar,[534] and other stories out of Plutarch,[535] which they never tire of; a shelf full of English history, from the chronicles of Brut[536] and Arthur,[537] down to the royal Henries,[538] which men hear eagerly; and a string of doleful tragedies, merry Italian tales,[539] and Spanish voyages,[540] which all the London prentices know. All the mass has been treated, with more or less skill, by every playwright, and the prompter has the soiled and tattered manuscripts. It is now no longer possible to say who wrote them first. They have been the property of the

Theater so long, and so many rising geniuses have enlarged or altered them, inserting a speech, or a whole scene, or adding a song, that no man can any longer claim copyright in this work of numbers. Happily, no man wishes to. They are not yet desired in that way. We have few readers, many spectators and hearers. They had best lie where they are.

5. Shakspeare, in common with his comrades, esteemed the mass of old plays, waste stock, in which any experiment could be freely tried. Had the *prestige* [541] which hedges about a modern tragedy existed, nothing could have been done. The rude warm blood of the living England circulated in the play, as in street-ballads, and gave body which he wanted to his airy and majestic fancy. The poet needs a ground in popular tradition on which he may work, and which, again, may restrain his art within the due temperance. It holds him to the people, supplies a foundation for his edifice; and, in furnishing so much work done to his hand, leaves him at leisure, and in full strength for the audacities of his imagination. In short, the poet owes to his legend what sculpture owed to the temple. Sculpture in Egypt, and in Greece, grew up in subordination to architecture. It was the ornament of the temple wall: at first, a rude relief carved on pediments, then the relief became bolder, and a head or arm was projected from the wall, the groups being still arranged with reference to the building, which serves also as a frame to hold the figures; and when, at last, the greatest freedom of style and treatment was reached, the prevailing genius of architecture still enforced a certain calmness and continence in the statue. As soon as the statue was begun for itself, and with no reference to the temple or palace, the art began to decline: freak, extravagance, and exhibition, took the place of the old temperance. This balance-wheel, which the sculptor found in architecture, the perilous irritability of poetic talent found in the accumulated dramatic materials to which the people were already wonted, and which had a certain excellence which no single genius,[542] however extraordinary, could hope to create.

6. In point of fact, it appears that Shakspeare did owe debts in all directions, and was able to use whatever he found; and the amount of indebtedness may be inferred from Malone's[543] laborious computations in regard to the First, Second, and Third parts of Henry VI., in which, "out of 6043 lines, 1771 were written by some author preceding Shakspeare; 2373 by him, on the foundation laid by his predecessors; and 1899 were entirely his own." And the proceeding investigation hardly leaves a single drama of his absolute invention. Malone's sentence is an important piece of external history. In Henry VIII, I think I see plainly the cropping out of the original rock on which his own finer stratum was laid. The first play was written by a superior, thoughtful man, with a vicious ear. I can mark his lines, and know well their cadence. See Wolsey's soliloquy,[544] and the following

scene from Cromwell,[545] where,—instead of the meter of Shakspeare, whose secret is, that the thought constructs the tune, so that reading for the sense will best bring out the rhythm,—here the lines are constructed on a given tune, and the verse has even a trace of pulpit eloquence. But the play contains, through all its length, unmistakable traits of Shakspeare's hand, and some passages, as the account of the coronation,[546] are like autographs. What is odd, the compliment to Queen Elizabeth[547] is in bad rhythm.[548]

7. Shakspeare knew that tradition supplies a better fable than any invention can. If he lost any credit of design, he augmented his resources; and, at that day, our petulant demand for originality was not so much pressed. There was no literature for the million. The universal reading, the cheap press, were unknown. A great poet, who appears in illiterate times, absorbs into his sphere all the light which is anywhere radiating. Every intellectual jewel, every flower of sentiment, it is his fine office to bring to his people; and he comes to value his memory[549] equally with his invention. He is therefore little solicitous whence his thoughts have been derived; whether through translation, whether through tradition, whether by travel in distant countries, whether by inspiration; from whatever source, they are equally welcome to his uncritical audience. Nay, he borrows very near home. Other men say wise things as well as he; only they say a good many foolish things, and do not know when they have spoken wisely. He knows the sparkle of the true stone, and puts it in high place, wherever he finds it. Such is the happy position of Homer,[550] perhaps; of Chaucer,[551] of Saadi.[552] They felt that all wit was their wit. And they are librarians and historiographers, as well as poets. Each romancer was heir and dispenser of all the hundred tales of the world,—

"Presenting Thebes'[553] and Pelops' line
And the tale of Troy divine."

The influence of Chaucer is conspicuous in all our early literature; and, more recently, not only Pope[554] and Dryden[555] have been beholden to him, but, in the whole society of English writers, a large unacknowledged debt is easily traced. One is charmed with the opulence which feeds so many pensioners. But Chaucer is a huge borrower.[556] Chaucer, it seems, drew continually, through Lydgat[557] and Caxton,[558] from Guido di Colonna,[559] whose Latin romance of the Trojan war was in turn a compilation from Dares Phrygius,[560] Ovid,[561] and Statius.[562] Then Petrarch,[563] Boccaccio,[564] and the Provençal poets,[565] and his benefactors: the Romaunt of the Rose[566] is only judicious translation from William of Lorris and John of Meung: Troilus and Creseide,[567] from Lollius of Urbino: The Cock and the Fox,[568] from the *Lais* of Marie: The

House of Fame,[569] from the French or Italian: and poor Gower[570] he uses as if he were only a brick-kiln or stone-quarry, out of which to build his house. He steals by this apology,—that what he takes has no worth where he finds it, and the greatest where he leaves it. It has come to be practically a sort of rule in literature, that a man, having once shown himself capable of original writing, is entitled thenceforth to steal from the writings of others at discretion. Thought is the property of him who can entertain it; and of him who can adequately place it. A certain awkwardness marks the use of borrowed thoughts; but, as soon as we have learned what to do with them, they become our own.

8. Thus, all originality is relative. Every thinker is retrospective. The learned member of the legislature, at Westminister,[571] or at Washington, speaks and votes for thousands. Show us the constituency, and the now invisible channels by which the senator is made aware of their wishes, the crowd of practical and knowing men, who, by correspondence or conversation, are feeding him with evidence, anecdotes, and estimates, and it will bereave his fine attitude and resistance of something of their impressiveness. As Sir Robert Peel[572] and Mr. Webster[573] vote, so Locke[574] and Rousseau[575] think for thousands; and so there were foundations all around Homer,[576] Menu,[577] Saada,[578] or Milton,[579] from which they drew; friends, lovers, books, traditions, proverbs,—all perished,—which, if seen, would go to reduce the wonder. Did the bard speak with authority? Did he feel himself overmatched by any companion? The appeal is to the consciousness of the writer. Is there at last in his breast a Delphi[580] whereof to ask concerning any thought or thing whether it be verily so, yea or nay? and to have answer, and rely on that? All the debts which such a man could contract to other wit, would never disturb his consciousness of originality: for the ministrations of books, and of other minds, are a whiff of smoke to that most private reality with which he has conversed.

9. It is easy to see that what is best written or done by genius, in the world, was no man's work, but came by wide social labor, when a thousand wrought like one, sharing the same impulse. Our English Bible[581] is a wonderful specimen of the strength and music of the English language. But it was not made by one man, or at one time; but centuries and churches brought it to perfection. There never was a time when there was not some translation existing. The Liturgy,[582] admired for its energy and pathos, is an anthology of the piety of ages and nations, a translation of the prayers and forms of the Catholic church,—these collected, too, in long periods, from the prayers and meditations of every saint and sacred writer all over the world. Grotius[583] makes the like remark in respect to the Lord's Prayer,

that the single clauses of which it is composed were already in use, in the time of Christ, in the rabbinical forms.[584] He picked out the grains of gold. The nervous language of the Common Law,[585] the impressive forms of our courts, and the precision and substantial truth of the legal distinctions, are the contribution of all the sharp-sighted, strong-minded men who have lived in the countries where these laws govern. The translation of Plutarch gets its excellence by being translation on translation. There never was a time when there was none. All the truly idiomatic and national phrases are kept, and all others successively picked out, and thrown away. Something like the same process had gone on, long before, with the originals of these books. The world takes liberties with world-books. Vedas,[586] Æsop's Fables,[587] Pilpay,[588] Arabian Nights,[589] Cid,[590] Iliad,[591] Robin Hood,[592] Scottish Minstrelsy,[593] are not the work of single men. In the composition of such works, the time thinks, the market thinks, the mason, the carpenter, the merchant, the farmer, the fop, all think for us. Every book supplies its time with one good word; every municipal law, every trade, every folly of the day, and the generic catholic genius who is not afraid or ashamed to owe his originality to the originality of all, stands with the next age as the recorder and embodiment of his own.

10. We have to thank the researches of antiquaries, and the Shakspeare Society,[594] for ascertaining the steps of the English drama, from the Mysteries[595] celebrated in churches and by churchmen, and the final detachment from the church, and the completion of secular plays, from Ferrex and Porrex,[596] and Gammer Gurton's Needle,[597] down to the possession of the stage by the very pieces which Shakspeare altered, remodelled, and finally made his own. Elated with success, and piqued by the growing interest of the problem, they have left no book-stall unsearched, no chest in a garret unopened, no file of old yellow accounts to decompose in damp and worms, so keen was the hope to discover whether the boy Shakspeare poached[598] or not, whether he held horses at the theater-door, whether he kept school, and why he left in his will only his second-best bed to Ann Hathaway, his wife.

11. There is somewhat touching in the madness with which the passing age mischooses the object on which all candles shine, and all eyes are turned; the care with which it registers every trifle touching Queen Elizabeth,[599] and King James,[600] and the Essexes,[601] Leicesters,[602] Burleighs,[603] and Buckinghams[604]; and lets pass without a single valuable note the founder of another dynasty, which alone will cause the Tudor dynasty[605] to be remembered,—the man who carries the Saxon race in him by the inspiration which feeds him, and on whose thoughts the foremost people of the world are now for some ages to be nourished, and minds to receive

this and not another bias. A popular player,—nobody suspected he was the poet of the human race; and the secret was kept as faithfully from poets and intellectual men, as from courtiers and frivolous people. Bacon,[606] who took the inventory of the human understanding for his times, never mentioned his name. Ben Jonson,[607] though we have strained his few words of regard and panegyric, had no suspicion of the elastic fame whose first vibrations he was attempting. He no doubt thought the praise he has conceded to him generous, and esteemed himself, out of all question, the better poet of the two.

12. If it need wit to know wit, according to the proverb, Shakspeare's time should be capable of recognizing it. Sir Henry Wotton[608] was born four years after Shakspeare, and died twenty-three years after him; and I find, among his correspondents and acquaintances, the following persons:[609] Theodore Beza, Isaac Casaubon, Sir Philip Sidney, Earl of Essex, Lord Bacon, Sir Walter Raleigh, John Milton, Sir Henry Vane, Isaac Walton, Dr. Donne, Abraham Cowley, Berlarmine, Charles Cotton, John Pym, John Hales, Kepler, Vieta, Albericus Gentilis, Paul Sarpi, Arminius; with all of whom exists some token of his having communicated, without enumerating many others, whom doubtless[610] he saw,—Shakspeare, Spenser, Jonson, Beaumont, Massinger, two Herberts, Marlow, Chapman and the rest. Since the constellation of great men who appeared in Greece in the time of Pericles,[611] there was never any such society;—yet their genius failed them to find out the best head in the universe. Our poet's mask was impenetrable. You cannot see the mountain near. It took a century to make it suspected; and not until two centuries had passed, after his death, did any criticism which we think adequate begin to appear. It was not possible to write the history of Shakspeare till now; for he is the father of German literature: it was on the introduction of Shakspeare into German, by Lessing,[612] and the translation of his works by Wieland[613] and Schlegel,[614] that the rapid burst of German literature was most intimately connected. It was not until the nineteenth century, whose speculative genius is a sort of living Hamlet,[615] that the tragedy of Hamlet could find such wondering readers. Now, literature, philosophy, and thought, are Shakspearized. His mind is the horizon beyond which, at present, we do not see. Our ears are educated to music by his rhythm. Coleridge[616] and Goethe[617] are the only critics who have expressed our convictions with any adequate fidelity; but there is in all cultivated minds a silent appreciation of his superlative power and beauty, which, like Christianity, qualifies the period.

14. The Shakspeare Society have inquired in all directions, advertised the missing facts, offered money for any information that will lead to proof; and with what result? Beside some important illustration of the history of

the English stage, to which I have adverted, they have gleaned a few facts touching the property, and dealings in regard to property, of the poet. It appears that, from year to year, he owned a larger share in the Blackfriars' Theater[618]: its wardrobe and other appurtenances were his: and he bought an estate in his native village, with his earnings, as writer and shareholder; that he lived in the best house in Stratford;[619] was intrusted by his neighbors with their commissions in London, as of borrowing money, and the like; and he was a veritable farmer. About the time when he was writing Macbeth,[620] he sues Philip Rogers, in the borough-court of Stratford, for thirty-five shillings, ten pence, for corn delivered to him at different times; and, in all respects, appears as a good husband with no reputation for eccentricity or excess. He was a good-natured sort of man, an actor and shareholder in the theater, not in any striking manner distinguished from other actors and managers. I admit the importance of this information. It is well worth the pains that have been taken to procure it.

15. But whatever scraps of information concerning his condition these researches may have rescued, they can shed no light upon that infinite invention which is the concealed magnet of his attraction for us. We are very clumsy writers of history. We tell the chronicle of parentage, birth, birth-place, schooling, schoolmates, earning of money, marriage, publication of books, celebrity, death; and when we have come to an end of this gossip no ray of relation appears between it and the goddess-born; and it seems as if, had we dipped at random into the "Modern Plutarch," and read any other life there, it would have fitted the poems as well. It is the essence of poetry to spring, like the rainbow daughter of Wonder, from the invisible, to abolish the past, and refuse all history. Malone, Warburton, Dyce, and Collier,[621] have wasted their oil. The famed theaters, Covent Garden, Drury Lane, the Park, and Tremont,[622] have vainly assisted. Betterton, Garrick, Kemble, Kean, and Macready,[623] dedicate their lives to this genius; him they crown, elucidate, obey, and express. The genius knows them not. The recitation begins; one golden word leaps out immortal from all this painted pedantry, and sweetly torments us with invitations to its own inaccessible homes. I remember, I went once to see the Hamlet of a famed performer,[624] the pride of the English stage; and all I then heard, and all I now remember, of the tragedian, was that in which the tragedian had no part; simply, Hamlet's question to the ghost, —

"What may this mean,[625]
That thou, dead corse, again in complete steel
Revisit'st thus the glimpses of the moon?"

That imagination which dilates the closet he writes in to the world's dimension, crowds it with agents in rank and order, as quickly reduces the big reality to be the glimpses of the moon. These tricks of his magic spoil for us the illusions of the green-room. Can any biography shed light on the localities into which the Midsummer Night's Dream[626] admits me? Did Shakspeare confide to any notary or parish recorder, sacristan, or surrogate, in Stratford, the genesis of that delicate creation? The forest of Arden,[627] the nimble air of Scone Castle,[628] the moonlight of Portia's villa,[629] "the antres vast[630] and desarts idle," of Othello's captivity,—where is the third cousin, or grand-nephew, the chancellor's file of accounts, or private letter, that has kept one word of those transcendent secrets? In fine, in this drama, as in all great works of art,—in the Cyclopean architecture[631] of Egypt and India; in the Phidian sculpture[632]; the Gothic ministers[633]; the Italian painting[634]; the Ballads of Spain and Scotland,[635]—the Genius draws up the ladder after him, when the creative age goes up to heaven, and gives way to a new, which sees the works, and ask in vain for a history.

16. Shakspeare is the only biographer of Shakspeare; and even he can tell nothing, except to the Shakspeare in us; that is, to our most apprehensive and sympathetic hour. He cannot step from off his tripod,[636] and give us anecdotes of his inspirations. Read the antique documents extricated, analyzed, and compared, by the assiduous Dyce and Collier; and now read one of those skyey sentences,—aerolites,—which seem to have fallen out of heaven, and which, not your experience, but the man within the breast, has accepted, as words of fate; and tell me if they match; if the former account in any manner for the latter; or, which gives the most historical insight into the man.

17. Hence, though our external history is so meager, yet, with Shakspeare for biographer, instead of Aubrey[637] and Rowe,[638] we have really the information which is material, that which describes character and fortune, that which, if we were about to meet the man and deal with him, would most import us to know. We have his recorded convictions on those questions which knock for answer at every heart,—on life and death, on love, on wealth and poverty, on the prizes of life, and the ways whereby we come at them; on the characters of men, and the influences, occult and open, which affect their fortunes; and on those mysterious and demoniacal powers which defy our science, and which yet interweave their malice and their gift in our brightest hours. Who ever read the volume of the Sonnets, without finding that the poet had there revealed, under masks that are no masks to the intelligent, the lore of friendship and of love; the confusion of sentiments in the most susceptible, and, at the same time, the most intellectual of men? What trait of his private mind has he hidden in his dramas? One can discern, in his ample pictures of the gentleman and the king, what forms and humanities pleased him; his delight in troops of friends, in large hospitality,

in cheerful giving. Let Timon,[639] let Warwick,[640] let Antonio[641] the merchant, answer for his great heart. So far from Shakspeare's being the least known, he is the one person, in all modern history, known to us. What point of morals, of manners, of economy, of philosophy, of religion, of taste, of the conduct of life, has he not settled? What mystery has he not signified his knowledge of? What office, or function, or district of man's work, has he not remembered? What king has he not taught state, as Talma[642] taught Napoleon? What maiden has not found him finer than her delicacy? What lover has he not out-loved? What sage has he not outseen? What gentleman has he not instructed in the rudeness of his behavior?

18. Some able and appreciating critics think no criticism on Shakspeare valuable, that does not rest purely on the dramatic merit; that he is falsely judged as poet and philosopher. I think as highly as these critics of his dramatic merit, who still think it secondary. He was a full man, who liked to talk; a brain exhaling thoughts and images, which, seeking vent, found the drama next at hand. Had he been less, we should have had to consider how well he filled his place, how good a dramatist he was,—and he is the best in the world. But it turns out, that what he has to say is of that weight, as to withdraw some attention from the vehicle; and he is like some saint whose history is to be rendered into all languages, into verse and prose, into songs and pictures, and cut up into proverbs; so that the occasion which gave the saint's meaning the form of a conversation, or of a prayer, or of a code of laws, is immaterial, compared with the universality of its application. So it fares with the wise Shakspeare and his book of life. He wrote the airs for all our modern music: he wrote the text of modern life; the text of manners: he drew the man of England and Europe; the father of the man in America: he drew the man, and described the day, and what is done in it: he read the hearts of men and women, their probity, and their second thought, and wiles; the wiles of innocence, and the transitions by which virtues and vices slide into their contraries: he could divide the mother's part from the father's part in the face of the child, or draw the fine demarcations of freedom and of fate: he knew the laws of repression which make the police of nature: and all the sweets and all the terrors of human lot lay in his mind as truly but as softly as the landscape lies on the eye. And the importance of this wisdom of life sinks the form, as of Drama or Epic, out of notice. 'Tis like making a question concerning the paper on which a king's message is written.

19. Shakspeare is as much out of the category of eminent authors, as he is out of the crowd. He is inconceivably wise; the others, conceivably. A good reader can, in a sort, nestle into Plato's brain, and think from thence; but not into Shakspeare's. We are still out of doors. For executive faculty, for creation, Shakspeare is unique. No man can imagine it better. He was the

farthest reach of subtlety compatible with an individual self,—the subtilest of authors, and only just within the possibility of authorship. With this wisdom of life, is the equal endowment of imaginative and of lyric power. He clothed the creatures of his legend with form and sentiments, as if they were people who had lived under his roof; and few real men have left such distinct characters as these fictions. And they spoke in language as sweet as it was fit. Yet his talents never seduced him into an ostentation, nor did he harp on one string. An omnipresent humanity[643] coördinates all his faculties. Give a man of talents a story to tell, and his partiality will presently appear. He has certain observations, opinions, topics, which have some accidental prominence, and which he disposes all to exhibit. He crams this part, and starves that other part, consulting not the fitness of the thing, but his fitness and strength. But Shakspeare has no peculiarity, no importunate topic; but all is duly given; no veins, no curiosities: no cow-painter, no bird-fancier, no mannerist is he: he has no discoverable egotism: the great he tells greatly; the small, subordinately. He is wise without emphasis or assertion; he is strong, as nature is strong, who lifts the land into mountain slopes without effort, and by the same rule as she floats a bubble in the air, and likes as well to do the one as the other. This makes that equality of power in farce, tragedy, narrative, and love-songs; a merit so incessant, that each reader is incredulous of the perception of other readers.

20. This power of expression, or of transferring the inmost truth of things into music and verse, makes him the type of the poet, and has added a new problem to metaphysics. This is that which throws him into natural history, as a main production of the globe, and as announcing new eras and ameliorations. Things were mirrored in his poetry without loss or blur; he could paint the fine with precision, the great with compass: the tragic and the comic indifferently, and without any distortion or favor. He carried his powerful execution into minute details, to a hair point; finishes an eyelash or a dimple as firmly as he draws a mountain; and yet these, like nature's, will bear the scrutiny of the solar microscope.

21. In short, he is the chief example to prove that more or less of production, more or fewer pictures, is a thing indifferent. He had the power to make one picture. Daguerre[644] learned how to let one flower etch its image on his plate of iodine; and then proceeds at leisure to etch a million. There are always objects; but there was never representation. Here is perfect representation, at last; and now let the world of figures sit for their portraits. No recipe can be given for the making of a Shakspeare; but the possibility of the translation of things into song is demonstrated.

22. His lyric power lies in the genius of the piece. The sonnets, though their excellence is lost in the splendor of the dramas, are as inimitable as they: and it is not a merit of lines, but a total merit of the piece; like the tone of voice of some incomparable person, so is this a speech of poetic beings, and any clause as unproducible now as a whole poem.

23. Though the speeches in the plays, and single lines, have a beauty which tempts the ear to pause on them for their euphuism,[645] yet the sentence is so loaded with meaning, and so linked with its foregoers and followers, that the logician is satisfied. His means are as admirable as his ends; every subordinate invention, by which he helps himself to connect some irreconcilable opposites, is a poem too. He is not reduced to dismount and walk, because his horses are running off with him in some distant direction; he always rides.

24. The finest poetry was first experienced: but the thought has suffered a transformation since it was an experience. Cultivated men often attain a good degree of skill in writing verses; but it is easy to read, through their poems, their personal history: any one acquainted with parties can name every figure: this is Andrew, and that is Rachael. The sense thus remains prosaic. It is a caterpillar with wings, and not yet a butterfly. In the poet's mind, the fact has gone quite over into the new element of thought, and has lost all that is exuvial. This generosity bides with Shakspeare. We say, from the truth and closeness of his pictures, that he knows the lesson by heart. Yet there is not a trace of egotism.

25. One more royal trait properly belongs to the poet. I mean his cheerfulness, without which no man can be a poet,—for beauty is his aim. He loves virtue, not for its obligation, but for its grace: he delights in the world, in man, in woman, for the lovely light that sparkles from them. Beauty, the spirit of joy and hilarity, he sheds over the universe. Epicurus[646] relates, that poetry hath such charms that a lover might forsake his mistress to partake of them. And the true bards have been noted for their firm and cheerful temper. Homer lies in sunshine; Chaucer is glad and erect; and Saadi says, "It was rumored abroad that I was penitent; but what had I to do with repentance?" Not less sovereign and cheerful,—much more sovereign and cheerful, is the tone of Shakspeare. His name suggests joy and emancipation to the heart of men. If he should appear in any company of human souls, who would not march in his troop? He touches nothing that does not borrow health and longevity from his festal style.

26. And now, how stands the account of man with this bard and benefactor, when in solitude, shutting our ears to the reverberations of his

fame, we seek to strike the balance? Solitude has austere lessons; it can teach us to spare both heroes and poets; and it weighs Shakspeare also, and finds him to share the halfness and imperfection of humanity.

27. Shakspeare, Homer, Dante,[647] Chaucer, saw the splendor of meaning that plays over the visible world; knew that a tree had another use than for apples, and corn another than for meal, and the ball of the earth, than for tillage and roads: that these things bore a second and finer harvest to the mind, being emblems of its thoughts, and conveying in all their natural history a certain mute commentary on human life. Shakspeare employed them as colors to compose his picture. He rested in their beauty; and never took the step which seemed inevitable to such genius, namely, to explore the virtue which resides in these symbols, and imparts this power,—what is that which they themselves say? He converted the elements, which waited on his command, into entertainments. He was master of the revels[648] to mankind. Is it not as if one should have, through majestic powers of science, the comets given into his hand, or the planets and their moons, and should draw them from their orbits to glare with the municipal fireworks on a holiday night, and advertise in all towns, "very superior pyrotechny this evening!" Are the agents of nature, and the power to understand them, worth no more than a street serenade, or the breath of a cigar? One remembers again the trumpet-text in the Koran,[649]—"The heavens and the earth, and all that is between them, think ye we have created them in jest?" As long as the question is of talent and mental power, the world of men has not his equal to show. But when the question is to life, and its materials, and its auxiliaries, how does he profit me? What does it signify? It is but a Twelfth Night,[650] or Midsummer Night's Dream, or a Winter Evening's Tale: what signifies another picture more or less? The Egyptian verdict[651] of the Shakspeare Societies comes to mind, that he was a jovial actor and manager. I cannot marry this fact to his verse. Other admirable men have led lives in some sort of keeping with their thought; but this man, in wide contrast. Had he been less, had he reached only the common measure of great authors, of Bacon, Milton, Tasso,[652] Cervantes,[653] we might leave the fact in the twilight of human fate: but, that this man of men, he who gave to the science of mind a new and larger subject than had ever existed, and planted the standard of humanity some furlongs forward into Chaos,—that he should not be wise for himself,—it must even go into the world's history, that the best poet led an obscure and profane life, using his genius for the public amusement.

28. Well, other men, priest and prophet, Israelite,[654] German,[655] and Swede,[656] beheld the same objects: they also saw through them that which was contained. And to what purpose? The beauty straightway

vanished; they read commandments, all-excluding mountainous duty; an obligation, a sadness, as of piled mountains, fell on them, and life became ghastly, joyless, a pilgrim's progress,[657] a probation, beleaguered round with doleful histories, of Adam's fall[658] and curse, behind us; with doomsdays and purgatorial[659] and penal fires before us; and the heart of the seer and the heart of the listener sank in them.

29. It must be conceded that these are half-views of half-men. The world still wants its poet-priest, a reconciler, who shall not trifle with Shakspeare the player, nor shall grope in graves with Swedenborg the mourner; but who shall see, speak, and act, with equal inspiration. For knowledge will brighten the sunshine; right is more beautiful than private affection; and love is compatible with universal wisdom.

PRUDENCE[660]

What right have I to write on Prudence, whereof I have little, and that of the negative sort? My prudence consists in avoiding and going without, not in the inventing of means and methods, not in adroit steering, not in gentle repairing. I have no skill to make money spend well, no genius in my economy, and whoever sees my garden discovers that I must have some other garden. Yet I love facts, and hate lubricity[661] and people without perception. Then I have the same title to write on prudence that I have to write on poetry or holiness. We write from aspiration and antagonism, as well as from experience. We paint those qualities which we do not possess. The poet admires the man of energy and tactics; the merchant breeds his son for the church or the bar; and where a man is not vain and egotistic you shall find what he has not by his praise. Moreover it would be hardly honest in me not to balance these fine lyric words of Love and Friendship[662] with words of coarser sound, and whilst my debt to my senses is real and constant, not to own it in passing.

Prudence is the virtue of the senses. It is the science of appearances. It is the outmost action of the inward life. It is God taking thought for oxen. It moves matter after the laws of matter. It is content to seek health of body by complying with physical conditions, and health of mind by the laws of the intellect.

The world of the senses is a world of shows; it does not exist for itself, but has a symbolic character; and a true prudence or law of shows recognizes the co-presence of other laws and knows that its own office is subaltern; knows that it is surface and not centre where it works. Prudence is false when detached. It is legitimate when it is the Natural History of the soul incarnate, when it unfolds the beauty of laws within the narrow scope of the senses.

There are all degrees of proficiency in knowledge of the world. It is sufficient to our present purpose to indicate three. One class lives to the utility of the symbol, esteeming health and wealth a final good. Another class live above this mark of the beauty of the symbol, as the poet and artist and the naturalist and man of science. A third class live above the beauty of the symbol to the beauty of the thing signified; these are wise men. The first class have common sense; the second, taste; and the third, spiritual perception. Once in a long time, a man traverses the whole scale, and sees and enjoys the symbol solidly, then also has a clear eye for its beauty, and lastly, whilst he pitches his tent on this sacred volcanic isle of nature, does not offer to build houses and barns thereon reverencing the splendor of the God which he sees bursting through each chink and cranny.

The world is filled with the proverbs[663] and acts and winkings of a base prudence, which is a devotion to matter, as if we possessed no other faculties than the palate, the nose, the touch, the eye and ear; a prudence which adores the Rule of Three, which never subscribes, which gives never, which seldom lends, and asks but one question of any project,—Will it bake bread? This is a disease like a thickening of the skin until the vital organs are destroyed. But culture, revealing the high origin of the apparent world and aiming at the perfection of the man as the end, degrades everything else, as health and bodily life, into means. It sees prudence not to be a several faculty, but a name for wisdom and virtue conversing with the body and its wants. Cultivated men always feel and speak so as if a great fortune, the achievement of a civil or social measure, great personal influence, a graceful and commanding address, had their value as proofs of the energy of the spirit. If a man lose his balance and immerse himself in any trades or pleasures for their own sake, he may be a good wheel or pin,[664] but he is not a cultivated man.

The spurious prudence, making the senses final, is the god of sots and cowards, and is the subject of all comedy. It is nature's joke, and therefore literature's. The true prudence limits this sensualism by admitting the knowledge of an internal and real world. This recognition once made,—the order of the world and the distribution of affairs and times being studied with the co-perception of their subordinate place, will reward any degree of attention. For, our existence, thus apparently attached in nature to the sun and the returning moon and the periods which they mark; so susceptible to climate and to country, so alive to social good and evil, so fond of splendor and so tender to hunger and cold and debt,—reads all its primary lessons out of these books.

Prudence does not go behind nature and ask whence it is? It takes the laws of the world whereby man's being is conditioned, as they are, and keeps these laws that it may enjoy their proper good. It respects space and time, climate, want, sleep, the law of polarity,[665] growth and death. There revolve, to give bound and period to his being on all sides, the sun and moon, the great formalists in the sky: here lies stubborn matter, and will not swerve from its chemical routine. Here is a planted globe, pierced and belted with natural laws and fenced and distributed externally with civil partitions and properties which impose new restraints on the young inhabitant.

We eat of the bread which grows in the field. We live by the air which blows around us and we are poisoned by the air that is too cold or too hot, too dry or too wet. Time, which shows so vacant, indivisible and divine in its coming, is slit and peddled into trifles and tatters. A door is to be painted, a lock to be repaired. I want wood or oil, or meal, or salt; the house smokes, or I have a headache; then the tax; and an affair to be transacted with a man without heart or brains, and the stinging recollection of an injurious or very awkward word,—these eat up the hours. Do what we can, summer will have its flies.[666] If we walk in the woods we must feed mosquitoes. If we go a-fishing we must expect a wet coat. Then climate is a great impediment to idle persons. We often resolve to give up the care of the weather, but still we regard the clouds and the rain.

We are instructed by these petty experiences which usurp the hours and years. The hard soil and four months of snow make the inhabitant of the northern temperate zone wiser and abler than his fellow who enjoys the fixed smile of the tropics. The islander may ramble all day at will. At night he may sleep on a mat under the moon, and wherever a wild date-tree grows, nature has, without a prayer even, spread a table for his morning meal. The northerner is perforce a householder. He must brew, bake, salt and preserve his food. He must pile wood and coal. But as it happens that not one stroke can labor lay to without some new acquaintance with nature; and as nature is inexhaustibly significant, the inhabitants of these climates[667] have always excelled the southerner in force. Such is the value of these matters that a man who knows other things can never know too much of these. Let him have accurate perceptions. Let him, if he have hands, handle; if eyes, measure and discriminate; let him accept and hive every fact of chemistry, natural history and economics; the more he has, the less is he willing to spare any one. Time is always bringing the occasions that disclose their value. Some wisdom comes out of every natural and innocent action. The domestic man, who loves no music so well as his kitchen clock and the airs which the logs sing to him as they burn on the hearth, has solaces which others never dream of. The application of means to ends ensures victory and the songs of victory not less in a farm or a shop than in the tactics of party or of war. The good husband finds method as efficient in the packing of fire-wood in a shed or in the harvesting of fruits in the cellar, as in Peninsular campaigns[668] or the files of the Department of State. In the rainy day he builds a work-bench, or gets his tool-box set in the corner of the barn-chamber, and stored with nails, gimlet, pincers, screwdriver and chisel. Herein he tastes an old joy of youth and childhood, the cat-like love of garrets, presses and corn-chambers, and of the conveniences of long housekeeping. His garden or his poultry-yard—very paltry places it may be—tells him many pleasant anecdotes. One might find argument for optimism in the abundant flow of this saccharine element of pleasure in every suburb and extremity of the good world. Let a man keep the law—any law,—and his way will be strown with satisfactions. There is more difference in the quality of our pleasures than in the amount.

On the other hand, nature punishes any neglect of prudence. If you think the senses final, obey their law. If you believe in the soul, do not clutch at sensual sweetness before it is ripe on the slow tree of cause and effect. It is vinegar to the eyes to deal with men of loose and imperfect perception. Dr. Johnson is reported to have said,[669]—"If the child says he looked out of this window, when he looked out of that,—whip him." Our American character is marked by a more than average delight in accurate perception, which is shown by the currency of the by-word, "No mistake."

But the discomfort of unpunctuality, of confusion of thought about facts, inattention to the wants of to-morrow, is of no nation. The beautiful laws of time and space, once dislocated by our inaptitude, are holes and dens. If the hive be disturbed by rash and stupid hands, instead of honey it will yield us bees. Our words and actions to be fair must be timely. A gay and pleasant sound is the whetting of the scythe in the mornings of June; yet what is more lonesome and sad than the sound of a whetstone or mower's rifle[670] when it is too late in the season to make hay? Scatter brained and "afternoon men" spoil much more than their own affairs in spoiling the temper of those who deal with them. I have seen a criticism on some paintings, of which I am reminded when I see the shiftless and unhappy men who are not true to their senses. The last Grand Duke of Weimar,[671] a man of superior understanding, said: "I have sometimes remarked in the presence of great works of art, and just now especially in Dresden, how much a certain property contributes to the effect which gives life to the figures, and to the life an irresistible truth. This property is the hitting, in all the figures we draw, the right centre of gravity. I mean the placing the figures firm upon their feet, making the hands grasp, and fastening the eyes on the spot where they should look. Even lifeless figures, as vessels and stools—let them be drawn ever so correctly—lose all effect so soon as they lack the resting upon their centre of gravity, and have a certain swimming and oscillating appearance. The Raphael in the Dresden gallery[672] (the only great affecting picture which I have seen) is the quietest and most passionless piece you can imagine; a couple of saints who worship the Virgin and child. Nevertheless it awakens a deeper impression than the contortions of ten crucified martyrs. For, beside all the resistless beauty of form, it possesses in the highest degree the property of the perpendicularity of all the figures." This perpendicularity we demand of all the figures in this picture of life. Let them stand on their feet, and not float and swing. Let us know where to find them. Let them discriminate between what they remember and what they dreamed. Let them call a spade a spade.[673] Let them give us facts, and honor their own senses with trust.

But what man shall dare task another with imprudence? Who is prudent? The men we call greatest are least in this kingdom. There is a certain fatal dislocation in our relation to nature, distorting all our modes of living and making every law our enemy, which seems at last to have aroused all the wit and virtue in the world to ponder the question of Reform. We must call the highest prudence to counsel, and ask why health and beauty and genius should now be the exception rather than the rule of human nature? We do not know the properties of plants and animals and the laws of nature, through our sympathy with the same; but this remains the dream of poets. Poetry and prudence should be coincident. Poets should be lawgivers; that is, the boldest lyric inspiration should not chide and insult, but should announce and lead the civil code and the day's work. But now the two things seem irreconcilably parted. We have violated law upon law until we stand amidst ruins, and when by chance we espy a coincidence between reason and the phenomena, we are surprised. Beauty should be the dowry of every man and woman, as invariably as sensation; but it is rare. Health or sound organization should be universal. Genius should be the child of genius, and every child should be inspired; but now it is not to be predicted of any child, and nowhere is it pure. We call partial half lights, by courtesy, genius; talent which converts itself to money; talent which glitters to-day that it may dine and sleep well to-morrow; and society is officered by *men of parts*,[674] as they are properly called, and not by divine men. These use their gifts to refine luxury, not to abolish it. Genius is always ascetic; and piety, and love. Appetite shows to the finer souls as a disease, and they find beauty in rites and bounds that resist it.

We have found out[675] fine names to cover our sensuality withal, but no gifts can raise intemperance. The man of talent affects to call his transgressions of the laws of the senses trivial and to count them nothing considered with his devotion to his art. His art rebukes him. That never taught him lewdness, nor the love of wine, nor the wish to reap where he had not sowed. His art is less for every deduction from his holiness, and less for every defect of common sense. On him who scorned the world, as he said, the scorned world wreaks its revenge. He that despiseth small things will perish by little and little. Goethe's Tasso[676] is very likely to be a pretty fair historical portrait, and that is true tragedy. It does not seem to me so genuine grief when some tyrannous Richard III.[677] oppresses and slays a score of innocent persons, as when Antonio and Tasso, both apparently right, wrong each other. One living after the maxims of this world and consistent and true to them, the other fired with all divine sentiments, yet grasping also at the pleasures of sense, without submitting to their law. That is a grief we all feel, a knot we cannot untie. Tasso's is no infrequent case in modern biography. A man of genius, of an ardent temperament, reckless of physical laws, self-indulgent, becomes presently unfortunate, querulous, a "discomfortable cousin," a thorn to himself and to others.

The scholar shames us by his bifold[678] life. Whilst something higher than prudence is active, he is admirable; when common sense is wanted, he is an encumbrance. Yesterday, Cæsar[679] was not so great; to-day, Job[680] not so miserable. Yesterday, radiant with the light of an ideal world in which he lives, the first of men, and now oppressed by wants and by sickness, for which he must thank himself, none is so poor to do him reverence. He resembles the opium eaters whom travellers describe as frequenting the bazaars of Constantinople, who skulk about all day, the most pitiful drivellers, yellow, emaciated, ragged, sneaking; then at evening, when the bazaars are open, they slink to the opium-shop, swallow their morsel and become tranquil, glorious and great. And who has not seen the tragedy of imprudent genius struggling for years with paltry pecuniary difficulties, at last sinking, chilled, exhausted and fruitless, like a giant slaughtered by pins?

Is it not better that a man should accept the first pains and mortifications of this sort, which nature is not slack in sending him, as hints that he must expect no other good than the just fruit of his own labor and self-denial? Health, bread, climate, social position, have their importance, and he will give them their due. Let him esteem Nature a perpetual counsellor, and her perfections the exact measure of our deviations. Let him make the night night, and the day day. Let him control the habit of expense. Let him see that as much wisdom may be expended on a private economy as on an empire, and as much wisdom may be drawn from it. The laws of the world are written out for him on every piece of money in his hand. There is nothing he will not be the better for knowing, were it only the wisdom of Poor Richard,[681] or the State-street[682] prudence of buying by the acre to sell by the foot; or the thrift of the agriculturist, to stick[683] in a tree between whiles, because it will grow whilst he sleeps; or the prudence which consists in husbanding little strokes of the tool, little portions of time, particles of stock and small gains. The eye of prudence may never shut. Iron, if kept at the ironmonger's, will rust; beer, if not brewed in the right state of the atmosphere, will sour; timber of ships will rot at sea, or if laid up high and dry, will strain, warp and dry-rot. Money, if kept by us, yields no rent and is liable to loss; if invested, is liable to depreciation of the particular kind of stock. Strike, says the smith, the iron is white. Keep the rake, says the haymaker, as nigh the scythe as you can, and the cart as nigh the rake. Our Yankee trade is reputed to be very much on the extreme of this prudence. It saves itself by its activity. It takes bank notes, — good, bad, clean, ragged, and saves itself by the speed with which it passes them off. Iron cannot rust, nor beer sour, nor timber rot, nor calicoes go out of fashion, nor money stocks depreciate, in the few swift moments in which the Yankee suffers any one of them to remain in his possession. In skating over thin ice our safety is in our speed.

Let him learn a prudence of a higher strain. Let him learn that everything in nature, even motes and feathers, go by law and not by luck, and that what he sows he reaps. By diligence and self-command let him put the bread he eats at his own disposal, and not at that of others, that he may not stand in bitter and false relations to other men; for the best good of wealth is freedom. Let him practise the minor virtues.[684] How much of human life is lost in waiting! Let him not make his fellow creatures wait. How many words and promises are promises of conversation! Let his be words of fate. When he sees a folded and sealed scrap of paper float around the globe in a pine ship and come safe to the eye for which it was written, amidst a swarming population, let him likewise feel the admonition to integrate his being across all these distracting forces, and keep a slender human word among the storms, distances and accidents that drive us hither and thither, and, by persistency, make the paltry force of one man reappear to redeem its pledge after months and years in the most distant climates.

We must not try to write the laws of any one virtue, looking at that only. Human nature loves no contradictions, but is symmetrical. The prudence which secures an outward well-being is not to be studied by one set of men, whilst heroism and holiness are studied by another, but they are reconcilable. Prudence concerns the present time, persons, property and existing forms. But as every fact hath its roots in the soul, and, if the soul were changed, would cease to be, or would become some other thing, therefore the proper administration of outward things will always rest on a just apprehension of their cause and origin; that is, the good man will be the wise man, and the single-hearted the politic man. Every violation of truth is not only a sort of suicide in the liar, but is a stab at the health of human society. On the most profitable lie the course of events presently lays a destructive tax; whilst frankness proves to be the best tactics, for it invites frankness, puts the parties on a convenient footing and makes their business a friendship. Trust men and they will be true to you; treat them greatly and they will show themselves great, though they make an exception in your favor to all their rules of trade.

So, in regard to disagreeable and formidable things, prudence does not consist in evasion or in flight, but in courage. He who wishes to walk in the most peaceful parts of life with any serenity must screw himself up to resolution. Let him front the object of his worst apprehension, and his stoutness will commonly make his fears groundless. The Latin proverb says,[685] "in battles the eye is first overcome." The eye is daunted and greatly exaggerates the perils of the hour. Entire self-possession may make a battle very little more dangerous to life than a match at foils or at football. Examples are cited by soldiers of men who have seen the cannon pointed and the fire given to it, and who have stepped aside from the path of the ball. The terrors of the storm are chiefly confined to the parlor and the cabin. The drover, the sailor, buffets it all day, and his health renews itself at as vigorous a pulse under the sleet as under the sun of June.

In the occurrence of unpleasant things among neighbors, fear comes readily to heart and magnifies the consequence of the other party; but it is a bad counsellor. Every man is actually weak and apparently strong. To himself he seems weak; to others formidable. You are afraid of Grim; but Grim also is afraid of you. You are solicitous of the good will of the meanest person, uneasy at his ill will. But the sturdiest offender of your peace and of the neighborhood, if you rip up *his* claims, is as thin and timid as any; and the peace of society is often kept, because, as children say, one is afraid and the other dares not. Far off, men swell, bully and threaten: bring them hand to hand, and they are a feeble folk.

It is a proverb that "courtesy costs nothing"; but calculation might come to value love for its profit. Love is fabled to be blind, but kindness is necessary to perception; love is not a hood, but an eye-water. If you meet a sectary or a hostile partisan, never recognize the dividing lines, but meet on what common ground remains,—if only that the sun shines and the rain rains for both,—the area will widen very fast, and ere you know it, the boundary mountains on which the eye had fastened have melted into air. If he set out to contend,[686] almost St. Paul will lie, almost St. John will hate. What low, poor, paltry, hypocritical people an argument on religion will make of the pure and chosen souls. Shuffle they will and crow, crook and hide, feign to confess here, only that they may brag and conquer there, and not a thought has enriched either party, and not an emotion of bravery, modesty, or hope. So neither should you put yourself in a false position to your contemporaries by indulging a vein of hostility and bitterness. Though your views are in straight antagonism[687] to theirs, assume an identity of sentiment, assume that you are saying precisely that which all think, and in the flow of wit and love roll out your paradoxes in solid column, with not the infirmity of a doubt. So at least shall you get an adequate deliverance. The natural emotions of the soul are so much better than the voluntary ones that you will never do yourself justice in dispute. The thought is not then taken hold of by the right handle, does not show itself proportioned and in its true bearings, but bears extorted, hoarse, and half witness. But assume a consent and it shall presently be granted, since really and underneath their all external diversities, all men are of one heart and mind.

Wisdom will never let us stand with any man or men on an unfriendly footing. We refuse sympathy and intimacy with people, as if we waited for some better sympathy and intimacy to come. But whence and when? To-morrow will be like to-day. Life wastes itself whilst we are preparing to live. Our friends and fellow-workers die off from us. Scarcely can we say we see new men, new women, approaching us. We are too old to regard fashion, too old to expect patronage of any greater or more powerful. Let us suck the sweetness of those affections and consuetudes[688] that grow near us. These old shoes are easy to the feet. Undoubtedly we can easily pick faults in our company, can easily whisper names prouder and that tickle the fancy more. Every man's imagination hath its friends; and pleasant would life be with such companions. But if you cannot have them on good mutual terms, you cannot have them. If not the Deity but our ambition hews and shapes the new relations, their virtue escapes, as strawberries lose their flavor in garden beds.

Thus truth, frankness, courage, love, humility, and all the virtues range themselves on the side of prudence, or the art of securing a present well-being. I do not know if all matter will be found to be made of one element, as oxygen or hydrogen, at last, but the world of manners and actions is wrought of one stuff, and begin where we will[689] we are pretty sure in a short space to be mumbling our ten commandments.

CIRCLES[690]

The eye is the first circle; the horizon which it forms is the second; and throughout nature this primary picture is repeated without end. It is the highest emblem in the cipher of the world. St. Augustine[691] described the nature of God as a circle whose centre was everywhere and its circumference nowhere. We are all our lifetime reading the copious sense of this first of forms. One moral we have already deduced in considering the circular or compensatory character of every human action. Another analogy we shall now trace, that every action admits of being outdone. Our life is an apprenticeship to the truth that around every circle another can be drawn; that there is no end in nature, but every end is a beginning; that there is always another dawn risen on mid-noon,[692] and under every deep a lower deep opens.

This fact, as far as it symbolizes the moral fact of the Unattainable, the flying Perfect, around which the hands of man can never meet, at once the inspirer and the condemner of every success, may conveniently serve us to connect many illustrations of human power in every department.

There are no fixtures in nature. The universe is fluid and volatile. Permanence is but a word of degrees. Our globe seen by God is a transparent law, not a mass of facts. The law dissolves the fact and holds its fluid. Our culture is the predominance of an idea which draws after it all this train of cities and institutions. Let us rise into another idea; they will disappear. The Greek sculpture[693] is all melted away, as if it had been statues of ice: here and there a solitary figure or fragment remaining, as we see flecks and scraps of snow left in cold dells and mountain clefts in June and July. For the genius that created it creates now somewhat else. The Greek letters[694] last a little longer, but are already passing under the same sentence and tumbling into the inevitable pit which the creation of new thought opens for all that is old. The new continents are built out of the ruins of an old planet; the new races fed out of the decomposition of the foregoing. New arts destroy the old.[695] See the investment of capital in aqueducts, made useless by hydraulics; fortifications, by gunpowder; roads and canals, by railways; sails, by steam; steam, by electricity.

You admire this tower of granite, weathering the hurts of so many ages. Yet a little waving hand built this huge wall, and that which builds is better than that which is built. The hand that built can topple it down much faster. Better than the hand and nimbler was the invisible thought which wrought through it; and thus ever, behind the coarse effect, is a fine cause, which, being narrowly seen, is itself the effect of a finer cause. Everything looks permanent until its secret is known. A rich estate appears to women and children a firm and lasting fact; to a merchant, one easily created out of any materials, and easily lost. An orchard, good tillage, good grounds, seem a fixture, like a gold mine, or a river, to a citizen; but to a large farmer, not much more fixed than the state of the crop. Nature looks provokingly stable and secular, but it has a cause like all the rest; and when once I comprehend that, will these fields stretch so immovably wide, these leaves hang so individually considerable? Permanence is a word of degrees. Every thing is medial. Moons are no more bounds to spiritual power than bat-balls.

The key to every man is his thought. Sturdy and defying though he look, he has a helm which he obeys, which is the idea after which all his facts are classified. He can only be reformed by showing him a new idea which commands his own. The life of man is a self-evolving circle,[696] which, from a ring imperceptibly small, rushes on all sides outwards to new and larger circles, and that without end. The extent to which this generation of circles, wheel without wheel, will go, depends on the force or truth of the individual soul. For it is the inert effort of each thought, having formed itself into a circular wave of circumstance, as for instance an empire, rules of an art, a local usage, a religious rite, to heap itself on that ridge and to solidify and hem in the life. But if the soul is quick and strong it bursts over that boundary on all sides and expands another orbit on the great deep, which also runs up into a high wave, with attempt again to stop and to bind. But the heart refuses to be imprisoned;[697] in its first and narrowest pulses it already tends outward with a vast force and to immense and innumerable expansions.

Every ultimate fact is only the first of a new series. Every general law only a particular fact of some more general law presently to disclose itself. There is no outside, no inclosing wall, no circumference to us. The man finishes his story,—how good! how final! how it puts a new face on all things! He fills the sky. Lo, on the other side rises also a man and draws a circle around the circle we had just pronounced the outline of the sphere. Then already is our first speaker not man, but only a first speaker. His only redress is forthwith to draw a circle outside of his antagonist. And so men do by themselves. The result of to-day, which haunts the mind and cannot be escaped will presently be abridged into a word, and the principle that seemed to explain nature will itself be included as one example of a bolder generalization. In the thought of to-morrow there is a power to upheave all thy creed, all the creeds, all the literatures of the nations, and marshal thee to a heaven which no epic dream has yet depicted. Every man is not so much a workman in the world as he is a suggestion of that he should be. Men walk as prophecies of the next age.

Step by step we scale this mysterious ladder; the steps are actions, the new prospect is power. Every several result is threatened and judged by that which follows. Every one seems to be contradicted by the new; it is only limited by the new. The new statement is always hated by the old, and, to those dwelling in the old, comes like an abyss of scepticism. But the eye soon gets wonted to it, for the eye and it are effects of one cause; then its innocency and benefit appear, and presently, all its energy spent, it pales and dwindles before the revelation of the new hour.

Fear not the new generalization. Does the fact look crass[698] and material, threatening to degrade thy theory of spirit? Resist it not; it goes to refine and raise thy theory of matter just as much.

There are no fixtures to men, if we appeal to consciousness. Every man supposes himself not to be fully understood; and if there is any truth in him, if he rests at last on the divine soul, I see not how it can be otherwise. The last chamber, the last closet, he must feel was never opened; there is always a residuum unknown, unanalyzable. That is, every man believes that he has a greater possibility.

Our moods do not believe in each other. To-day I am full of thoughts and can write what I please. I see no reason why I should not have the same thought, the same power of expression, to-morrow. What I write, whilst I write it, seems the most natural thing in the world: but yesterday I saw a dreary vacuity in this direction in which now I see so much; and a month hence, I doubt not, I shall wonder who he was that wrote so many continuous pages. Alas for this infirm faith, this will not strenuous, this vast ebb of a vast flow! I am God in nature; I am a weed by the wall.

The continual effort to raise himself above himself,[699] to work a pitch above his last height, betrays itself in a man's relations. We thirst for approbation, yet cannot forgive the approver. The sweet of nature is love; yet if I have a friend I am tormented by my imperfections. The love of me accuses the other party. If he were high enough[700] to slight me, then could I love him, and rise by my affection to new heights. A man's growth is seen in the successive choirs of his friends. For every friend whom he loses for truth, he gains a better. I thought as I walked in the woods and mused on any friends, why should I play with them this game of idolatry? I know and see too well, when not voluntarily blind, the speedy limits of persons called high and worthy. Rich, noble and great they are by the liberality of our speech, but truth is sad. O blessed Spirit, whom I forsake for these, they are not thee! Every personal consideration that we allow costs us heavenly state. We sell the thrones of angels for a short and turbulent pleasure.

How often must we learn this lesson? Men cease to interest us when we find their limitations. The only sin is limitation. As soon as you once come up with a man's limitations, it is all over with him. Has he talents? has he enterprises? has he knowledge? It boots not. Infinitely alluring and attractive was he to you yesterday, a great hope, a sea to swim in; now, you have found his shores, found it a pond, and you care not if you never see it again.

Each new step we take in thought reconciles twenty seemingly discordant facts, as expressions of one law. Aristotle and Plato[701] are reckoned the respective heads of two schools. A wise man will see that Aristotle platonizes. By going one step farther back in thought, discordant opinions are reconciled by being seen to be two extremes of one principle, and we can never go so far back as to preclude a still higher vision.

Beware when the great God lets loose a thinker on this planet. Then all things are at risk. It is as when a conflagration has broken out in a great city, and no man knows what is safe, or where it will end. There is not a piece of science but its flank may be turned to-morrow; there is not any literary reputation, not the so-called eternal names of fame, that may not be revised and condemned. The very hopes of man, the thoughts of his heart, the religion of nations, the manners and morals of mankind are all at the mercy of a new generalization. Generalization is always a new influx of the divinity into the mind. Hence the thrill that attends it.

Valor consists in the power of self-recovery, so that a man cannot have his flank turned, cannot be out-generalled, but put him where you will, he stands. This can only be by his preferring truth to his past apprehension of truth, and his alert acceptance of it from whatever quarter; the intrepid conviction that his laws, his relations to society, his Christianity, his world, may at any time be superseded and decease.

There are degrees in idealism. We learn first to play with it academically, as the magnet was once a toy. Then we see in the heyday of youth and poetry that it may be true, that it is true in gleams and fragments. Then, its countenance waxes stern and grand, and we see that it must be true. It now shows itself ethical and practical. We learn that God is; that he is in me; and that all things are shadows of him. The idealism of Berkeley[702] is only a crude statement of the idealism of Jesus, and that again is a crude statement of the fact that all nature is the rapid efflux of goodness executing and organizing itself. Much more obviously is history and the state of the world at any one time directly dependent on the intellectual classification then existing in the minds of men. The things which are dear to men at this hour are so on account of the ideas which have emerged on their mental horizon, and which cause the present order of things, as a tree bears its apples. A new degree of culture would instantly revolutionize the entire system of human pursuits.

Conversation is a game of circles. In conversation we pluck up the *termini* [703] which bound the common of silence on every side. The parties are not to be judged by the spirit they partake and even express under this Pentecost.[704] To-morrow they will have receded from this high-water mark. To-morrow you shall find them stooping under the old pack-saddles. Yet let us enjoy the cloven flame whilst it glows on our walls. When each new speaker strikes a new light, emancipates us from the oppression of the last speaker to oppress us with the greatness and exclusiveness of his own thought, then yields us to another redeemer, we seem to recover our rights, to become men. O, what truths profound and executable only in ages and orbs, are supposed in the announcement of every truth! In common hours, society sits cold and statuesque. We all stand waiting, empty,—knowing, possibly, that we can be full, surrounded by mighty symbols which are not symbols to us, but prose and trivial toys. Then cometh the god and converts the statues into fiery men, and by a flash of his eye burns up the veil which shrouded all things, and the meaning of the very furniture, of cup and saucer, of chair and clock and tester, is manifest. The facts which loomed so large in the fogs of yesterday,—property, climate, breeding, personal beauty and the like, have strangely changed their proportions. All that we reckoned settled shakes and rattles; and literatures, cities, climates, religions, leave their foundations and dance before our eyes. And yet here again see the swift circumscription! Good as is discourse, silence is better, and shames it. The length of the discourse indicates the distance of thought betwixt the speaker and the hearer. If they were at a perfect understanding in any part, no words would be necessary thereon. If at one in all parts, no words would be suffered.

Literature is a point outside of our hodiernal[705] circle through which a new one may be described. The use of literature is to afford us a platform whence we may command a view of our present life, a purchase by which we may move it. We fill ourselves with ancient learning, install ourselves the best we can in Greek, in Punic,[706] in Roman houses, only that we may wiselier see French, English and American houses and modes of living. In like manner[707] we see literature best from the midst of wild nature, or from the din of affairs, or from a high religion. The field cannot be well seen from within the field. The astronomer must have his diameter of the earth's orbit as a base to find the parallax of any star.

Therefore we value the poet. All the argument and all the wisdom is not in the encyclopædia, or the treatise on metaphysics, or the Body of Divinity, but in the sonnet or the play. In my daily work I incline to repeat my old steps, and do not believe in remedial force, in the power of change and reform. But some Petrarch[708] or Ariosto,[709] filled with the new wine of his imagination, writes me an ode or a brisk romance, full of daring thought and action. He smites and arouses me with his shrill tones, breaks up my whole chain of habits, and I open my eye on my own possibilities. He claps wings to the sides of all the solid old lumber of the world, and I am capable once more of choosing a straight path in theory and practice.

We have the same need to command a view of the religion of the world. We can never see Christianity from the catechism:—from the pastures, from a boat in the pond, from amidst the songs of wood-birds we possibly may. Cleansed by the elemental light and wind, steeped in the sea of beautiful forms which the field offers us, we may chance to cast a right glance back upon biography. Christianity is rightly dear to the best of mankind; yet was there never a young philosopher whose breeding had fallen into the Christian church by whom that brave text of Paul's was not specially prized, "Then shall also the Son be subject unto Him who put all things under him, that God may be all in all."[710] Let the claims and virtues of persons be never so great and welcome, the instinct of man presses eagerly onward to the impersonal and illimitable, and gladly arms itself against the dogmatism of bigots with this generous word out of the book itself.

The natural world may be conceived of as a system of concentric circles, and we now and then detect in nature slight dislocations which apprize us that this surface on which we now stand is not fixed, but sliding. These manifold tenacious qualities,[711] this chemistry and vegetation, these metals and animals, which seem to stand there for their own sake, are means and methods only, are words of God, and as fugitive as other words. Has the naturalist or chemist learned his craft, who has explored the gravity of atoms and the elective affinities, who has not yet discerned the deeper law whereof this is only a partial or approximate statement, namely that like draws to like, and that the goods which belong to you gravitate to you and need not be pursued with pains and cost? Yet is that statement approximate also, and not final. Omnipresence is a higher fact. Not through subtle subterranean channels need friend and fact be drawn to their counterpart, but, rightly considered, these things proceed from the eternal generation of the soul. Cause and effect are two sides of one fact.

The same law of eternal procession ranges all that we call the virtues, and extinguishes each in the light of a better. The great man will not be prudent in the popular sense; all his prudence will be so much deduction from his grandeur. But it behooves each to see, when he sacrifices prudence, to what god he devotes it; if to ease and pleasure, he had better be prudent still; if to a great trust, he can well spare his mule and panniers who has a winged chariot instead. Geoffrey draws on his boots to go through the woods, that his feet may be safer from the bite of snakes; Aaron never thinks of such a peril. In many years neither is harmed by such an accident. Yet it seems to me that with every precaution you take against such an evil you put yourself into the power of the evil. I suppose that the highest prudence is the lowest prudence. Is this too sudden a rushing from the centre to the verge of our orbit? Think how many times we shall fall back into pitiful calculations before we take up our rest in the great sentiment, or make the verge of to-day the new centre. Besides, your bravest sentiment is familiar to the humblest men. The poor and the low have their way of expressing the last facts of philosophy as well as you. "Blessed be nothing" and "The worse things are, the better they are" are proverbs which express the transcendentalism of common life.

One man's justice is another's injustice; one man's beauty another's ugliness; one man's wisdom another's folly; as one beholds the same objects from a higher point of view. One man thinks justice consists in paying debts, and has no measure in his abhorrence of another who is very remiss in this duty and makes the creditor wait tediously. But that second man has his own way of looking at things; asks himself which debt must I pay first, the debt to the rich, or the debt to the poor? the debt of money, or the debt of thought to mankind, of genius to nature? For you, O broker, there is no other principle but arithmetic. For me, commerce is of trivial import; love, faith, truth of character, the aspiration of man, these are sacred; nor can I detach one duty, like you, from all other duties, and concentrate my forces mechanically on the payment of moneys. Let me live onward; you shall find that, though slower, the progress of my character will liquidate all these debts without injustice to higher claims. If a man should dedicate himself to the payment of notes, would not this be injustice? Owes he no debt but money? And are all claims on him to be postponed to a landlord's or a banker's?

There is no virtue which is final; all are initial. The virtues of society are vices of the saint. The terror of reform is the discovery that we must cast away our virtues, or what we have always esteemed such, into the same pit that has consumed our grosser vices.

Forgive his crimes, forgive his virtues too,
Those smaller faults, half converts to the right.[712]

It is the highest power of divine moments that they abolish our contritions also. I accuse myself of sloth and unprofitableness day by day; but when these waves of God flow into me I no longer reckon lost time. I no longer poorly compute my possible achievement by what remains to me of the month or the year; for these moments confer a sort of omnipresence and omnipotence which asks nothing of duration, but sees that the energy of the mind is commensurate with the work to be done, without time.

And thus, O circular philosopher, I hear some reader exclaim, you have arrived at a fine pyrrhonism,[713] at an equivalence and indifferency of all actions, and would fain teach us that *if we are true*, forsooth, our crimes may be lively stones out of which we shall construct the temple of the true God.

I am not careful to justify myself. I own I am gladdened[714] by seeing the predominance of the saccharine principle throughout vegetable nature, and not less by beholding in morals that unrestrained inundation of the principle of good into every chink and hole that selfishness has left open, yea into selfishness and sin itself; so that no evil is pure, nor hell itself without its extreme satisfactions. But lest I should mislead any when I have my own head and obey my whims, let me remind the reader that I am only an experimenter. Do not set the least value on what I do, or the least discredit on what I do not, as if I pretended to settle anything as true or false. I unsettle all things. No facts are to me sacred; none are profane; I simply experiment, an endless seeker with no Past at my back.

Yet this incessant movement and progression which all things partake could never become sensible to us but by contrast to some principle of fixture or stability in the soul. Whilst the eternal generation of circles proceeds, the eternal generator abides. That central life is somewhat superior to creation, superior to knowledge and thought, and contains all its circles. For ever it labors to create a life and thought as large and excellent as itself; but in vain; for that which is made instructs how to make a better.

Thus there is no sleep, no pause, no preservation, but all things renew, germinate and spring. Why should we import rags and relics into the new hour? Nature abhors the old, and old age seems the only disease: all others run into this one. We call it by many names, — fever, intemperance, insanity, stupidity and crime: they are all forms of old age: they are rest, conservatism, appropriation, inertia; not newness, not the way onward. We grizzle every day. I see no need of it. Whilst we converse with what is above us, we do not grow old, but grow young. Infancy, youth, receptive, aspiring, with religious eye looking upward, counts itself nothing and abandons itself to the instruction flowing from all sides. But the man and woman of seventy assume to know all; throw up their hope; renounce aspiration; accept the actual for the necessary and talk down to the young. Let them then become organs of the Holy Ghost; let them be lovers; let them behold truth; and their eyes are uplifted, their wrinkles smoothed, they are perfumed again with hope and power. This old age ought not to creep on a human mind. In nature every moment is new; the past is always swallowed and forgotten; the coming only is sacred. Nothing is secure but life, transition, the energizing spirit. No love can be bound by oath or covenant to secure it against a higher love. No truth so sublime but it may be trivial to-morrow in the light of new thoughts. People wish to be settled: only as far as they are unsettled is there any hope for them.

Life is a series of surprises. We do not guess to-day the mood, the pleasure, the power of to-morrow, when we are building up our being. Of lower states, — of acts of routine and sense, we can tell somewhat, but the masterpieces of God, the total growths and universal movements of the soul, he hideth; they are incalculable. I can know that truth is divine and helpful; but how it shall help me I can have no guess, for *so to be* is the sole inlet of *so to know*. The new position of the advancing man has all the powers of the old, yet has them all new. It carries in its bosom all the energies of the past, yet is itself an exhalation of the morning. I cast away in this new moment all my once hoarded knowledge, as vacant and vain. Now for the first time seem I to know any thing rightly. The simplest words, — we do not know what they mean except when we love and aspire.

The difference between talents and character is adroitness to keep the old and trodden round, and power and courage to make a new road to new and better goals. Character makes an overpowering present, a cheerful, determined hour, which fortifies all the company by making them see that much is possible and excellent that was not thought of. Character dulls the impression of particular events. When we see the conqueror we do not think much of any one battle or success. We see that we had exaggerated the difficulty. It was easy to him. The great man is not convulsible or tormentable. He is so much that events pass over him without much impression. People say sometimes, "See what I have overcome; see how cheerful I am; see how completely I have triumphed over these black events." Not if they still remind me of the black event, — they have not yet conquered. Is it conquest to be a gay and decorated sepulchre, or a half-crazed widow, hysterically laughing? True conquest is the causing the black event to fade and disappear as an early cloud of insignificant result in a history so large and advancing.

The one thing which we seek with insatiable desire is to forget ourselves, to be surprised out of our propriety, to lose our sempiternal[715] memory and to do something without knowing how or why; in short to draw a new circle. Nothing great was ever achieved without enthusiasm. The way of life is wonderful. It is by abandonment. The great moments of history are the facilities of performance through the strength of ideas, as the works of genius and religion. "A man," said Oliver Cromwell,[716] "never rises so high as when he knows not whither he is going." Dreams and drunkenness, the use of opium and alcohol are the semblance and counterfeit of this oracular genius, and hence their dangerous attraction for men. For the like reason they ask the aid of wild passions, as in the gaming and war, ape in some manner these flames and generosities of the heart.

NOTES

THE AMERICAN SCHOLAR

[1] **Games of strength.** The public games of Greece were athletic and intellectual contests of various kinds. There were four of importance: the Olympic, held every four years; the Pythian, held every third Olympic year; and the Nemean and Isthmian, held alternate years between the Olympic periods. These great national festivals exercised a strong influence in Greece. They were a secure bond of union between the numerous independent states and did much to help the nation to repel its foreign invaders. In Greece the accomplished athlete was reverenced almost as a god, and cases have been recorded where altars were erected and sacrifices made in his honor. The extreme care and cultivation of the body induced by this national spirit is one of the most significant features of Greek culture, and one which might wisely be imitated in the modern world.

[2] **Troubadours.** In southern France during the eleventh century, wandering poets went from castle to castle reciting or singing love-songs, composed in the old Provençal dialect, a sort of vulgarized Latin. The life in the great feudal chateaux was so dull that the lords and ladies seized with avidity any amusement which promised to while away an idle hour. The troubadours were made much of and became a strong element in the development of the Southern spirit. So-called Courts of Love were formed where questions of an amorous nature were discussed in all their bearings; learned opinions were expressed on the most trivial matters, and offenses were tried.

Some of the Provençal poetry is of the highest artistic significance, though the mass of it is worthless high-flown trash.

[3] At the time this oration was delivered (1837), many of the authors who have since given America a place in the world's literature were young men writing their first books. "We were," says James Russell Lowell, "still socially and intellectually moored to English thought, till Emerson cut the cable and gave us a chance at the dangers and glories of blue water."

[4] **Pole-star.** Polaris is now the nearest conspicuous star to the north pole of the celestial equator. Owing to the motion of the pole of the celestial

equator around that of the ecliptic, this star will in course of time recede from its proud position, and the brilliant star Vega in the constellation Harp will become the pole-star.

[5] It is now a well-recognized fact in the development of animal life that as any part of the body falls into disuse it in time disappears. Good examples of this are the disappearance of powerful fangs from the mouth of man, the loss of power in the wings of barnyard fowls; and, *vice versa*, as new uses for a member arise, its structure changes to meet the new needs. An example of this is the transformation from the hoof of a horse through the cloven hoofs of the cow to the eventual development of highly expert fingers in the monkey and man. Emerson assumed the doctrine of evolution to be sufficiently established by the anatomical evidence of gradual development. In his own words: "Man is no up-start in the creation. His limbs are only a more exquisite organization—say rather the finish—of the rudimental forms that have been already sweeping the sea and creeping in the mud. The brother of his hand is even now cleaving the arctic sea in the fin of the whale, and innumerable ages since was pawing the marsh in the flipper of the saurian." A view afterwards condensed into his memorable couplet:

> "Striving to be man, the worm
> Mounts through all the spires of form."

[6] **Stint.** A prescribed or allotted task, a share of labor.

[7] **Ridden.** Here used in the sense of dominated.

[8] **Monitory pictures.** Instructive warning pictures.

[9] The Greek stoic philosopher Epictetus is the author of this saying, not "the old oracle." It occurs in the Encheiridion, or manual, a work put together by a pupil of Epictetus. The original saying of Epictetus is as follows: "Every thing has two handles, the one by which it may be borne, the other by which it may not. If your brother acts unjustly, do not lay hold of the act by that handle wherein he acts unjustly, for this is the handle which cannot be borne: but lay hold of the other, that he is your brother, that he was nurtured with you, and you will lay hold of the thing by that handle by which it can be borne."

[10] Every day, the sun (shines).

[11] **Beholden.** Emerson here uses this past participle with its original meaning instead of in its present sense of "indebted."

[12] Here we have a reminder of Emerson's pantheism. He means the inexplicable continuity "of what I call God, and fools nature," as Browning expressed it.

[13] His expanding knowledge will become a creator.

[14] **Know thyself.** Plutarch ascribes this saying to Plato. It is also ascribed to Pythagoras, Chilo, Thales, Cleobulus, Bias, and Socrates; also to Phemonië, a mythical Greek poetess of the ante-Homeric period. Juvenal (Satire XI. 27) says that this precept descended from heaven. "Know thyself" and "Nothing too much" were inscribed upon the Delphic oracle.

"Know then thyself, presume not God to scan;
The proper study of mankind is man."

[15] Observe the brisk movement of these sentences. How they catch and hold the attention, giving a new impulse to the reader's interest!

[16] Nature abhors a vacuum.

[17] **Noxious.** Harmful.

[18] **John Locke** (1632-1704), an English philosopher whose work was of especial significance in the development of modern philosophy. The work he is best known by is the exhaustive "Essay on the Human Understanding," in which he combated the theory of Descartes, that every man has certain "innate ideas." The innate-idea theory was first proved by the philosopher Descartes in this way. Descartes began his speculations from a standpoint of absolute doubt. Then he said, "I think, therefore I am," and from this formula he built up a number of ideas innate to the human mind, ideas which we cannot but hold. Locke's "Essay on the Human Understanding" did much to discredit Descartes' innate ideas, which had been very generally accepted in Europe before.

[19] **Francis Bacon**, Baron Verulam, Viscount Saint Alban's (1561-1626), a famous English statesman and philosopher. He occupied high public offices, but in 1621 was convicted of taking bribes in his office of Lord Chancellor. He pleaded guilty and was sentenced to imprisonment and a fine of forty thousand pounds. Both these sentences were remitted, however. In the seventeenth century, judicial corruption was so common that Bacon's offence was not considered so gross as it would now be. As a philosopher Bacon's rank has been much disputed. While some claim that to his improved method of studying nature are chiefly to be attributed the prodigious strides taken by modern science, others deny him all merit in this respect. His best known works are: "The Novum Organum," a philosophical treatise; "The Advancement of Learning," a remarkable argument in favor of scholarship; and the short essays on subjects of common interest, usually printed under the simple title "Bacon's Essays."

[20] **Third Estate.** The thirteenth century was the age when the national assemblies of most European countries were putting on their definite shape. In most of them the system of *estates* prevailed. These in most countries were three—nobles, clergy, and commons, the commons being the third estate. During the French Revolution the Third Estate, or Tiers Etat, asserted its rights and became a powerful factor in French politics, choosing its own leaders and effecting the downfall of its oppressors.

[21] **Restorers of readings.** Men who spend their lives trying to improve and correct the texts of classical authors, by comparing the old editions with each other and picking out the version which seem most in accordance with the authors' original work.

[22] **Emendators.** The same as restorers of readings.

[23] **Bibliomaniacs.** Men with a mania for collecting rare and beautiful books. Not a bad sort of mania, though Emerson never had any sympathy for it.

[24] To many readers Emerson's own works richly fulfill this obligation. He himself lived continually in such a lofty mental atmosphere that no one can come within the circle of his influence without being stimulated and elevated.

[25] Genius, the possession of a thoroughly active soul, ought not to be the special privilege of favorites of fortune, but the right of every sound man.

[26] They stunt my mental growth. A man should not accept another man's conclusions, but merely use them as steps on his upward path.

[27] If you do not employ such talent as you have in original labor, in bearing the mental fruit of which you are capable, then you do not vindicate your claim to a share in the divine nature.

[28] **Disservice.** Injury.

[29] In original composition of any sort our efforts naturally flow in the channels worn for us by the first dominating streams of early genius. The conventional is the continual foe of all true art.

[30] Emerson is continually stimulating us to look at things in new ways. Here, for instance, at once the thought comes: "Is it not perhaps possible that the transcendent genius of Shakespeare has been rather noxious than beneficent in its influence on the mind of the world? Has not the all-pervading Shakespearian influence flooded and drowned out a great deal of original genius?"

[31] That is,—when in his clear, seeing moments he can distil some drops of truth from the world about him, let him not waste his time in studying other men's records of what they have seen.

[32] While Emerson's verse is frequently unmusical, in his prose we often find passages like this instinct with the fairest poetry.

[33] **Geoffrey Chaucer** (1340-1400). The father of English poetry. Chaucer's chief work is the "Canterbury Tales," a series of stories told by pilgrims traveling in company to Canterbury. Coleridge, the poet, wrote of Chaucer: "I take unceasing delight in Chaucer; his manly cheerfulness is especially delicious to me in my old age. How exquisitely tender he is, yet how free from the least touch of sickly melancholy or morbid drooping." Chaucer's poetry is above all things fresh. It breathes of the morning of literature. Like Homer he had at his command all the riches of a new language undefiled by usage from which to choose.

"Dan Chaucer, well of English undefyled,
On Fame's eternall beadroll worthie to be fyled."

[34] **Andrew Marvell** (1620-1678). An eminent English patriot and satirist. As a writer he is chiefly known by his "Rehearsal Transposed," written in answer to a fanatical defender of absolute power. When a young man he was assistant to the poet Milton, who was then Latin secretary to Oliver Cromwell. Marvell's wit and distinguished abilities rendered him formidable to the corrupt administration of Charles II., who attempted without success to buy his friendship. Emerson's literary perspective is a bit unusual when he speaks of Marvell as "one of the great English poets." Marvell hardly ranks with Chaucer, Shakespeare, and Milton.

[35] **John Dryden** (1631-1700). A celebrated English poet. Early in life he wrote almost entirely for the stage and achieved great success. In the latter part of his life, however, according to Macaulay, he "turned his powers in a new direction with success the most splendid and decisive. The first rank in poetry was beyond his reach, but he secured the most honorable place in the second.... With him died the secret of the old poetical diction of England,—the art of producing rich effects by familiar words."

[36] **Plato** (429-347 B.C.). One of the most illustrious philosophers of all time. Probably no other philosopher has contributed so much as Plato to the moral and intellectual training of the human race. This pre-eminence is due not solely to his transcendent intellect, but also in no small measure to his poetic power and to that unrivaled grace of style which led the ancients to say that if Jove should speak Greek he would speak like Plato. He was a remarkable example of that universal culture of body and mind which

characterized the last period of ancient Greece. He was proficient in every branch of art and learning and was such a brilliant athlete that he contended in the Isthmian and Pythian games.

[37] **Gowns.** The black gown worn occasionally in America and always in England at the universities; the distinctive academic dress is a cap and gown.

[38] **Pecuniary foundations.** Gifts of money for the support of institutions of learning.

[39] **Wit** is here used in its early sense of intellect, good understanding.

[40] **Valetudinarian.** A person of a weak, sickly constitution.

[41] **Mincing.** Affected.

[42] **Preamble.** A preface or introduction.

[43] **Dumb abyss.** That vast immensity of the universe about us which we can never understand.

[44] **I** comprehend its laws; I lose my fear of it.

[45] Silkworms feed on mulberry-leaves. Emerson describes what science calls "unconscious cerebration."

[46] **Ripe fruit.** Emerson's ripe fruit found its way into his diary, where it lay until he needed it in the preparation of some lecture or essay.

[47] I. Corinthians xv. 53.

[48] **Empyrean.** The region of pure light and fire; the ninth heaven of ancient astronomy.

> "The deep-domed empyrean
> Rings to the roar of an angel onset."

[49] **Ferules.** According to the methods of education fifty years ago, it was quite customary for the teacher to punish a school-child with his ferule or ruler.

[50] Oliver Wendell Holmes cites this last sentence as the most extreme development of the distinctively Emersonian style. Such things must be read not too literally but rapidly, with alert attention to what the previous train of thought has been.

[51] **Savoyards.** The people of Savoy, south of Lake Geneva in Switzerland.

[52] Emerson's style is characterized by the frequent use of pithy epigrams like this.

[53] **Sir Isaac Newton** (1642-1727). A great English philosopher and mathematician. He is famous as having discovered the law of gravitation.

[54] **Unhandselled.** Uncultivated, without natural advantages. A handsel is a gift.

[55] **Druids.** The ancient priesthood of the Britons in Cæsar's time. They had immense power among these primitive peoples. They were the judges as well as the priests and decided all questions. It is believed that they made human sacrifices to their gods in the depths of the primeval forest, but not much is known of their rites.

[56] **Berserkers.** Berserker was a redoubtable hero in Scandinavian mythology, the grandson of the eight-handed Starkodder and the beautiful Alfhilde. He had twelve sons who inherited the wild-battle frenzy, or berserker rage. The sagas, the great Scandinavian epics, are full of stories of heroes who are seized with this fierce longing for battle, murder, and sudden death. The name means bear-shirt and has been connected with the old *were-wolf* tradition, the myth that certain people were able to change into man-devouring wolves with a wolfish mad desire to rend and kill.

[57] **Alfred**, surnamed the Great (848-901), king of the West Saxons in England. When he ascended the throne his country was in a deplorable condition from the repeated inroads of northern invaders. He eventually drove them out and established a secure government. England owes much to the efforts of Alfred. He not only fought his country's battles, but also founded schools, translated Latin books into his native tongue, and did much for the intellectual improvement of his people.

[58] **The hoe and the spade.** "In spite of Emerson's habit of introducing the names of agricultural objects into his writing ('Hay, corn, roots, hemp, flax, apples, wool, and wood' is a line from one of his poems), his familiarity therewith is evidently not so great as he would lead one to imagine. 'Take care, papa,' cried his little son, seeing him at work with a spade, 'you will dig your leg.'"

[59] **John Flamsteed** (1646-1719). An eminent English astronomer. He appears to have been the first to understand the theory of the equation of time. He passed his life in patient observation and determined the position of 2884 stars.

[60] **Sir William Herschel** (1738-1822). One of the greatest astronomers that any age or nation has produced. Brought up to the profession of music, it was not until he was thirty years old that he turned his attention to astronomy. By rigid economy he obtained a telescope, and in 1781

discovered the planet Uranus. This great discovery gave him great fame and other substantial advantages. He was made private astronomer to the king and received a pension. His discoveries were so far in advance of his time, they had so little relation with those of his predecessors, that he may almost be said to have created a new science by revealing the immensity of the scale on which the universe is constructed.

[61] **Nebulous.** In astronomy a nebula is a luminous patch in the heavens far beyond the solar system, composed of a mass of stars or condensed gases.

[62] **Fetich.** The word seems to have been applied by Portuguese sailors and traders on the west coast of Africa to objects worshiped by the natives, which were regarded as charms or talismans. Of course the word here means an object of blind admiration and devotion.

[63] **Cry up,** to praise, extol.

[64] **Ancient and honorable.** Isaiah ix. 15.

[65] **Complement.** What is needed to complete or fill up some quantity or thing.

[66] **Signet.** Seal. Emerson is not always felicitous in his choice of metaphors.

[67] **Macdonald.** In Cervantes' "Don Quixote," Sancho Panza, the squire to the "knight of the metaphysical countenance," tells a story of a gentleman who had asked a countryman to dine with him. The farmer was pressed to take his seat at the head of the table, and when he refused out of politeness to his host, the latter became impatient and cried: "Sit there, clod-pate, for let me sit wherever I will, that will still be the upper end, and the place of worship to thee." This saying is commonly attributed to Rob Roy, but Emerson with his usual inaccuracy in such matters places it in the mouth of Macdonald,—which Macdonald is uncertain.

[68] **Carolus Linnæus** (1707-1778). A great Swedish botanist. He did much to make botany the orderly science it now is.

[69] **Sir Humphry Davy** (1778-1829). The most famous of English chemists. The most important to mankind of his many discoveries was the safety-lamp to be used in mines where there is danger of explosion from fire-damp.

[70] **Baron George Cuvier** (1769-1832). An illustrious French philosopher, statesman, and writer who made many discoveries in the realm of natural history, geology and philosophy.

[71] **The moon.** The tides are caused by the attraction of the moon and the sun. The attraction of the moon for the water nearest the moon is somewhat greater than the attraction of the earth's center. This causes a slight bulging of the water toward the moon and a consequent high tide.

[72] Emerson frequently omits the principal verb of his sentences as here: "In a century *there may exist* one or two men."

[73] This obscurely constructed sentence means: "For their acquiescence in a political and social inferiority the poor and low find some compensation in the immense moral capacity thereby gained."

[74] "**They**" refers to the hero or poet mentioned some twenty lines back.

[75] **Comprehendeth.** Here used in the original sense *to include.* The perfect man should be so thoroughly developed at every point that he will possess a share in the nature of every man.

[76] By the Classic age is generally meant the age of Greece and Rome; and by the Romantic is meant the middle ages.

[77] **Introversion.** Introspection is the more usual word to express the analytic self-searching so common in these days.

[78] **Second thoughts.** Emerson uses the word here in the same sense as the French *arrière-pensée*, a mental reservation.

[79]

"And thus the native hue of resolutionIs
sicklied o'er with the pale cast of thought."
Hamlet, Act III, Sc. 1.

[80] **Movement.** The French Revolution.

[81] Let every common object be credited with the diviner attributes which will class it among others of the same importance.

[82] **Oliver Goldsmith** (1728-1774). An eminent English poet and writer. He is best known by the comedy "She Stoops to Conquer," the poem "The Deserted Village," and the "Vicar of Wakefield." "Of all romances in miniature," says Schlegel, the great German critic, "the 'Vicar of Wakefield' is the most exquisite." It is probably the most popular English work of fiction in Germany.

[83] **Robert Burns** (1759-1796). A celebrated Scottish poet. The most striking characteristics of Burns' poetry are simplicity and intensity, in which he is scarcely, if at all, inferior to any of the greatest poets that have ever lived.

[84] **William Cowper** (1731-1800). One of the most popular of English poets. His poem "The Task" was probably more read in his day than any poem of equal length in the language. Cowper also made an excellent translation of Homer.

[85] **Johann Wolfgang von Goethe** (1749-1832). The most illustrious name in German literature; a great poet, dramatist, novelist, philosopher, and critic. The Germans regard Goethe with the same veneration we accord to Shakespeare. The colossal drama "Faust" is the most splendid product of his genius, though he wrote a large number of other plays and poems.

[86] **William Wordsworth** (1770-1850). By many considered the greatest of modern English poets. His descriptions of the ever-varying moods of nature are the most exquisite in the language. Matthew Arnold in his essay on Emerson says: "As Wordsworth's poetry is, in my judgment, the most important work done in verse in our language during the present century, so Emerson's 'Essays' are, I think, the most important work done in prose."

[87] **Thomas Carlyle** (1795-1881). A famous English essayist, historian, and speculative philosopher. It is scarcely too much to say that no other author of this century has exerted a greater influence not merely upon the literature but upon the mind of the English nation than Carlyle. Emerson was an intimate friend of Carlyle, and during the greater part of his life maintained a correspondence with the great Englishman. An interesting description of their meeting will be found among the "Critical Opinions" at the beginning of the work.

[88] **Alexander Pope** (1688-1744). The author of the "Essay on Criticism," "Rape of the Lock," the "Essay on Man," and other famous poems. Pope possessed little originality or creative imagination, but he had a vivid sense of the beautiful and an exquisite taste. He owed much of his popularity to the easy harmony of his verse and the keenness of his satire.

[89] **Samuel Johnson** (1709-1784). One of the eminent writers of the eighteenth century. He wrote "Lives of the Poets," poems, and probably the most remarkable work of the kind ever produced by a single person, an English dictionary.

[90] **Edward Gibbon** (1737-1794). One of the most distinguished of English historians. His great work is the "Decline and Fall of the Roman Empire." Carlyle called Gibbon, "the splendid bridge from the old world to the new."

[91] **Emanuel Swedenborg** (1688-1772). A great Swedish theologian, naturalist, and mathematician, and the founder of a religious sect which

has since his death become prominent among the philosophical schools of Christianity.

[92] **Johann Heinrich Pestalozzi** (1746-1827). A Swiss teacher and educational reformer of great influence in his time.

COMPENSATION

[93] These lines are printed under the title of *Compensation* in Emerson's collected poems. He has also another poem of eight lines with the same title.

[94] **Documents**, data, facts.

[95] This doctrine, which a little observation would confute, is still taught by some.

[96] **Doubloons**, Spanish and South American gold coins of the value of about $15.60 each.

[97] **Polarity**, that quality or condition of a body by virtue of which it exhibits opposite or contrasted properties in opposite or contrasted directions.

[98] **Systole and diastole**, the contraction and dilation of the heart and arteries.

[99] **They are increased** and consequently want more.

[100] **Intenerate**, soften.

[101] **White House**, the popular name of the presidential mansion at Washington.

[102] Explain the phrase *eat dust*.

[103] **Overlook**, oversee, superintend.

[104] **Res nolunt**, etc. Translated in the previous sentence.

[105] **The world ... dew.** Explain the thought. What gives the earth its shape?

[106] **The microscope ... little.** This statement is not in accordance with the facts, if we are to understand *perfect* in the sense which the next sentence would suggest.

[107] Emerson has been considered a pantheist.

[108]Οἱ κύβοι, etc. The translation follows in the text. This old proverb is quoted by Sophocles, (Fragm. lxxiv. 2) in the form:

Ἀεὶ γὰρ εὖ πίπτουσιν οἱ Διὸς κύβοι,

Emerson uses it in *Nature* in the form "Nature's dice are always loaded."

[109] **Amain,** with full force, vigorously.

[110] The proverb is quoted by Horace, Epistles, I, x. 24:

"Naturam expelles furca, tamen usque recurret."

A similar thought is expressed by Juvenal, Seneca, Cicero, and Aristophanes.

[111] **Augustine,** Confessions, B. I.

[112] **Jupiter,** the supreme god of the Romans, the Zeus of the Greeks.

[113] **Tying up the hands.** The expression is used figuratively, of course.

[114] The supreme power in England is vested in Parliament.

[115] **Prometheus** stole fire from heaven to benefit the race of men. In punishment for this Jupiter chained him to a rock and set an eagle to prey upon his liver. Some unknown and terrible danger threatened Jupiter, the secret of averting which only Prometheus knew. For this secret Jupiter offered him his freedom.

[116] **Minerva,** goddess of wisdom, who sprang full-armed from the brain of Jupiter. The secret which she held is told in the following lines.

[117] **Aurora,** goddess of the dawn. Enamored of Tithonus, she persuaded Jupiter to grant him immortality, but forgot to ask for him immortal youth. Read Tennyson's poem on *Tithonus*.

[118] **Achilles,** the hero of Homer's *Iliad*. His mother Thetis, to render him invulnerable, plunged him into the waters of the Styx. The heel by which she held him was not washed by the waters and remained vulnerable. Here he received a mortal wound.

[119] **Siegfried,** hero of the Nibelungenlied, the old German epic poem. Having slain a dragon, he bathed in its blood and became covered with an invulnerable horny hide, only one small spot between his shoulders which was covered by a leaf remaining vulnerable. Into this spot the treacherous Hagen plunged his lance.

[120] **Nemesis,** a Greek female deity, goddess of retribution, who visited the righteous anger of the gods upon mortals.

[121] **The Furies** or Eumenides, stern and inexorable ministers of the vengeance of the gods.

[122] **Ajax and Hector,** Greek and Trojan heroes in the Trojan War. See Homer's *Iliad*. Achilles slew Hector and, lashing him to his chariot with the

belt which Ajax had given Hector, dragged him round the walls of Troy. Ajax committed suicide with the sword which Hector had presented to him.

[123] **Thasians,** inhabitants of the island of Thasus. The story here told of the rival of the athlete Theagenes is found in Pausanias' *Description of Greece,* Book VI. chap. xi.

[124] Shakespeare, the greatest of English writers, seems to have succeeded entirely or almost entirely in removing the personal element from his writings.

[125] **Hellenic,** Greek.

[126] **Tit for tat,** etc. This paragraph is composed of a series of proverbs.

[127] **Edmund Burke** (1729?-1797), illustrious Irish statesman, orator, and author.

[128] **Pawns,** the pieces of lowest rank in chess.

[129] What is the meaning of *obscene* here? Compare the Latin.

[130] **Polycrates,** a tyrant of Samos, who was visited with such remarkable prosperity that he was advised by a friend to break the course of it by depriving himself of some valued possession. In accordance with this advice he cast into the sea an emerald ring which he considered his rarest treasure. A few days later a fisherman presented the monarch with a large fish inside of which the ring was found. Soon after this Polycrates fell into the power of an enemy and was nailed to a cross.

[131] **Scot and lot,** "formerly, a parish assessment laid on subjects according to their ability. Now, a phrase for obligations of every kind regarded collectively." (Webster.)

[132] Read Emerson's essay on *Gifts.*

[133] **Worm worms,** breed worms.

[134] Compare the old proverb "Murder will out." See Chaucer, *N.P.T.,* 232 and 237, and *Pr. T.,* 124.

[135]

"Et semel emissum volat irrevocabile verbum."
Horace, *Epist.,* I. XVIII. 65.

[136] **Stag in the fable.** See *Æsop,* lxvi. 184, *Cerva et Leo;* Phædrus I. 12. *Cervus ad fontem;* La Fontaine, vi. 9, *Le Cerf se Voyant dans l'eau.*

[137] See the quotation from St. Bernard farther on.

[138] **Withholden,** old participle of *withhold,* now *withheld.*

[139] What is the etymology of the word *mob*?

[140] **Optimism and Pessimism.** The meanings of these two opposites are readily made out from the Latin words from which they come.

[141] **St. Bernard de Clairvaux** (1091-1153), French ecclesiastic.

[142] **Jesus.** Holmes writes of Emerson: "Jesus was for him a divine manifestation, but only as other great human souls have been in all ages and are to-day. He was willing to be called a Christian just as he was willing to be called a Platonist.... If he did not worship the 'man Christ Jesus' as the churches of Christendom have done, he followed his footsteps so nearly that our good Methodist, Father Taylor, spoke of him as more like Christ than any man he had known."

[143] The first *his* refers to Jesus, the second to Shakespeare.

[144] **Banyan.** What is the characteristic of this tree that makes it appropriate for this figure?

SELF-RELIANCE

[145] **Ne te,** etc. "Do not seek for anything outside of thyself." From Persius, *Sat.* I. 7. Compare Macrobius, *Com. in Somn. Scip.,* I. ix. 3, and Boethius, *De Consol. Phil.,* IV. 4.

[146] *Epilogue to Beaumont and Fletcher's Honest Man's Fortune.*

[147] These lines appear in Emerson's *Quatrains* under the title *Power.*

[148] **Genius.** See the paragraph on genius in Emerson's lecture on *The Method of Nature,* one sentence of which runs: "Genius is its own end, and draws its means and the style of its architecture from within, going abroad only for audience, and spectator."

[149] "The man that stands by himself, the universe stands by him also." — Emerson, *Behavior.*

[150] **Plato** (429-347 b.c.), (See note 36.)

[151] **Milton** (1608-1674), the great English epic poet, author of *Paradise Lost.*

"O mighty-mouth'd inventor of harmonies,
O skill'd to sing of Time or Eternity,
God-gifted organ-voice of England,
Milton, a name to resound for ages."
Tennyson.

[152] "The great poet makes feel our own wealth." — Emerson, *The Over-Soul.*

[153] **Then most when,** most at the time when.

[154] "The imitator dooms himself to hopeless mediocrity." — Emerson, *Address to the Senior Class in Divinity College, Cambridge.*

[155]

"For words, like Nature, half reveal
And half conceal the soul within."
Tennyson, *In Memoriam,* V. I.

[156] **Trust thyself.** This is the theme of the present essay, and is a lesson which Emerson is never tired of teaching. In *The American Scholar* he says:

"In self-trust all the virtues are comprehended." In the essay on *Greatness:*

"Self-respect is the early form in which greatness appears.... Stick to your own.... Follow the path your genius traces like the galaxy of heaven for you to walk in."

Carlyle says:

"The fearful unbelief is unbelief in yourself."

[157] **Chaos** (Χάος), the confused, unorganized condition in which the world was supposed to have existed before it was reduced to harmony and order; hence, utter confusion and disorder.

[158] **These,** *i.e.,* children, babes, and brutes.

[159] **Four or five.** Supply the noun.

[160] **Nonchalance,** a French word meaning *indifference, coolness.*

[161] **Pit in the playhouse,** formerly, the seats on the floor below the level of the stage. These cheap seats were occupied by a class who did not hesitate to express their opinions of the performances.

[162] **Eclat,** a French word meaning *brilliancy of success, striking effect.*

[163] "Lethe, the river of oblivion." — *Paradise Lost.* Oblivion, forgetfulness.

[164] **Who.** What is the construction?

[165] **Nonconformist,** one who does not conform to established usages or opinions. Emerson considers conformity and consistency as the two terrors that scare us from self-trust. (See note 182.)

[166] **Explore if it be goodness**, investigate for himself and see if it be really goodness.

"Prove all things; hold fast that which is good."
Paul, *I. Thes.* v. 21.

[167] **Suffrage**, approval.

"What stronger breastplate than a heart untainted?
Thrice is he arm'd that hath his quarrel just;
And he but naked, though lock'd up in steel,
Whose conscience with injustice is corrupted."
Shakespeare, *II. Henry VI.*, III. 2.

[168] "There is nothing either good or bad, but thinking makes it so." —*Hamlet*, ii. 2.

[169] **Barbadoes**, an island in the Atlantic Ocean, one of the Lesser Antilles. The negroes, composing by far the larger part of the population, were formerly slaves.

[170] He had rather have his actions ascribed to whim and caprice than to spend the day in explaining them.

[171] **Diet and bleeding**, special diet and medical care, used figuratively, of course.

[172] Read Emerson's essay on *Greatness*.

[173] **The precise man**, precisely what kind of man.

[174] "By their fruits ye shall know them." —*Matthew*, vii. 16 and 20.

[175] **With**, notwithstanding, in spite of.

[176] **Of the bench**, of an impartial judge.

[177] **Bound their eyes with ... handkerchief**, in this game of blindman's-buff.

[178] "Pin thy faith to no man's sleeve; hast thou not two eyes of thy own?" —Carlyle.

[179] Give examples of men who have been made to feel the displeasure of the world for their nonconformity.

[180] "Nihil tam incertum nec tam inæstimabile est quam animi multitudinis." —Livy, xxxi. 34.

"Mobile mutatur semper cum principe vulgus."
Claudianus, *De IV. Consul. Honorii*, 302.

[181] *The other terror.* The first, conformity, has just been treated.

[182] **Consistency.** Compare, on the other hand, the well-known saying, "Consistency, thou art a jewel."

[183] **Orbit,** course in life.

[184] **Somewhat,** something.

[185] See *Genesis,* xxxix. 12.

[186] **Pythagoras** (fl. about 520 b.c.), a Greek philosopher. His society was scattered and persecuted by the fury of the populace.

[187] **Socrates** (470?-399 b.c.), the great Athenian philosopher, whose teachings are the subject of most of Plato's writings, was accused of corrupting the youth, and condemned to drink hemlock.

[188] **Martin Luther** (1483-1546) preached against certain abuses of the Roman Catholic Church and was excommunicated by the Pope. He became the leader of the Protestant Reformation.

[189] **Copernicus** (1473-1543) discovered the error of the old Ptolemaic system of astronomy and showed that the sun is the centre of our planetary system. Fearing the persecution of the church, he hesitated long to publish his discovery, and it was many years after his death before the world accepted his theory.

[190] **Galileo** (1564-1642), the famous Italian astronomer and physicist, discoverer of the satellites of Jupiter and the rings of Saturn, was thrown into prison by the Inquisition.

[191] **Sir Isaac Newton.** (See note 53.)

[192] **Andes,** the great mountain system of South America.

[193] **Himmaleh,** Himalaya, the great mountain system of Asia.

[194] **Alexandrian stanza.** The Alexandrian line consists of twelve syllables (iambic hexameter). Neither the acrostic nor the Alexandrine has the property assigned to it here. A palindrame reads the same forward as backward, as:

"Madam, I'm Adam";"
Signa te signa; temere me tangis et angis";

or the inscription on the church of St. Sophia, Constantinople:

Νίψον ἀνοήματα μὴ μόναν ὄψιν

[195] The reference is to sailing vessels, of course.

[196] **Scorn eyes**, scorn observers.

[197] **Chatham**, William Pitt, Earl of Chatham (1708-1778), this distinguished statesman and orator. He became very popular as a statesman and was known as "The Great Commoner."

[198] **Adams.** The reference is presumably to Samuel Adams (1722-1803), a popular leader and orator in the cause of American freedom. He was a member of the Continental Congress and a signer of the Declaration of Independence. Emerson may have in mind, however, John Adams (1735-1826), second president of the United States.

[199] **Spartan.** The ancient Spartans were noted for their courage and fortitude.

[200] **Julius Cæsar** (100-44 b.c.), the great Roman general, statesman, orator, and author.

[201] **St. Anthony** (251-356), Egyptian founder of monachism, the system of monastic seclusion.

[202] **George Fox** (1624-1691), English founder of the Society of Friends or Quakers.

[203] **John Wesley** (1703-1791), English founder of the religious sect known as Methodists.

[204] **Thomas Clarkson** (1760-1846), English philanthropist and abolitionist.

[205] **Scipio** (235-184 b.c.), the great Roman general who defeated Hannibal and decided the fate of Carthage. The quotation is from *Paradise Lost*, Book IX., line 610.

[206] In the story of *Abou Hassan* or *The Sleeper Awakened* in the *Arabian Nights* Abou Hassan awakes and finds himself treated in every respect as the Caliph Haroun Al-raschid. Shakespeare has made use of a similar trick in *Taming of the Shrew*, where Christopher Sly is put to bed drunk in the lord's room and on awaking is treated as a lord.

[207] **Alfred the Great** (849-901), King of the West Saxons. He was a wise king, a great scholar, and a patron of learning.

[208] **Scanderbeg**, George Castriota (1404-1467), an Albanian chief who embraced Christianity and carried on a successful war against the Turks.

[209] **Gustavus Adolphus** (1594-1632), King of Sweden, the hero of Protestantism in the Thirty Years' War.

[210] **Hieroglyphic,** a character in the picture-writing of the ancient Egyptian priests; hence, hidden sign.

[211] **Parallax,** an angle used in astronomy in calculating the distance of a heavenly body. The parallax decreases as the distance of the body increases.

[212] The child has the advantage of the experience of all his ancestors. Compare Tennyson's line in *Locksley Hall:*

"I the heir of all the ages, in the foremost files of time."

[213] "Why should we grope among the dry bones of the past, or put the living generation into masquerade out of its faded wardrobe? The sun shines to-day also." — Emerson, *Introd. to Nature, Addresses, etc.*

[214] Explain the thought in this sentence.

[215] **Judas Iscariot,** who betrayed Jesus.

[216] **Agent,** active, acting.

[217] An allusion to the Mohammedan custom of removing the shoes before entering a mosque.

[218] Of a truth, men are mystically united; a mystic bond of brotherhood makes all men one.

[219] **Thor and Woden.** Woden or Odin was the chief god of Scandinavian mythology. Thor, his elder son, was the god of thunder. From these names come the names of the days Wednesday and Thursday.

[220] Explain the meaning of this sentence.

[221] **You, or you,** addressing different persons.

[222] "The truth shall make you free." — *John,* viii. 32.

[223] **Antinomianism,** the doctrine that the moral law is not binding under the gospel dispensation, faith alone being necessary to salvation.

[224] "There is no sorrow I have thought more about than that — to love what is great, and try to reach it, and yet to fail." George Eliot, *Middlemarch,* lxxvi.

[225] Explain the use of *it* in these expressions.

[226] **Stoic,** a disciple of the Greek philosopher Zeno, who taught that men should be free from passion, unmoved by joy and grief, and should submit without complaint to the inevitable.

[227] **Word made flesh,** see *John,* i. 14.

[228] **Healing to the nations,** see *Revelation,* xxii. 2.

[229] **In what prayers do men allow themselves** to indulge?

[230]

"Prayer is the soul's sincere desire,
Uttered or unexpressed,
The motion of a hidden fire
That trembles in the breast."
Montgomery, *What is Prayer?*

[231] **Caratach** (Caractacus) is a historical character in Fletcher's (1576-1625) tragedy of *Bonduca* (Boadicea).

[232] **Zoroaster,** a Persian philosopher, founder of the ancient Persian religion. He flourished long before the Christian era.

[233] "Speak thou with us, and we will hear: but let not God speak with us, lest we die." — *Exodus,* xx. 19. Compare also the parallel passage in *Deuteronomy,* v. 25-27.

[234] **John Locke.** (See note 18.)

[235] **Lavoisier** (1743-1794), celebrated French chemical philosopher, discoverer of the composition of water.

[236] **James Hutton** (1726-1797), great Scotch geologist, author of the *Theory of the Earth.*

[237] **Jeremy Bentham** (1748-1832), English philosopher, jurist, and legislative reformer.

[238] **Fourier** (1772-1837), French socialist, founder of the system of Fourierism.

[239] **Calvinism,** the doctrines of John Calvin (1509-1564). French theologian and Protestant reformer. A cardinal doctrine of Calvinism is predestination.

[240] **Quakerism,** the doctrines of the Quakers or Friends, a society founded by George Fox (1624-1691).

[241] **Emanuel Swedenborg** (1688-1772), Swedish theosophist, founder of the New Jerusalem Church. He is taken by Emerson in his *Representative Men* as the type of the mystic, and is often mentioned in his other works.

[242] "Though we travel the world over to find the beautiful, we must carry it with us, or we find it not." — Emerson, *Art.*

[243] **Thebes,** a celebrated ruined city of Upper Egypt.

[244] **Palmyra,** a ruined city of Asia situated in an oasis of the Syrian desert, supposed to be the Tadmor built by Solomon in the wilderness (*II. Chr.*, viii. 4).

[245]

> "Vain, very vain, my weary search to find
> That bliss which only centers in the mind....
> Still to ourselves in every place consign'd,
> Our own felicity we make or find."
>   Goldsmith (and Johnson),
>   *The Traveler*, 423-32.

> "He that has light within his own clear breast
> May sit i' th' center, and enjoy bright day;
> But he that hides a dark soul, and foul thoughts,
> Benighted walks under the mid-day sun;
> Himself in his own dungeon."
>   Milton, *Comus*, 381-5.

Compare also *Paradise Lost*, I, 255-7.

[246] **Vatican,** the palace of the pope in Rome, with its celebrated library, museum, and art gallery.

[247] **Doric,** the oldest, strongest, and simplest of the three styles of Grecian architecture.

[248] **Gothic,** a pointed style of architecture, prevalent in western Europe in the latter part of the middle ages.

[249] **Never imitate.** Emerson insists on this doctrine.

[250] **Shakespeare** (1564-1616), the great English poet and dramatist. He is mentioned in Emerson's writings more than any other character in history, and is taken as the type of the poet in his *Representative Men*.

"O mighty poet! Thy works are not as those of other men, simply and merely great works of art; but are also like the phenomena of nature, like the sun and the sea, the stars and the flowers,—like frost and snow, rain and dew, hailstorm and thunder, which are to be studied with entire submission of our own faculties, and in the perfect faith that in them there can be no too much or too little, nothing useless or inert,—but that, the further we press in our discoveries, the more we shall see proofs of design and self-supporting arrangement where the careless eye had seen nothing but accident!"—De Quincy.

[251] **Benjamin Franklin** (1706-1790), American philosopher, statesman, diplomatist, and author. He discovered the identity of lightning with electricity, invented the lightning-rod, went on several diplomatic missions to Europe, was one of the committee that drew up the Declaration of Independence, signed the treaty of Paris, and compiled *Poor Richard's Almanac.*

[252] **Francis Bacon** (1561-1626), a famous English philosopher and statesman. He became Lord Chancellor under Elizabeth. He is best known by his *Essays*; he wrote also the *Novum Organum* and the *Advancement of Learning.*

[253] **Sir Isaac Newton.** (See note 53.)

[254] **Scipio.** (See note 205.)

[255] **Phidias** (500?-432? b.c.), famous Greek sculptor.

[256] **Egyptians.** He has in mind the pyramids.

[257] The Pentateuch is attributed to Moses.

[258] **Dante** (1265-1321), the greatest of Italian poets, author of the *Divina Commedia.*

[259] **Foreworld**, a former ideal state of the world.

[260] **New Zealander**, inhabitant of New Zealand, a group of two islands lying southeast of Australia.

[261] **Geneva**, a city of Switzerland, situated at the southwestern extremity of Lake Geneva.

[262] **Greenwich nautical almanac.** The meridian of the Royal Observatory at Greenwich, near London, is the prime meridian for reckoning the longitude of the world. The nautical almanac is a publication containing astronomical data for the use of navigators and astronomers. What is the name of the corresponding publication of the U.S. Observatory at Washington?

[263] Get the meaning of these astronomical terms.

[264] **Plutarch.** (50?-120? a.d.), Greek philosopher and biographer, author of *Parallel Lives,* a series of Greek and Roman biographies. Next after Shakespeare and Plato he is the author most frequently mentioned by Emerson. Read the essay of Emerson on Plutarch.

[265] **Phocion** (402-317 b.c.), Athenian statesman and general. (See note 364.)

[266] **Anaxagoras** (500-426 b.c.), Greek philosopher of distinction.

[267] Diogenes (400?-323?), Greek cynic philosopher who affected great contempt for riches and honors and the comforts of civilized life, and is said to have taken up his residence in a tub.

[268] **Henry Hudson** (— — - 1611), English navigator and explorer, discoverer of the bay and river which bear his name.

[269] **Bering** or **Behring** (1680-1741), Danish navigator, discoverer of Behring Strait.

[270] **Sir William Edward Parry** (1790-1855), English navigator and Arctic explorer.

[271] **Sir John Franklin** (1786-1846?), celebrated English navigator and Arctic explorer, lost in the Arctic seas.

[272] **Christopher Columbus** (1445?-1506), Genoese navigator and discoverer of America. His ship, the Santa Maria, appears small and insignificant in comparison with the modern ocean ship.

[273] **Napoleon Bonaparte** (1769-1821), Emperor of France, one of the greatest military geniuses the world has ever seen. He was defeated in the battle of Waterloo by the Duke of Wellington, and died in exile on the isle of St. Helena. Emerson takes him as a type of the man of the world in his *Representative Men*: "I call Napoleon the agent or attorney of the middle class of modern society.... He was the agitator, the destroyer of prescription, the internal improver, the liberal, the radical, the inventor of means, the opener of doors and markets, the subverter of monopoly and abuse.... He had the virtues of the masses of his constituents: he had also their vices. I am sorry that the brilliant picture has its reverse."

[274] **Comte de las Cases** (not Casas) (1766-1842), author of *Mémorial de Sainte-Hélène*.

[275] **Ali**, Arabian caliph, surnamed the "Lion of God," cousin and son-in-law of Mohammed. He was assassinated about 661.

[276] The county of Essex in England has several namesakes in America.

[277] **Fortune**. In Roman mythology Fortune, the goddess of fortune or chance, is represented as standing on a ball or wheel.

> "Nec metuis dubio Fortunæ stantis in orbe
> Numen, et exosæ verba superba deæ?"
> Ovid, *Tristia*, v., 8, 8.

FRIENDSHIP

[278] Most of Emerson's *Essays* were first delivered as lectures, in practically the form in which they afterwards appeared in print. The form and style, it is true, were always carefully revised before publication; this Emerson called 'giving his thoughts a Greek dress.' His essay on *Friendship*, published in the First Series of *Essays* in 1841 was not, so far as we know, delivered as a lecture; parts of it, however, were taken from lectures which Emerson delivered on *Society, The Heart,* and *Private Life.*

In connection with his essay on *Friendship*, the student should read the two other notable addresses on the same subject, one the speech by Cicero, the famous Roman orator, and the other the essay by Lord Bacon, the great English author.

[279] **Relume.** Is this a common word? Define it.

[280] **Pass my gate.** The walk opposite Emerson's house on the 'Great Road' to Boston was a favorite winter walk for Concord people. Along it passed the philosophic Alcott and the imaginative Hawthorne, as well as famous townsmen, and school children.

[281] **My friends have come to me**, etc.: Compare with Emerson's views here expressed the noble passage in his essay on *The Over-Soul*: "Every friend whom not thy fantastic will but the great and tender heart in thee craveth, shall lock thee in his embrace. And this because the heart in thee is the heart of all; not a valve, not a wall, not an intersection is there anywhere in nature, but one blood rolls uninterruptedly in endless circulation through all men, as the water of the globe is all one sea, and, truly seen, its tide is one."

[282] **Bard.** Poet: originally one who composed and sang to the music of a harp verses in honor of heroes and heroic deeds.

[283] **Hymn, ode, and epic.** Define each of these three kinds of poetry.

[284] **Apollo.** In classic mythology, the sun god who presided over music, poetry, and art; he was the guardian and leader of the Muses.

[285] **Muses.** In classic mythology, the nine sisters who presided over music, poetry, art, and science. They were Clio the muse of history, Euterpe of music, especially the flute, Thalia of comedy, Melpomene of tragedy, Terpsichore of dancing, Erato of erotic poetry, mistress of the lyre, Polyhymnia of sacred poetry, Urania of astronomy, Calliope of eloquence and epic poetry.

[286] **Genius.** According to an old belief, a spirit that watched over a person to control, guide and aid him.

[287] **"Crush the sweet poison,"** etc. This is a quotation from *Comus*, a poem by Milton.

[288] **Systole and diastole.** (See note 98.)

[289] **Friendship, like the immortality**, etc. See on what a high plane Emerson places this relation of friendship. In 1840 he wrote in a letter: "I am a worshiper of friendship, and cannot find any other good equal to it. As soon as any man pronounces the words which approve him fit for that great office, I make no haste; he is holy; let me be holy also; our relations are eternal; why should we count days and weeks?"

[290] **Elysian temple.** Temple of bliss. In Greek mythology, Elysium was the abode of the blessed after death.

[291] **An Egyptian skull.** Plutarch says that at an Egyptian feast a skull was displayed, either as a hint to make the most of the pleasure which can be enjoyed but for a brief space, or as a warning not to set one's heart upon transitory things.

[292] **Conscious of a universal success**, etc. Emerson wrote in his journal: "My entire success, such as it is, is composed wholly of particular failures."

[293] **Extends the old leaf.** Compare Emerson's lines:

"When half-gods go
The gods arrive."

[294] **A texture of wine and dreams.** What does Emerson mean by this phrase? Explain the whole sentence.

[295] **"The valiant warrior,"** etc. The quotation is from Shakespeare's *Sonnet*, xxv.

[296] **Naturlangsamkeit.** A German word meaning slowness. The slowness of natural development.

[297] **Olympian.** One who took part in the great Greek games held every four years on the plain of Olympia. The racing, wrestling and other contests of strength and skill were accompanied by sacrifices to the gods, processions, and banquets. There was a sense of dignity and almost of worship about the games. The Olympic games have been recently revived, and athletes from all countries of the world contest for the prizes—simple garlands of wild olive.

[298] **I knew a man who**, etc. The allusion is to Jonas Very, a mystic and poet, who lived at Salem, Massachusetts.

[299] **Paradox.** Define this word. Explain its application to a friend.

[300] **My author says**, etc. The quotation is from *A Consideration upon Cicero*, by the French author, Montaigne. Montaigne was one of Emerson's favorite authors from his boyhood: of the essays he says, "I felt as if I myself, had written this book in some former life, so sincerely it spoke my thoughts."

[301] **Cherub.** What is the difference between a cherub and a seraph?

[302] **Curricle.** A two-wheeled carriage, especially popular in the eighteenth century.

[303] **This law of one to one.** Emerson felt that this same law applied to nature. He wrote in his journal: "Nature says to man, 'one to one, my dear.'"

[304] **Crimen quos**, etc. The Latin saying is translated in the preceding sentence.

[305] **Nonage.** We use more commonly the word, "minority."

[306] **Janus-faced.** The word here means simply two-faced, without the idea of deceit usually attached to it. In Roman mythology, Janus, the doorkeeper of heaven was the protector of doors and gateways and the patron of the beginning and end of undertakings. He was the god of the rising and setting of the sun, and was represented with two faces, one looking to the east and the other to the west. His temple at Rome was kept open in time of war and closed in time of peace.

[307] **Harbinger.** A forerunner; originally an officer who rode in advance of a royal person to secure proper lodgings and accommodations.

[308] **Empyrean.** Highest and purest heaven; according to the ancients, the region of pure light and fire.

HEROISM

[309] **Title.** Probably this essay is, essentially at least, the lecture on *Heroism* delivered in Boston in the winter of 1837, in the course of lectures on *Human Culture*.

[310] **Motto.** This saying of Mahomet's was the only motto prefixed to the essay in the first edition. In later editions, Emerson prefixed, according to his custom, some original lines;

"Ruby wine is drunk by knaves,
Sugar spends to fatten slaves,
Rose and vine-leaf deck buffoons,
Thunder clouds are Jove's festoons,
Drooping oft in wreaths of dread
Lightning-knotted round his head:
The hero is not fed on sweets,
Daily his own heart he eats;
Chambers of the great are jails,
And head-winds right for royal sails."

[311] **Elder English dramatists.** The dramatists who preceded Shakespeare. In his essay on *Shakespeare; or, the Poet,* Emerson enumerates the foremost of these, — "Kyd, Marlowe, Greene, Jonson, Chapman, Dekker, Webster, Heywood, Middleton, Peele, Ford, Massinger, Beaumont and Fletcher."

[312] **Beaumont and Fletcher.** Francis Beaumont and John Fletcher were two dramatists of the Elizabethan age. They wrote together and their styles were so similar that critics are unable to identify the share of each in their numerous plays.

[313] **Rodrigo, Pedro, or Valerio.** Favorite names for heroes among the dramatists. Rodrigo Diaz de Bivar, known usually by the title of the Cid, was the national hero of Spain, famous for his exploits against the Moors. Don Pedro was the Prince of Arragon in Shakespeare's play, *Much Ado About Nothing.*

[314] **Bonduca, Sophocles, the Mad Lover, and Double Marriage.** The first, third and fourth are names of plays by Beaumont and Fletcher. In the case of the second, Emerson, by a lapse of memory, gives the name of one of the chief characters instead of the name of the play—*The Triumph of Honor* in a piece called *Four Plays in One.* It is from this play by Beaumont and Fletcher that the passage in the essay is quoted.

[315] **Adriadne's crown.** According to Greek mythology, the crown of Adriadne was, for her beauty and her sufferings, put among the stars. She was the daughter of Minos, King of Crete; she gave Theseus the clue by means of which he escaped from the labyrinth and she was afterwards abandoned by him.

[316] **Romulus.** The reputed founder of the city of Rome.

[317] **Laodamia, Dion.** Read these two poems by Wordsworth, the great English poet, and tell why you think Emerson mentioned them here.

[318] **Scott.** Sir Walter Scott, a famous Scotch author.

[319] **Lord Evandale, Balfour of Burley.** These are characters in Scott's novel, *Old Mortality.* The passage referred to by Emerson is in the forty-second chapter.

[320] **Thomas Carlyle.** Carlyle was a great admirer of heroes, asserting that history is the biography of great men. One of his most popular books is *Heroes and Hero-Worship,* on a plan similar to that of Emerson's *Representative Men.*

[321] **Robert Burns.** A Scotch lyric poet. Emerson was probably thinking of the patriotic song, *Scots wha hae wi' Wallace bled.*

[322] **Harleian Miscellanies.** A collection of manuscripts published in the eighteenth century, and named for Robert Harley, the English statesman who collected them.

[323] **Lutzen.** A small town in Prussia. The battle referred to was fought in 1632 and in it the Swedes under Gustavus Adolphus gained a great victory over vastly superior numbers. Nearly two hundred years later another battle was fought at Lutzen, in which Napoleon gained a victory over the allied Russians and Prussians.

[324] **Simon Ockley.** An English scholar of the seventeenth century whose chief work was a *History of the Saracens.*

[325] **Oxford.** One of the two great English universities.

[326] **Plutarch.** (See note 264.)

[327] **Brasidas.** This hero, described by Plutarch, was a Spartan general who lived about four hundred years before Christ.

[328] **Dion.** A Greek philosopher who ruled the city of Syracuse in the fourth century before Christ.

[329] **Epaminondas.** A Greek general and statesman of the fourth century before Christ.

[330] **Scipio.** (See note 205.)

[331] **Stoicism.** The stern and severe philosophy taught by the Greek philosopher Zeno; he taught that men should always seek virtue and be indifferent to pleasure and happiness. This belief, carried to the extreme of severity, exercised a great influence on many noble Greeks and Romans.

[332] **Heroism is an obedience**, etc. In one of his poems Emerson says:

"So nigh is grandeur to our dust,
So near is God to man,
When Duty whispers low, 'Thou must,'
The youth replies, 'I can.'"

[333] **Plotinus.** An Egyptian philosopher who taught in Rome during the third century. It was said that he so exalted the mind that he was ashamed of his body.

[334] **Indeed these humble considerations**, etc. The passage, like many which Emerson quotes, is rendered inexactly. The Prince says to Poins: "Indeed these humble considerations make me out of love with my greatness. What a disgrace it is to me to remember thy name! or to know thy face to-morrow! or to take note how many pairs of silk stockings thou hast, that is, these and those that were thy peach-colored ones! or to bear the inventory of thy shirts, as, one for superfluity and another for use!" Shakespeare's *Henry IV.*, Part II. 2, 2.

[335] **Ibn Hankal.** Ibn Hankul, an Arabian geographer and traveler of the tenth century. He wrote an account of his twenty years' travels in Mohammedan countries; in 1800 this was translated into English by Sir William Jones under the title of *The Oriental Geography of Ibn Hankal.* In that volume this anecdote is told in slightly different words.

[336] **Bokhara.** Where is Bokhara? It corresponds to the ancient Sogdiana.

[337] **Bannocks.** Thick cakes, made usually of oatmeal. What does Emerson mean by this sentence? Probably no person ever met his visitors, many of whom were "exacting and wearisome," and must have been unwelcome, with more perfect courtesy and graciousness than Emerson.

[338] **John Eliot.** Give as full an account as you can of the life and works of this noble Apostle to the Indians of the seventeenth century.

[339] **King David**, etc. See First Chronicles, 11, 15-19.

[340] **Brutus.** Marcus Junius Brutus, a Roman patriot of the first century before Christ, who took part in the assassination of Julius Cæsar.

[341] **Philippi.** A city of Macedonia near which in the year 42 B.C. were fought two battles in which the republican army under Brutus and Cassius was defeated by Octavius and Antony, friends of Cæsar.

[342] **Euripides.** A Greek tragic poet of the fifth century before Christ.

[343] **Scipio.** (See note 205.) Plutarch in his *Morals* gives another version of the story: "When Paetilius and Quintus accused him of many

crimes before the people; 'on this very day,' he said, 'I conquered Hannibal and Carthage. I for my part am going with my crown on to the Capitol to sacrifice; and let him that pleaseth stay and pass his vote upon me.' Having thus said, he went his way; and the people followed him, leaving his accusers declaiming to themselves."

[344] **Socrates.** (See note 187.)

[345] **Prytaneum.** A public hall at Athens.

[346] **Sir Thomas More.** An English statesman and author who was beheaded in 1535 on a charge of high treason. The incident to which Emerson refers is one which showed his "pleasant wit" undisturbed by the prospect of death. As the executioner was about to strike, More moved his head carefully out of reach of the ax. "Pity that should be cut," he said, "that has never committed treason."

[347] **Blue Laws.** Any rigid Sunday laws or religious regulations. The term is usually applied to the early laws of New Haven and Connecticut which regulated personal and religious conduct.

[348] **Epaminondas.** (See note 329.)

[349] **Olympus.** A mountain of Greece, the summit of which, according to Greek mythology, was the home of the gods.

[350] **Jerseys.** Consult a history of the United States for a full account of Washington's campaign in New Jersey.

[351] **Milton.** (See note 151.)

[352] **Pericles.** A famous Greek statesman of the fifth century before Christ, in whose age Athens was preëminent in naval and military affairs and in letters and art.

[353] **Xenophon.** A Greek historian of the fourth century before Christ.

[354] **Columbus.** Give an account of his life.

[355] **Bayard.** Chevalier de Bayard was a French gentleman of the fifteenth century. He is the French national hero, and is called "The Knight without fear and without reproach."

[356] **Sidney.** Probably Sir Philip Sidney, an English gentleman and scholar of the sixteenth century who is the English national hero as Bayard is the French; another brave Englishman was Algernon Sidney, a politician and patriot of the seventeenth century.

[357] **Hampden.** John Hampden was an English statesman and patriot who was killed in the civil war of the seventeenth century.

[358] **Colossus.** The Colossus of Rhodes was a gigantic statue—over a hundred feet in height—of the Rhodian sun god. It was one of the seven wonders of the world; it was destroyed by an earthquake about two hundred years before Christ.

[359] **Sappho.** A Greek poet of the seventh century before Christ. Her fame remains, though most of her poems have been lost.

[360] **Sevigné.** Marquise de Sevigné was a French author of the seventeenth century.

[361] **De Staël.** Madame de Staël was a French writer whose books and political opinions were condemned by Napoleon.

[362] **Themis.** A Greek goddess. The personification of law, order, and justice.

[363] **A high counsel**, etc. Such was the advice given to the Emerson boys by their aunt, Miss Mary Moody Emerson: "Scorn trifles, lift your aims; do what you are afraid to do; sublimity of character must come from sublimity of motive." Upon her monument are inscribed Emerson's words about her: "She gave high counsels. It was the privilege of certain boys to have this immeasurably high standard indicated to their childhood, a blessing which nothing else in education could supply."

[364] **Phocion.** A Greek general and statesman of the fourth century before Christ who advised the Athenians to make peace with Philip of Macedon. He was put to death on a charge of treason.

[365] **Lovejoy.** Rev. Elijah Lovejoy, a Presbyterian clergyman of Maine who published a periodical against slavery. In 1837 an Illinois mob demanded his printing press, which he refused to give up. The building containing it was set on fire and when Lovejoy came out he was shot.

[366] **Let them rave**, etc. These lines are misquoted, being evidently given from memory, from Tennyson's *Dirge*. In the poem occur these lines:

"Let them rave.
Thou wilt never raise thine head
From the green that folds thy grave—
Let them rave."

MANNERS

[367] The essay on *Manners* is from the Second Series of *Essays*, published in 1844, three years after the First Series. The essays in this volume, like those in the first, were, for the most part, made up of Emerson's lectures, rearranged and corrected. The lecture on *Manners* had been delivered in

the winter of 1841. He had given another lecture on the same subject about four years before, and several years later he treated of the same subject in his essay on *Behavior* in *The Conduct of Life*. You will find it interesting to read *Behavior* in connection with this essay.

[368] **Feejee islanders.** Since this essay was written, the people of the Feejee, or Fiji, Islands have become Christianized, and, to a large extent, civilized.

[369] **Gournou.** This description is found in *A Narrative of the Operations and Recent Discoveries within the Pyramids*, by Belzoni, an Italian traveler and explorer.

[370] **Borgoo.** A province of Africa.

[371] **Tibboos, Bornoos.** Tribes of Central Africa, mentioned in Heeren's *Historical Researches*.

[372] **Honors himself with architecture.** Architecture was a subject in which Emerson was deeply interested. Read his poem, *The Problem*.

[373] **Chivalry.** Chivalry may be considered "as embodying the Middle Age conception of the ideal life of ... the Knights"; the word is often used to express "the ideal qualifications of a knight, as courtesy, generosity, valor, and dexterity in arms." Fully to understand the order of Knighthood and the ideals of chivalry, you must read the history of Europe in the Middle Ages.

[374] **Sir Philip Sidney.** (See note 356.)

[375] **Sir Walter Scott.** (1771-1832). His historical novels dealing with the Middle Ages have some fine pictures of the chivalrous characters in which he delighted.

[376] **Masonic sign.** A sign of secret brotherhood, like the sign given by one Mason to another.

[377] **Correlative abstract.** Corresponding abstract name. Sir Philip Sidney, himself the ideal gentleman, used the word "gentlemanliness." He said: "Gentlemanliness is high-erected thoughts seated in a heart of courtesy."

[378] **Gentilesse.** Gentle birth and breeding. Emerson was very fond of the passage on "gentilesse" in Chaucer's *Wife of Bath's Tale*.

[379] **Feudal Ages.** The Middle Ages in Europe during which the feudal system prevailed. According to this, land was held by its owners on condition of certain duties, especially military service, performed for a superior lord.

[380] **God knows,** etc. Why is this particularly true of a republic such as the United States?

[381] **The incomparable advantage of animal spirits.** Why does Emerson regard this as of such importance? In his journals he frequently comments on his own lack of animal spirits, and says that it unfits him for general society and for action.

[382] **The sense of power.** "I like people who can do things," wrote Emerson in his journal.

[383] **Lundy's Lane.** Give a full account of this battle in the War of 1812.

[384] **Men of the right Cæsarian pattern.** Men versatile as was Julius Cæsar, the Roman, famous as a general, statesman, orator, and writer.

[385] **Timid maxim.** Why does Emerson term this saying "timid"?

[386] **Lord Falkland.** Lucius Cary, Viscount Falkland, was an English politician who espoused the royalist side; he was killed in battle in the Civil War.

[387] **Saladin.** A famous sultan of Egypt and Syria who lived in the twelfth century. Scott describes him as possessing an ideal knightly character and introduces him, disguised as a physician and also as a wandering soldier in his historical romance, *The Talisman.*

[388] **Sapor.** A Persian monarch of the fourth century who defeated the Romans in battle.

[389] **The Cid.** See "Rodrigo," in *Heroism*, 313.

[390] **Julius Cæsar.** See note on "Cæsarian," 384.

[391] **Scipio.** (See note 205.)

[392] **Alexander.** Alexander, King of Macedon, surnamed the Great. In the fourth century before Christ he made himself master of the known world.

[393] **Pericles.** See note on *Heroism*, 352.

[394] **Diogenes.** (See note 267.)

[395] **Socrates.** (See note 187.)

[396] **Epaminondas.** (See note 329.)

[397] **My contemporaries.** Emerson probably had in mind, among others, his friend, the gentle philosopher, Thoreau.

[398] **Fine manners.** "I think there is as much merit in beautiful manners as in hard work," said Emerson in his journal.

[399] **Napoleon.** (See note 273.)

[400] **Noblesse.** Nobility. Why does Emerson use here the French word?

[401] **Faubourg St. Germain.** A once fashionable quarter of Paris, on the south bank of the Seine; it was long the headquarters of the French royalists.

[402] **Cortez.** Consult a history of the United States for an account of this Spanish soldier, the conqueror of Mexico.

[403] **Nelson.** Horatio Nelson, an English admiral, who won many great naval victories and was killed in the battle of Trafalgar in 1805.

[404] **Mexico.** The scene of Cortez's victories.

[405] **Marengo.** The scene of a battle in Italy in 1800, in which Napoleon defeated the Austrians with a larger army and made himself master of northern Italy.

[406] **Trafalgar.** A cape on the southern coast of Spain, the scene of Nelson's last great victory, in which the allied French and Spanish fleets were defeated.

[407] **Mexico, Marengo, and Trafalgar.** Is this the order in which you would expect these words to occur? Why not?

[408] **Estates of the realm.** Orders or classes of people with regard to political rights and powers. In modern times, the nobility, the clergy, and the people are called "the three estates."

[409] **Tournure.** Figure; turn of dress,—and so of mind.

[410] **Coventry.** It is said that the people of Coventry, a city in England, at one time so disliked soldiers that to send a military man there meant to exclude him from social intercourse; hence the expression "to send to Coventry" means to exclude from society.

[411] **"If you could see Vich Ian Vohr with his tail on."** Vich Ian Vohr is a Scotch chieftain in Scott's novel, *Waverley*. One of his dependents says to Waverley, the young English officer: "If you Saxon duinhé-wassal [English gentleman] saw but the Chief with his tail on." "With his tail on?" echoed Edward in some surprise. "Yes—that is, with all his usual followers when he visits those of the same rank." See *Waverley*, chapter 16.

[412] **Mercuries.** The word here means simply messengers. According to Greek mythology, Mercury was the messenger of the gods.

[413] **Herald's office.** In England the Herald's College, or College of Arms, is a royal corporation the chief business of which is to grant armorial bearings, or coats of arms, and to trace and preserve genealogies. What does Emerson mean by comparing certain circles of society to this corporation?

[414] **Amphitryon.** Host; it came to have this meaning from an incident in the story of Amphitryon, a character in Greek legend. At one time Jupiter assumed the form of Amphitryon and gave a banquet. The real Amphitryon came in and asserted that he was master of the house. In the French play, founded on this story, the question is settled by the assertion of the servants and guests that "he who gives the feast is the host."

[415] **Tuileries.** An old royal residence in Paris which was burned in 1871.

[416] **Escurial**, or escorial. A celebrated royal edifice near Madrid in Spain.

[417] **Hide ourselves as Adam**, etc. See Genesis iii. 8.

[418] **Cardinal Caprara.** An Italian cardinal, Bishop of Milan, who negotiated the famous concordat of 1801, an agreement between the Church and State regulating the relations between civil and ecclesiastical powers.

[419] **The pope.** Pope Pius VII.

[420] **Madame de Staël.** (See note 361.)

[421] **Mr. Hazlitt.** William Hazlitt, an English writer.

[422] **Montaigne.** A French essayist of the sixteenth century.

[423] **The hint of tranquillity and self-poise.** It is suggested that Emerson had here in mind a favorite passage of the German author, Richter, in which Richter says of the Greek statues: "The repose not of weariness but of perfection looks from their eyes and rests upon their lips."

[424] **A Chinese etiquette.** What does Emerson mean by this expression?

[425] **Recall.** In the first edition, Emerson had here the word "signify." Which is the better word and why?

[426] **Measure.** What meaning has this word here? Is this the sense in which we generally use it?

[427] **Creole natures.** What is a creole? What does Emerson mean by "Creole natures"?

[428] **Mr. Fox.** Charles James Fox, an English statesman and orator of the eighteenth century.

[429] **Burke.** Both Fox and Burke opposed the taxation of the American colonies and sympathized with their resistance; it was on the subject of the French Revolution that the two friends clashed.

[430] **Sheridan.** Richard Brinsley Sheridan, an Irish dramatist, member of the famous Literary Club to which both Fox and Burke belonged.

[431] **Circe.** According to Greek legend, Circe was a beautiful enchantress. Men who partook of the draught she offered, were turned to swine.

[432] **Captain Symmes.** The only real personage of this group. He asserted that there was an opening to the interior of the earth which was stocked with plants and animals.

[433] **Clerisy.** What word would we be more apt to use here?

[434] **St. Michael's (Square).** St. Michael's was an order instituted by Louis XI. of France.

[435] **Cologne water.** A perfumed water first made at the city of Cologne in Germany, from which it took its name.

[436] **Poland.** This kingdom of Europe was, in the eighteenth century, taken possession of and divided among its powerful neighbors, Russia, Prussia, and Austria.

[437] **Philhellene.** Friend of Greece.

[438] **As Heaven and Earth are fairer far**, etc. This passage is quoted from Book II. of Keats' *Hyperion*.

[439] **Waverley.** The Waverley novels, a name applied to all of Scott's novels from *Waverley*, the title of the first one.

[440] **Robin Hood.** An English outlaw and popular hero, the subject of many ballads.

[441] **Minerva.** In Roman mythology, the goddess of wisdom corresponding to the Greek Pallas-Athene.

[442] **Juno.** In Roman mythology, the wife of the supreme god Jupiter.

[443] **Polymnia.** In Greek mythology, one of the nine muses who presided over sacred poetry; the name is more usually written Polyhymia.

[444] **Delphic Sibyl.** In ancient mythology, the Sibyls were certain women who possessed the power of prophecy. One of these who made her abode at Delphi in Greece was called the Delphian, or Delphic, sibyl.

[445] **Hafiz.** A Persian poet of the fourteenth century.

[446] **Firdousi.** A Persian poet of the tenth century.

[447] **She was an elemental force**, etc. Of this passage Oliver Wendell Holmes said that Emerson "speaks of woman in language that seems to pant for rhythm and rhyme."

[448] **Byzantine.** An ornate style of architecture developed in the fourth and fifth centuries, marked especially by its use of gold and color.

[449] **Golden Book.** In a book, called "the Golden Book," were recorded the names of all the children of Venetian noblemen.

[450] **Schiraz.** A province of Persia famous especially for its roses, wine, and nightingales, and described by the poets as a place of ideal beauty.

[451] **Osman.** The name given by Emerson in his journal and essays to his ideal man, one subject to the same conditions as himself.

[452] **Koran.** The sacred book of the Mohammedans.

[453] **Jove.** Jupiter, the supreme god of Roman mythology.

[454] **Silenus.** In Greek mythology, the leader of the satyrs. This fable, which Emerson credits to tradition, was original.

[455] **Her owl.** The owl was the bird sacred to Minerva, the goddess of wisdom.

GIFTS

[456] This essay was first printed in the periodical called *The Dial*.

It was a part of Emerson's philosophic faith that there is no such thing as giving, — everything that belongs to a man or that he ought to have, will come to him. But in the ordinarily accepted sense of the word, Emerson was a gracious giver and receiver. In his family the old New England custom of New Year's presents was kept up to his last days. His presents were accompanied with verses to be read before the gift was opened.

[457] **Into chancery.** The phrase "in chancery," means in litigation, as an estate, in a court of equity.

[458] **Cocker.** Spoil, indulge, — a word now little used.

[459] **Fruits are acceptable gifts.** Emerson took especial pleasure in the beauty of fruits and the thought of how they had been evolved from useless, insipid seed cases.

[460] **To let the petitioner,** etc. We can hardly imagine Emerson's asking a gift or favor. He often quoted the words of Landor, an English writer: "The highest price you can pay for a thing is to ask for it."

[461] **Furies.** In Roman mythology, three goddesses who sought out and punished evil-doers.

[462] **A man's biography,** etc. Emerson wrote in his journal: "Long ago I wrote of *gifts* and neglected a capital example. John Thoreau, Jr. [who, like his brother Henry, was a lover of nature] one day put a bluebird's box on my barn,—fifteen years ago it must be,—and there it still is, with every summer a melodious family in it adorning the place and singing its praises. There's a gift for you which cost the giver no money, but nothing which he bought could have been as good."

[463] **Sin offering.** Under the Hebrew law, a sacrifice or offering for sin. See Leviticus xxiii. 19. Explain what Emerson means here by the word.

[464] **Blackmail.** What is "blackmail"? How may Christmas gifts, for instance, become a species of blackmail?

[465] **Brother, if Jove,** etc. In the Greek legend, Epimetheus gives this advice to his brother Prometheus. The lines are taken from a translation of *Works and Days,* by the Greek poet, Hesiod.

[466] **Timons.** Here used in the sense of wealthy givers. Timon, the hero of Shakespeare's play, *Timon of Athens,* wasted his fortune in lavish gifts and entertainments, and in his poverty was exposed to the ingratitude of those whom he had served. He became morose and died in miserable retirement.

[467] **It is a very onerous business,** etc. One of Emerson's favorite passages in the essays of Montaigne, a French writer, was this: "Oh, how am I obliged to Almighty God, who has been pleased that I should immediately receive all I have from his bounty, and particularly reserved all my obligation to himself! How instantly do I beg of his holy compassion that I may never owe a real thanks to anyone. O happy liberty in which I have thus far lived! May it continue with me to the last. I endeavor to have no need of any one."

When Emerson, in his old age, had his house injured by fire, his friends contributed funds to repair it and to send him to England. The gift was proffered graciously and accepted gratefully.

[468] **Buddhist.** A follower of Buddha, a Hindoo religious teacher of the fifth century before Christ.

NATURE

[469] **Nature.** Emerson's first published volume was a little book of essays, entitled *Nature*, which appeared in 1836. In the years which followed, he thought more deeply on the subject and, according to his custom, made notes about it and entries in his journals. In the winter of 1843 he delivered a lecture on *Relation to Nature*, and it is probable that this essay is built up from that. The plan of it, however, had been long in his mind: In 1840 he wrote in his journal: "I think I must do these eyes of mine the justice to write a new chapter on Nature. This delight we all take in every show of night or day or field or forest or sea or city, down to the lowest particulars, is not without sequel, though we be as yet only wishers and gazers, not at all knowing what we want. We are predominated here as elsewhere by an upper wisdom, and resemble those great discoverers who are haunted for years, sometimes from infancy, with a passion for the fact, or class of facts in which the secret lies which they are destined to unlock, and they let it not go until the blessing is won. So these sunsets and starlights, these swamps and rocks, these bird notes and animal forms off which we cannot get our eyes and ears, but hover still, as moths round a lamp, are no doubt a Sanscrit cipher covering the whole religious history of the universe, and presently we shall read it off into action and character. The pastures are full of ghosts for me, the morning woods full of angels."

[470] **There are days**, etc. The passage in Emerson's journal is hardly less beautiful. Under date of October 30, 1841, he wrote: "On this wonderful day when heaven and earth seem to glow with magnificence, and all the wealth of all the elements is put under contribution to make the world fine, as if Nature would indulge her offspring, it seemed ungrateful to hide in the house. Are there not dull days enough in the year for you to write and read in, that you should waste this glittering season when Florida and Cuba seem to have left their glittering seats and come to visit us with all their shining hours, and almost we expect to see the jasmine and cactus burst from the ground instead of these last gentians and asters which have loitered to attend this latter glory of the year? All insects are out, all birds come forth, the very cattle that lie on the ground seem to have great thoughts, and Egypt and India look from their eyes."

[471] **Halcyons.** Halcyon days, ones of peace and tranquillity; anciently, days of calm weather in mid-winter, when the halcyon, or kingfisher, was supposed to brood. It was fabled that this bird laid its eggs in a nest that floated on the sea, and that it charmed the winds and waves to make them calm while it brooded.

[472] **Indian Summer.** Calm, dry, hazy weather which comes in the autumn in America. The Century Dictionary says it was called Indian Summer because the season was most marked in the sections of the upper eastern Mississippi valley inhabited by Indians about the time the term became current.

[473] **Gabriel.** One of the seven archangels. The Hebrew name means "God is my strong one."

[474] **Uriel.** Another of the seven archangels; the name means "Light of God."

[475] **Converts all trees to wind-harps.** Compare with this passage the lines in Emerson's poem, *Woodnotes*:

"And the countless leaves of the pines are strings
Tuned to the lay the wood-god sings."

[476] **The village.** Concord, Massachusetts. Emerson's home the greater part of the time from 1832 till his death.

[477] **I go with my friend**, etc. With Henry Thoreau, the lover of Nature.

[478] **Our little river.** The Concord river.

[479] **Novitiate and probation.** Explain the meaning of these words, in the Roman Catholic Church. What does Emerson mean by them here?

[480] **Villegiatura.** The Italian name for a season spent in country pleasures.

[481] **Hanging gardens.** The hanging gardens of Babylon were one of the seven wonders of the world.

[482] **Versailles.** A royal residence near Paris, with beautiful formal gardens.

[483] **Paphos.** A beautiful city on the island of Cyprus, where was situated a temple of Astarte, or Venus.

[484] **Ctesiphon.** One of the chief cities of ancient Persia, the site of a magnificent royal palace.

[485] **Notch Mountains.** Probably the White Mountains near Crawford Notch, a deep, narrow valley which is often called "The Notch."

[486] **Æolian harp.** A stringed instrument from which sound is drawn by the passing of the wind over its strings. It was named for Æolus, the god of the winds, in Greek mythology.

[487] **Dorian.** Dorus was one of the four divisions of Greece: the word is here used in a general sense for Grecian.

[488] **Apollo.** In Greek and Roman mythology, the sun god, who presided over music, poetry, and healing.

[489] **Diana.** In Roman mythology, the goddess of the moon devoted to the chase.

[490] **Edens.** Beautiful, sinless places, — like the garden of Eden.

[491] **Tempes.** Places like the lovely valley of Tempe in Thessaly, Greece.

[492] **Como Lake.** A lake of northern Italy, celebrated for its beauty.

[493] **Madeira Islands.** Where are these islands, famous for picturesque beauty and balmy atmosphere?

[494] **Common.** What is a common?

[495] **Campagna.** The plain near Rome.

[496] **Dilettantism.** Define this word and explain its use here.

[497] **"Wreaths" and "Flora's Chaplets."** About the time that Emerson was writing his essays, volumes of formal, artificial verses were very fashionable, more as parlor ornaments than as literature. Two such volumes were *A Wreath of Wild Flowers from New England* and *The Floral Offering* by Mrs. Frances Osgood, a New England writer.

[498] **Pan.** In Greek mythology, the god of woods, fields, flocks, and shepherds.

[499] **The multitude of false cherubs,** etc. Explain the meaning of this sentence. If true money were valueless, would people make false money?

[500] **Proteus.** In Greek mythology, a sea god who had the power of assuming different shapes. If caught and held fast, however, he was forced to assume his own shape and answer the questions put to him.

[501] **Mosaic ... Schemes.** The conception of the world as given in Genesis on which the law of Moses, the great Hebrew lawgiver, was founded.

[502] **Ptolemaic schemes.** The system of geography and astronomy taught in the second century by Ptolemy of Alexandria; it was accepted till the sixteenth century, when the Copernican system was established. Ptolemy believed that the sun, planets, and stars revolve around the earth; Copernicus taught that the planets revolve around the sun.

[503] **Flora.** In Roman mythology, the goddess of the spring and of flowers.

[504] **Fauna.** In Roman mythology, the goddess of fields and shepherds; she represents the fruitfulness of the earth.

[505] **Ceres.** The Roman goddess of grain and harvest, corresponding to the Greek goddess, Demeter.

[506] **Pomona.** The Roman goddess of fruit trees and gardens.

[507] **All duly arrive.** Emerson deducts from nature the doctrine of evolution. What is its teaching?

[508] **Plato.** (See note 36.)

[509] **Himalaya Mountain chains.** (See note 193.)

[510] **Franklin.** Give an account of Benjamin Franklin, the famous American scientist and patriot. What did he prove about lightening?

[511] **Dalton.** John Dalton was an English chemist who, about the beginning of the nineteenth century, perfected the atomic theory, that is, the theory that all chemical combinations take place in certain ways between the atoms, or ultimate particles, of bodies.

[512] **Davy.** (See note 69.)

[513] **Black.** Joseph Black, a Scotch chemist who made valuable discoveries about latent heat and carbon dioxide, or carbonic acid gas.

[514] **The astronomers said,** etc. Beginning with this passage, several pages of this essay was published in 1844, under the title of *Tantalus*, in the next to the last number of *The Dial*, which Emerson edited.

[515] **Centrifugal, centripetal.** Define these words.

[516] **Stoics.** See "Stoicism," 331.

[517] **Luther.** (See note 188.)

[518] **Jacob Behmen.** A German mystic of the sixteenth century; his name is usually written Boehme.

[519] **George Fox.** (See note 202.)

[520] **James Naylor.** An English religious enthusiast of the seventeenth century; he was first a Puritan and later a Quaker.

[521] **Operose.** Laborious.

[522] **Outskirt and far-off reflection**, etc. Compare with this passage Emerson's poem, *The Forerunners*.

[523] **[OE]dipus.** In Greek mythology, the King of Thebes who solved the riddle of the Sphinx, a fabled monster.

[524] **Prunella.** A widely scattered plant, called self-heal, because a decoction of its leaves and stems was, and to some extent is, valued as an application to wounds. An editor comments on the fact that during the last years of Emerson's life "the little blue self-heal crept into the grass before his study window."

SHAKESPEARE; OR, THE POET

[525] **Shakespeare; or the Poet** is one of seven essays on great men in various walks of life, published in 1850 under the title of *Representative Men*. These essays were first delivered as lectures in Boston in the winter of 1845, and were repeated two years later before English audiences. They must have been especially interesting to those Englishmen who had, seven years before, heard Emerson's friend, Carlyle, deliver his six lectures on great men whom he selected as representative ones. These lectures were published under the title of *Heroes and Hero-Worship*. You should read the latter part of Carlyle's lecture on *The Hero as Poet* and compare what he says about Shakespeare with Emerson's words. Both Emerson and Carlyle reverenced the great English poet as "the master of mankind." Even in serious New England, the plays of Shakespeare were found upon the bookshelf beside religious tracts and doctrinal treatises. There the boy Emerson found them and learned to love them, and the man Emerson loved them but the more. It was as a record of personal experiences that he wrote in his journal: "Shakespeare fills us with wonder the first time we approach him. We go away, and work and think, for years, and come again,—he astonishes us anew. Then, having drank deeply and saturated us with his genius, we lose sight of him for another period of years. By and by we return, and there he stands immeasurable as at first. We have grown wiser, but only that we should see him wiser than ever. He resembles a high mountain which the traveler sees in the morning and thinks he shall quickly near it and pass it and leave it behind. But he journeys all day till noon, till night. There still is the dim mountain close by him, having scarce altered its bearings since the morning light."

[526] **Genius.** Here instead of speaking as in *Friendship*, see note 286, of the genius or spirit supposed to preside over each man's life, Emerson mentions the guardian spirit of human kind.

[527] **Shakespeare's youth**, etc. It is impossible to appreciate or enjoy this essay without having some clear general information about the condition of the English people and English literature in the glorious

Elizabethan age in which Shakespeare lived. Consult, for this information, some brief history of England and a comprehensive English literature.

[528] **Puritans.** Strict Protestants who became so powerful in England that in the time of the Commonwealth they controlled the political and religious affairs of the country.

[529] **Anglican Church.** The Established Church of England; the Episcopal church.

[530] **Punch.** The chief character in a puppet show, hence the puppet show itself.

[531] **Kyd, Marlowe, Greene**, etc. For an account of these dramatists consult a text book on English literature. The English drama seems to have begun in the Middle Ages with what were called Miracle plays, which were scenes from Bible history; about the same time were performed the Mystery plays, which dramatized the lives of saints. These were followed by the Moralities, plays in which were personified abstract virtues and vices. The first step in the creation of the regular drama was taken by Heywood, who composed some farcical plays called Interludes. The people of the sixteenth century were fond of pageants, shows in which classical personages were introduced, and Masques, which gradually developed from pageants into dramas accompanied with music. About the middle of the sixteenth century, rose the English drama,—comedy, tragedy, and historical plays. The chief among the group of dramatists who attained fame before Shakespeare began to write were Kyd, Marlowe, Greene, and Peele. Ben Jonson and Beaumont and Fletcher rank next to Shakespeare among his contemporaries, and among the other dramatists of the period were Chapman, Dekker, Webster, Heywood, Middleton, Ford, and Massinger.

[532] **At the time when,** etc. Probably about 1585.

[533] **Tale of Troy.** Drama founded on the Trojan war. The subject of famous poems by Latin and Greek poets.

[534] **Death of Julius Cæsar.** An account of the plots which ended in the assassination of the great Roman general.

[535] **Plutarch.** See note on *Heroism*(264). Shakespeare, like the earlier dramatists, drew freely on Plutarch's *Lives* for material.

[536] **Brut.** A poetical version of the legendary history of Britain, by Layamon. Its hero is Brutus, a mythical King of Britain.

[537] **Arthur.** A British King of the sixth century, around whose life and deeds so many legends have grown up that some historians say he, too,

was a myth. He is the center of the great cycle of romances told in prose in Mallory's *Morte d'Arthur* and in poetry in Tennyson's *Idylls of the King*.

[538] **The royal Henries.** Among the dramas popular in Shakespeare's day which he retouched or rewrote are the historical plays. Henry IV., First and Second Parts; Henry V; Henry VI., First, Second, and Third Parts; and Henry VIII.

[539] **Italian tales.** Italian literature was very popular in Shakespeare's day, and authors drew freely from it for material, especially from the *Decameron*, a famous collection of a hundred tales, by Boccaccio, a poet of the fourteenth century.

[540] **Spanish voyages.** In the sixteenth century, Spain was still a power upon the high seas, and the tales of her conquests and treasures in the New World were like tales of romance.

[541] **Prestige.** Can you give an English equivalent for this French word?

[542] **Which no single genius,** etc. In the same way, some critics assure us, the poems credited to the Greek poet, Homer, were built up by a number of poets.

[543] **Malone.** An Irish critic and scholar of the eighteenth century, best known by his edition of Shakespeare's plays.

[544] **Wolsey's Soliloquy.** See Shakespeare's *Henry VIII.* iii, 2. Cardinal Wolsey was prime minister of England in the reign of Henry VIII.

[545] **Scene with Cromwell.** See *Henry VIII.* iii, 2. Thomas Cromwell was the son of an English blacksmith; he rose to be lord high chamberlain of England in the reign of Henry VIII., but, incurring the King's displeasure, was executed on a charge of treason.

[546] **Account of the coronation.** See *Henry VIII.* iv, 1.

[547] **Compliment to Queen Elizabeth.** See *Henry VIII.* v, 5.

[548] **Bad rhythm.** Too much importance must not be attached to these matters in deciding authorship, as critics disagree about them.

[549] **Value his memory,** etc. The Greeks, in appreciation of the value of memory to the poet, represented the Muses as the daughters of Mnemosyne, the goddess of memory.

[550] **Homer.** A Greek poet to whom is assigned the authorship of the two greatest Greek poems, the *Iliad* and the *Odyssey*; he is said to have lived about a thousand years before Christ.

[551] **Chaucer.** (See note 33.)

[552] **Saadi.** A Persian poet, supposed to have lived in the thirteenth century. His best known poems are his odes.

[553] **Presenting Thebes,** etc. This quotation is from Milton's poem, *Il Penseroso.* Milton here names the three most popular subjects of Greek tragedy,—the story of [OE]dipus, the ill-fated King of Thebes who slew his father; the tale of the descendants of Pelops, King of Pisa, who seemed born to woe—Agamemnon was one of his grandsons; the third subject was the tale of Troy and the heroes of the Trojan war,—called "divine" because the Greeks represented even the gods as taking part in the contest.

[554] **Pope.** (See note 88.)

[555] **Dryden.** (See note 35.)

[556] **Chaucer is a huge borrower.** Taine, the French critic, says on this subject: "Chaucer was capable of seeking out in the old common forest of the Middle Ages, stories and legends, to replant them in his own soil and make them send out new shoots.... He has the right and power of copying and translating because by dint of retouching he impresses ... his original work. He recreates what he imitates."

[557] **Lydgate.** John Lydgate was an English poet who lived a generation later than Chaucer; in his *Troy Book* and other poems he probably borrowed from the sources used by Chaucer; he called himself "Chaucer's disciple."

[558] **Caxton.** William Caxton, the English author, more famous as the first English printer, was not born until after Chaucer's death. The work from which Emerson supposes the poet to have borrowed Caxton's translation of *Recueil des Histoires de Troye,* the first printed English book, appeared about 1474.

[559] **Guido di Colonna.** A Sicilian poet and historian of the thirteenth century. Chaucer in his *House of Fame* placed in his vision "on a pillar higher than the rest, Homer and Livy, Dares the Phrygian, Guido Colonna, Geoffrey of Monmouth, and the other historians of the war of Troy."

[560] **Dares Phrygius.** A Latin account of the fall of Troy, written about the fifth century, which pretends to be a translation of a lost work on the fall of Troy by Dares, a Trojan priest mentioned in Homer's *Iliad.*

[561] **Ovid.** A Roman poet who lived about the time of Christ, whose best-known work is the *Metamorphoses,* founded on classical legends.

[562] **Statius.** A Roman poet of the first century after Christ.

[563] **Petrarch.** An Italian poet of the fourteenth century.

[564] **Boccaccio.** An Italian novelist and poet of the fourteenth century. See note on "Italian tales," 539. It is supposed that the plan of the *Decameron* suggested the similar but far superior plan of Chaucer's *Canterbury Tales.*

[565] **Provençal poets.** The poets of Provençe, a province of the southeastern part of France. In the Middle Ages it was celebrated for its lyric poets, called troubadours.

[566] **Romaunt of the Rose,** etc. Chaucer's *Romaunt of the Rose,* written during the period of French influence, is an incomplete and abbreviated translation of a French poem of the thirteenth century, *Roman de la Rose,* the first part of which was written by William of Loris and the latter by John of Meung, or Jean de Meung.

[567] **Troilus and Creseide,** etc. Chaucer ascribes the Italian poem which he followed in his *Troilus and Creseide* to an unknown "Lollius of Urbino"; the source of the poem, however, is *Il Filostrato,* by Boccaccio, the Italian poet already mentioned. Chaucer's poem is far more than a translation; more than half is entirely original, and it is a powerful poem, showing profound knowledge of the Italian poets, whose influence with him superseded the French poets.

[568] **The Cock and the Fox.** *The Nun's Priest's Tale* in the *Canterbury Tales* was an original treatment of the *Roman de Renart,* of Marie of France, a French poet of the twelfth century.

[569] **House of Fame,** etc. The plan of the *House of Fame,* written during the period of Chaucer's Italian influence, shows the influence of Dante; the general idea of the poem is from Ovid, the Roman poet.

[570] **Gower.** John Gower was an English poet, Chaucer's contemporary and friend; the two poets went to the same sources for poetic materials, but Chaucer made no such use of Gower's works as we would infer from this passage. Emerson relied on his memory for facts, and hence made mistakes, as here in the instances of Lydgate, Caxton, and Gower.

[571] **Westminster, Washington.** What legislative body assembles at Westminster Palace, London? What at Washington?

[572] **Sir Robert Peel.** An English statesman who died in 1850, not long after *Representative Men* was published.

[573] **Webster.** Daniel Webster, an American statesman and orator who was living when this essay was written.

[574] **Locke.** John Locke. (See note 18.)

[575] **Rousseau.** Jean Jacques Rousseau, a French philosopher of the eighteenth century.

[576] **Homer.** (See note 550.)

[577] **Menn.** Menn, or Mann, was in Sanscrit one of fourteen legendary beings; the one referred to by Emerson, Mann Vaivasvata was supposed to be the author of the laws of Mann, a collection made about the second century.

[578] **Saadi** or Sadi. (See note 552.)

[579] **Milton.** Of this great English poet and prose writer of the seventeenth century, Emerson says: "No man can be named whose mind still acts on the cultivated intellect of England and America with an energy comparable to that of Milton. As a poet Shakespeare undoubtedly transcends and far surpasses him in his popularity with foreign nations: but Shakespeare is a voice merely: who and what he was that sang, that sings, we know not."

[580] **Delphi.** Here, source of prophecy. Delphi was a city in Greece, where was the oracle of Apollo, the most famous of the oracles of antiquity.

[581] **Our English Bible.** The version made in the reign of King James I. by forty-seven learned divines is a monument of noble English.

[582] **Liturgy.** An appointed form of worship used in a Christian church,—here, specifically, the service of the Episcopal church. Emerson's mother had been brought up in that church, and though she attended her husband's church, she always loved and read her Episcopal prayer book.

[583] **Grotius.** Hugo Grotius was a Dutch jurist, statesman, theologian, and poet of the seventeenth century.

[584] **Rabbinical forms.** The forms used by the rabbis, Jewish doctors or expounders of the law.

[585] **Common law.** In a general sense, the system of law derived from England, in general use among English-speaking people.

[586] **Vedas.** The sacred books of the Brahmins.

[587] **Æsop's Fables.** Fables ascribed to Æsop, a Greek slave who lived in the sixth century before Christ.

[588] **Pilpay,** or Bidpai. Indian sage to whom were ascribed some fables. From an Arabic translation, these passed into European languages and were used by La Fontaine, the French fabulist.

[589] **Arabian Nights.** *The Arabian Nights' Entertainment or A Thousand and One Nights* is a collection of Oriental tales, the plan and name of which are very ancient.

[590] **Cid.** *The Romances of the Cid,* the story of the Spanish national hero, mentioned in note on *Heroism* 139:5, was written about the thirteenth century by an unknown author; it supplied much of the material for two Spanish chronicles and Spanish and French tragedies written later on the same subject.

[591] **Iliad.** The poem in which the Greek, poet, Homer, describes the siege and fall of Troy. Emerson here expresses the view adopted by many scholars that it was the work, not of one, but of many men.

[592] **Robin Hood.** The ballads about Robin Hood, an English outlaw and popular hero of the twelfth century.

[593] **Scottish Minstrelsy.** *The Minstrelsy of the Scottish Border,* a collection of original and collected poems, published by Sir Walter Scott in 1802.

[594] **Shakespeare Society.** The Shakespeare Society, founded in 1841, was dissolved in 1853. In 1874 The New Shakespeare Society was founded.

[595] **Mysteries.** See "Kyd, Marlowe, etc." 531.

[596] **Ferrex and Porrex,** or **Gorboduc.** The first regular English tragedy, by Thomas Norton and Thomas Sackville, printed in 1565.

[597] **Gammer Gurtor's Needle.** One of the first English comedies, written by Bishop Still and printed in 1575.

[598] **Whether the boy Shakespeare poached,** etc. For a fuller account of the facts of Shakespeare's life, of which some traditions and facts are mentioned here, consult some good biography of the poet.

[599] **Queen Elizabeth.** Dining her reign, 1558-1603, the English drama rose and attained its height, and there was produced a prose literature hardly inferior to the poetic.

[600] **King James.** King James VI. of Scotland and I. of England who was Elizabeth's kinsman and successor; he reigned in England from 1603 to 1625.

[601] **Essexes.** Walter Devereux was a brave English gentleman whom Elizabeth made Earl of Essex in 1572. His son Robert, the second Earl of Essex, was a favorite of Queen Elizabeth's.

[602] **Leicester.** The Earl of Leicester, famous in Shakespeare's time, was Robert Dudley, an English courtier, politician, and general, the favorite of Queen Elizabeth.

[603] **Burleighs** or Burghleys: William Cecil, baron of Burghley, was an English statesman, who, for forty years, was Elizabeth's chief minister.

[604] **Buckinghams.** George Villiers, the first duke of Buckingham, was an English courtier and politician, a favorite of James I. and Charles I.

[605] **Tudor dynasty.** The English dynasty of sovereigns descended on the male side from Owen Tudor. It began with Henry VII. and ended with Elizabeth.

[606] **Bacon.** Consult English literature and history for an account of the great statesman and author, Francis Bacon, "the wisest, brightest, meanest of mankind."

[607] **Ben Jonson**, etc. In his *Timber or Discoveries*, Ben Jonson, a famous classical dramatist contemporary with Shakespeare, says: "I loved the man and do honor his memory on this side idolatry as much as any. He was indeed honest and of an open and free nature: had an excellent fancy; brave notions and gentle expressions: wherein he flowed with that facility that sometimes it was necessary he should be stopped.... His wit was in his own power; would the rule of it had been so, too. Many times he fell into those things could not escape laughter.... But he redeemed his vices with his virtues. There was ever more in him to be praised than to be pardoned."

[608] **Sir Henry Wotton.** An English diplomatist and author of wide culture.

[609] **The following persons**, etc. The persons enumerated were all people of note of the seventeenth century. Sir Philip Sidney, Earl of Essex, Lord Bacon, Sir Walter Raleigh, John Milton, Sir Henry Vane, Isaac Walton, Dr. John Donne, Abraham Cowley, Charles Cotton, John Pym, and John Hales were Englishmen, scholars, statesmen, and authors. Theodore Beza was a French theologian; Isaac Casaubon was a French-Swiss scholar; Roberto Berlarmine was an Italian cardinal; Johann Kepler was a German astronomer; Francis Vieta was a French mathematician; Albericus Gentilis was an Italian jurist; Paul Sarpi was an Italian historian; Arminius was a Dutch theologian.

[610] **Many others whom doubtless**, etc. Emerson here enumerates some famous English authors of the same period, not mentioned in the preceeding list.

[611] **Pericles.** See note on *Heroism*, 352.

[612] **Lessing.** Gotthold Ephraim Lessing, a German critic and poet of the eighteenth century.

[613] **Wieland.** Christopher Martin Wieland was a German contemporary of Lessing's, who made a prose translation into German of Shakespeare's plays.

[614] **Schlegel.** August Wilhelm von Schlegel, a German critic and poet, who about the first of the nineteenth century translated some of Shakespeare's plays into classical German.

[615] **Hamlet.** The hero of Shakespeare's play of the same name.

[616] **Coleridge.** Samuel Taylor Coleridge, an English poet, author of critical lectures and notes on Shakespeare.

[617] **Goethe.** (See note 85.)

[618] **Blackfriar's Theater.** A famous London theater in which nearly all the great dramas of the Elizabethan age were performed.

[619] **Stratford.** Stratford-on-Avon, a little town in Warwickshire, England, where Shakespeare was born and where he spent his last years.

[620] **Macbeth.** One of Shakespeare's greatest tragedies, written about 1606.

[621] **Malone, Warburton, Dyce, and Collier.** English scholars of the eighteenth and nineteenth centuries who edited the works of Shakespeare.

[622] **Covent Garden, Drury Lane, the Park, and Tremont:** The leading London theaters in the eighteenth and nineteenth centuries.

[623] **Betterton, Garrick, Kemble, Kean, and Macready**, famous British actors of the Shakespearian parts.

[624] **The Hamlet of a famed performer**, etc. Macready. Emerson said to a friend: "I see you are one of the happy mortals who are capable of being carried away by an actor of Shakespeare. Now, whenever I visit the theater to witness the performance of one of his dramas, I am carried away by the poet."

[625] **What may this mean**, etc. *Hamlet*, I. 4.

[626] **Midsummer Night's Dream.** One of Shakespeare's plays.

[627] **The forest of Arden.** In which is laid, the scene of Shakespeare's play, *As You Like It*.

[628] **The nimble air of Scone Castle.** It was of the air of Inverness, not of Scone, that "the air nimbly and sweetly recommends itself unto our gentle senses." —*Macbeth*, i. 6.

[629] **Portia's villa.** See the moonlight scene, *Merchant of Venice*, v. 1.

[630] **The antres vost**, etc. See *Othello*, I. 3. "Antres" is an old word, meaning caves, caverns.

[631] **Cyclopean architecture.** In Greek mythology, the Cyclops were a race of giants. The term 'Cyclopean' is applied here to the architecture of Egypt and India, because of the majestic size of the buildings, and the immense size of the stones used, as if it would require giants to perform such works.

[632] **Phidian sculpture.** Phidias was a famous Greek sculptor who lived in the age of Pericles and beautified Athens with his works.

[633] **Gothic minsters.** Churches or cathedrals, built in the Gothic, or pointed, style of architecture which prevailed during the Middle Ages; it owed nothing to the Goths, and this term was originally used in reproach, in the sense of "barbarous."

[634] **The Italian painting.** In Italy during the fifteenth and sixteenth centuries pictorial art was carried to a degree of perfection unknown in any other time or country.

[635] **Ballads of Spain and Scotland.** The old ballads of these countries are noted for beauty and spirit.

[636] **Tripod.** Define this word, and explain its appropriateness here.

[637] **Aubrey.** John Aubrey, an English antiquarian of the seventeenth century.

[638] **Rowe.** Nicholas Rowe, an English author of the seventeenth century, who wrote a biography of Shakespeare.

[639] **Timon.** See note on *Gifts*, 466.

[640] **Warwick.** An English politician and commander of the fifteenth century, called "the King Maker." He appears in Shakespeare's plays, *Henry IV., V.,* and *VI.*

[641] **Antonio.** The Venetian Merchant in Shakespeare's play, *The Merchant of Venice.*

[642] **Talma.** François Joseph Talma was a French tragic actor, to whom Napoleon showed favor.

[643] **An omnipresent humanity,** etc. See what Carlyle has to say on this subject in his *Hero as Poet*.

[644] **Daguerre.** Louis Jacques Daguerre, a French painter, one of the inventors of the daguerreotype process, by means of which an image is fixed on a metal plate by the chemical action of light.

[645] **Euphuism.** The word here has rather the force of euphemism, an entirely different word. Euphuism was an affected ornate style of expression, so called from *Euphues*, by John Lyly, a sixteenth century master of that style.

[646] **Epicurus.** A Greek philosopher of the third century before Christ. He was the founder of the Epicurean school of philosophy which taught that pleasure should be man's chief aim and that the highest pleasure is freedom.

[647] **Dante.** (See note 258.)

[648] **Master of the revels,** etc. Emerson always expressed thankfulness for "the spirit of joy which Shakespeare had shed over the universe." See what Carlyle says in *The Hero as Poet*, about Shakespeare's "mirthfulness and love of laughter."

[649] **Koran.** The Sacred book of the Mohammedans.

[650] **Twelfth Night,** etc. The names of three bright, merry, or serene plays by Shakespeare.

[651] **Egyptian verdict.** Emerson used Egyptian probably in the sense of "gipsy." He compares such opinions to the fortunes told by the gipsies.

[652] **Tasso.** An Italian poet of the sixteenth century.

[653] **Cervantes.** A Spanish poet and romancer of the sixteenth century, the author of *Don Quixote*.

[654] **Israelite.** Such Hebrew prophets as Isaiah and Jeremiah.

[655] **German.** Such as Luther.

[656] **Swede.** Such as Swedenborg, the mystic philosopher of the eighteenth century of whom Emerson had already written in *Representative Men*.

[657] **A pilgrim's progress.** As described by John Bunyan, the English writer, in his famous *Pilgrim's Progress*.

[658] **Doleful histories of Adam's fall,** etc. The subject of *Paradise Lost*, the great poem by John Milton.

[659] **With doomsdays and purgatorial,** etc. As described by Dante in his *Divine Commedia,* an epic about hell, purgatory, and paradise.

PRUDENCE

[660] The essay on *Prudence* was given as a lecture in the course on *Human Culture,* in the winter of 1837-8. It was published in the first series of *Essays,* which appeared in 1841.

[661] **Lubricity.** The word means literally the state or quality of being slippery; Emerson uses it several times, in its derived sense of "instability."

[662] **Love and Friendship.** The subjects of the two essays preceding *Prudence,* in the volume of 1841.

[663] **The world is filled with the proverbs,** etc. Compare with this passage Emerson's words in *Compensation* on "the flights of proverbs, whose teaching is as true and as omnipresent as that of birds and flies."

[664] **A good wheel or pin.** That is, a part of a machine.

[665] **The law of polarity.** Having two opposite poles, the properties of the one of which are the opposite of the other.

[666] **Summer will have its flies.** Emerson discoursed with philosophic calm about the impediments and disagreeableness which beset every path; he also accepted them with serenity when he encountered them in his daily life.

[667] **The inhabitants of the climates,** etc. As a northerner, Emerson naturally felt that the advantage and superiority were with his own section. He expressed in his poems *Voluntaries* and *Mayday* views similar to those declared here.

[668] **Peninsular campaign.** Emerson here refers to the military operations carried on from 1808 to 1814 in Portugal, Spain, and southern France against the French, by the British, Spanish, and Portuguese forces commanded by Wellington. What was the "Peninsular campaign" in American history?

[669] **Dr. Johnson is reported to have said,** etc. Dr. Samuel Johnson was an eminent English scholar of the eighteenth century. In this, as in many other instances, Emerson quotes from his memory instead of from the book. The words of Dr. Johnson, as reported by his biographer Boswell, are: "Accustom your children constantly to this; if a thing happened at one window, and they, when relating it, say it happened at another, do not let it pass, but instantly check them; you do not know where deviation from truth will end."

[670] **Rifle.** A local name in England and New England for an instrument, on the order of a whetstone, used for sharpening scythes; it is made of wood, covered with fine sand or emery.

[671] **Last grand duke of Weimar.** Saxe-Weimar-Eisenach is a grand duchy of Germany. The grand duke referred to was Charles Augustus, who died in 1828. He was the friend and patron of the great German authors, Goethe, Schiller, Herder, and Wieland.

[672] **The Raphael in the Dresden gallery.** The Sistine Madonna, the most famous picture of the great Italian artist, Raphael.

[673] **Call a spade a spade.** Plutarch, the Greek historian, said, "These Macedonians ... call a spade a spade."

[674] **Parts.** A favorite eighteenth century term for abilities, talents.

[675] **We have found out**, etc. Emerson always insisted that morals and intellect should be united. He urged that power and insight are lessened by shortcomings in morals.

[676] **Goethe's Tasso.** A play by the German poet Goethe, founded on the belief that the imprisonment of Tasso was due to his aspiration to the hand of Leonora d'Este, sister of the duke of Ferrara. Tasso was a famous Italian poet of the seventeenth century.

[677] **Richard III.** An English king, the last of the Plantagenet line, the hero—or villain—of Shakespeare's historical play, Richard III.

[678] **Bifold.** Give a simpler word that means the same.

[679] **Cæsar.** Why is Cæsar the great Roman ruler, given as a type of greatness?

[680] **Job.** Why is Job, the hero of the Old Testament book of the same name, given as a type of misery?

[681] **Poor Richard.** *Poor Richard's Almanac,* published (1732-1757) by Benjamin Franklin was a collection of maxims inculcating prudence and thrift. These were given as the sayings of "Poor Richard."

[682] **State Street.** A street in Boston, Massachusetts, noted as a financial center.

[683] **Stick in a tree between whiles**, etc. "Jock, when ye hae naething else to do, ye may be aye sticking in a tree; it will be growing, Jock, when ye're sleeping." —Scott's *Heart of Midlothian.* It is said that these were the words of a dying Scotchman to his son.

[684] **Minor virtues.** Emerson suggests that punctuality and regard for a promise are two of these. Can you name others?

[685] **The Latin proverb says**, etc. This is quoted from Tacitus, the famous Roman historian.

[686] **If he set out to contend,** etc. In contention, Emerson holds, the best men would lose their characteristic virtues, —the fearless apostle Paul, his devotion to truth; the gentle disciple John, his loving charity.

[687] **Though your views are in straight antagonism,** &c. This was Emerson's own method, and by it he won a courteous hearing from those to whom his views were most objectionable.

[688] **Consuetudes.** Give a simpler word that has the same meaning.

[689] **Begin where we will,** etc. Explain what Emerson means by this expression.

CIRCLES

[690] This essay first appeared in the first series of *Essays,* published in 1841. Unlike most of the other essays in the volume, no earlier form of it exists, and it was probably not delivered first as a lecture.

Dr. Richard Garnett says in his *Life of Emerson:* "The object of this fine essay quaintly entitled *Circles* is to reconcile this rigidity of unalterable law with the fact of human progress. Compensation illustrates one property of a circle, which always returns to the point where it began, but it is no less true that around every circle another can be drawn.... Emerson followed his own counsel; he always keeps a reserve of power. His theory of *Circles* reappears without the least verbal indebtedness to himself in the splendid essay on *Love.*"

[691] **St. Augustine.** A celebrated father of the Latin church, who flourished in the fourth century. His most famous work is his *Confessions,* an autobiographical volume of religious meditations.

[692] **Another dawn risen on mid-noon.** "Another morn has risen on mid-noon." Milton, *Paradise Lost,* Book V.

[693] **Greek sculpture.** The greatest development of the art of sculpture that the world has ever known was that which took place in Greece, with Athens as the center, in the fifth century before Christ. The masterpieces which remain are the models on which modern art formed itself.

[694] **Greek letters.** In literature—in drama, philosophy and history— Greece attained an excellence as signal as in art. Emerson as a scholar, felt that the literature of Greece was more permanent than its art. Would an artist be apt to take this view?

[695] **New arts destroy the old,** etc. Tell the ways in which the improvements and inventions mentioned by Emerson have been superseded by others; give the reasons. Mention other similar cases of more recent date.

[696] **The life of man is a self-evolving circle,** etc. "Throw a stone into the stream, and the circles that propagate themselves are the beautiful type of all influence." — Emerson, in *Nature.*

[697] **The heart refuses to be imprisoned.** It is a superstition current in many countries that an evil spirit cannot escape from a circle drawn round it.

[698] **Crass.** Gross; coarse.

[699] **The continual effort to raise himself above himself,** etc.

"Unless above himself he can
Erect himself, how poor a thing is man!"
Samuel Daniel.

[700] **If he were high enough,** etc.

Have I a lover
Who is noble and free? —
I would he were nobler
Than to love me.
Emerson, *The Sphinx.*

[701] **Aristotle and Plato.** Plato was a famous Greek philosopher who flourished in the fourth century before Christ. He was the disciple of Socrates, the teacher of Aristotle, and the founder of the academic school of philosophy. His exposition of idealism was founded on the teachings of Socrates. Aristotle, another famous Greek philosopher, was for twenty years the pupil of Plato. He founded the peripatetic school of philosophy, and his writing dealt with all the then known branches of science.

[702] **Berkeley.** George Berkeley was a British clergyman of the eighteenth century. He was the author of works on philosophy which are marked by extreme subjective idealism.

[703] **Termini.** Boundaries or marks to indicate boundaries. In Roman mythology, Terminus was the god who presided over boundaries or landmarks. He is represented with a human head, but without feet or arms, — to indicate that he never moved from his place.

[704] **Pentecost.** One of three great Jewish festivals. On the day of Pentecost, the Holy Spirit descended upon the infant Christian church, with the gift of tongues. See Acts ii. 1-20.

[705] **Hodiernal.** Belonging to our present day.

[706] **Punic.** Of Carthage, a famous ancient city, and state of northern Africa. Carthage was the rival of Rome, but was, after long warfare, overcome in the second century before Christ.

[707] **In like manner,** etc. Emerson always urged that in order to get the best from all, one must pass from affairs to thought, society to solitude, books to nature.

"See thou bring not to field or stone
The fancies found in books;
Leave authors' eyes, and fetch your own,
To brave the landscape's look."
Emerson, *Waldeinsamkeit.*

[708] **Petrarch.** (See note 563.)

[709] **Ariosto.** A famous Italian author of the sixteenth century, who wrote comedies, satires, and a metrical romance, *Orlando Furioso.*

[710] **"Then shall also the Son"**, etc. See 1 Corinthians xv. 28: Does Emerson quote the passage verbatim?

[711] **These manifold tenacious qualities,** etc. It is remarked of Emerson that the idea of the symbolism of nature which he received from Plato, was the source of much of his pleasure in Swedenborg, the Swedish mystic philosopher. Emerson says in his volume on *Nature*: "The noblest ministry of nature is to stand as an apparition of God."

[712] **"Forgive his crimes,"** etc. This is quoted from *Night Thoughts* by the English didactic poet, Edward Young.

[713] **Pyrrhonism.** A doctrine held by a follower of Pyrrho, a Greek philosopher of the third century before Christ, who founded the sceptical school. He taught that it is impossible to attain truth, and that men should be indifferent to all external circumstances.

[714] **I own I am gladdened,** etc. Emerson always held fast to the consoling thought that there was no evil without good, none out of which Good did not or could not come.

[715] **Sempiternal.** Everlasting; eternal.

[716] **Oliver Cromwell.** An Englishman of the middle classes who became the military and civil leader of the English Revolution of the seventeenth century. He refused the title of king; but as Lord Protector of the English commonwealth, he exercised royal power.